THACKERAY'S
Contributions to the *MORNING CHRONICLE*

UNIVERSITY OF ILLINOIS PRESS, Urbana and London, 1966

WILLIAM MAKEPEACE THACKERAY: *Contributions to the MORNING CHRONICLE*

Edited by
GORDON N. RAY

PREFACE

For the decade before January, 1847, when *Vanity Fair* began to appear in monthly parts, William Makepeace Thackeray earned his living chiefly by anonymous contributions to a variety of magazines and newspapers. During his lifetime he himself collected much of this work for book publication, and after his death devoted Thackerayans published several volumes containing further gleanings from the field. But in this process one of the most important and long-lasting of his periodical connections, that with the London *Morning Chronicle*, was largely ignored. It may be surmised that Thackeray himself failed to reprint his *Morning Chronicle* articles because most of them were reviews of individual books, rather than wide-ranging essays. Later students of his work (apart from "Lewis Melville," who reprinted his review of Horne's *New Spirit of the Age*,[1] and Harold Strong Gulliver, who reprinted his review of Horace Smith's *Poetical Works* together with excerpts from his reviews of Jesse's *Life of George Brummell, Esq.* and Disraeli's *Coningsby*[2]) have entirely overlooked Thackeray's association with this newspaper.

Only with the appearance of my edition of Thackeray's *Letters* in 1945-46, indeed, was the extent of his contributions to the *Morning Chronicle* revealed. I there for the first time identified

---

[1] Thackeray, *Critical Papers in Literature,* ed. Lewis Melville (London, 1904), pp. 301-9.

[2] *Thackeray's Literary Apprenticeship* (Valdosta, Georgia, 1934), pp. 140-3, 237-9, 240-1.

as Thackeray's thirty-one additional contributions to this newspaper.[3] These are reprinted in this volume together with the four reviews previously attributed to him by Melville and Gulliver. Thus the reader will here find conveniently collected all of Thackeray's presently identifiable writing for the *Morning Chronicle* except for a pair of communications to the editor in 1850, which are readily accessible in his *Works*.[4] A literal text is given save for the silent correction of obvious errors. When it is remembered that these articles were printed from manuscript and that Thackeray probably saw proof of none of them, this practice will perhaps seem justified. Annotation has been held to a minimum, and some of what is provided will be found in the index.

G. N. R.

Urbana, Illinois
October, 1954

---

[3] *The Letters and Private Papers of William Makepeace Thackeray,* four volumes (Cambridge, 1945-6), II, 845-6. Cited hereafter as *Letters.*
[4] *The Oxford Thackeray,* ed. George Saintsbury, 17 volumes (Oxford, 1908), X, 583-92. Cited hereafter as *Works.*

CONTENTS

W M Thackeray

WILLIAM MAKEPEACE THACKERAY
(age 36)
FROM A DRAWING BY COUNT D'ORSAY IN 1848

INTRODUCTION

During the eighteen-thirties and eighteen-forties the *Morning Chronicle* was the chief rival of the *Times* for the title of London's principal newspaper. The *Chronicle's* liberal political policies made it far more congenial to Thackeray than its great rival, and for many years he endeavored unavailingly to obtain a place on its staff. As early as 1835 he hoped to become the *Chronicle's* Constantinople representative through the interest of its Paris correspondent Eyre Evans Crowe; and in 1839, encouraged by another staff member, John Payne Collier, he tried unsuccessfully to place political articles in the paper. Early in 1844 his efforts at last bore fruit. In March of that year he was confident of a post worth £300 a year with the *Chronicle*, "where my friends [John] Doyle & Crowe are working anxiously in my favour." In June he was tied to London by his work for the paper, which by this time netted him "£20 a month" and was "as safe as if I had an engagement." Only when he left for a Mediterranean trip in August were his contributions interrupted; and he resumed his work for the paper upon returning to London in February, 1845. By January of 1846 he was reporting to his stepfather that he had "£700 [a year] between Punch & the Chronicle." Even so, he was not satisfied with the articles which he wrote during this year. "The Chronicle & I must part company or I must cut down half the salary," he told his mother on 6 March. "They are most provokingly friendly all the time, and insist that I should neither resign nor disgorge—but how can one but act honorably by people who are so good-natured?" So encouraged he continued to contribute until the following January, when he

finally announced: "I am no longer a writer in the Chronicle."
And despite his immense success with *Vanity Fair* in the months
that followed, he resumed his articles sporadically in 1848,
attracted by the "good pay." "It is an awful bribe," he wrote,
"that 5 guineas an article."[1]

In the first months of his *Chronicle* connection Thackeray
sought to make his mark as a political writer. On 1 June 1844
we find him looking forward to "a day's work at the Emperor
of Russia about whose visit all the towns agog." But he shortly
had to admit: "I cant write the politics." And though he continued to try his hand occasionally at this subject, in the end he
was forced to grant "I am a very weak & poor politician." This
was a pity in Thackeray's view, since "the literary part is badly
paid;" but he consoled himself with the thought that at least his
"Chronicle articles are very well liked—they relieve the dullness
of that estimable paper." Yet Thackeray's readers may be profoundly grateful that he thus failed "to get within the guard of
the Chronicle" in political matters and had to limit himself to
"outside articles" (book reviews and art criticism) and "occasional jeux d'esprit."[2] Newspaper politics would today be of
little interest even from his hand, while his lively "outside articles"
remain almost as absorbing as when they were first written.

Moreover, it would be a hopeless task to seek out Thackeray's
political articles or news reports, since these subjects offer little
scope for the display of a writer's identifying idiosyncrasies.[3] A
very different situation obtains when the topic dealt with is
literature or painting. Here Thackeray's touch is often unmistakable. Certainly it is reassuring to have some articles definitely
tagged as his by references in his letters[4] and to be able to add
still other contributions by cross-references in the articles thus
identified.[5] But in the case of the articles reprinted in this

---

[1] *Letters*, I, 271, 281-7, 384, 398; II, 164, 170, 172, 225, 231, 264, 373, 442.

[2] The same, II, 171, 172, 225, 216.

[3] Two such articles, "Meeting on Kennington Common" and "Chartist Meeting," are reprinted in this volume; but this is possible only because they are specifically identified by references in *Letters*, II, 364-5.

[4] See *Letters*, II, 143, 145, 149, 234-5, 249, 364-5.

[5] Since we know that Thackeray wrote the *Chronicle* review of *Sybil*, for example, it follows that he wrote several related articles in which the penchant of contemporary imaginative writers for indulging in "comic

volume, the echoes of Thackeray's acknowledged writings are so numerous,[6] the parallels to his familiar opinions so obvious,[7] and his stylistic peculiarities so manifest, that no doubt as to the authorship of these articles remains, even without such specific evidence.

At the same time it is equally certain that there is much other work by him in the *Chronicle* which cannot now be identified. The articles reprinted here would not by themselves have brought him an income of £20 to £30 a month during the long period of his "floating connection" with that newspaper. Only thirty-one of the more than one hundred articles on literary and artistic subjects printed in the *Chronicle* between March and August, 1844, and February, 1845 and December, 1846, appear in the following pages. A number of others, for whatever reason less marked by his individual stamp, no doubt remain to be identified, should a file of the paper listing authors of individual contributions ever turn up.[8] But these additions, if they are ever made, should not materially alter the estimate of his work for the *Chronicle* which follows.

politics" is deplored, notably "Smythe's *Historic Fancies*," "Lever's *St. Patrick's Eve*," and "Christmas Books. No. III." Similarly, since Thackeray wrote "Christmas Books. No. III," he also wrote the first and second articles in this series.

[6] Here are a few such echoes among many: p. 51 below and *Works,* VI, 550, IX, 315; pp. 52-3 below and *Works,* IX, 121-2; p. 87 below and *Works,* VI, 538; p. 91 below and *Works,* VI, 567, 590, X, 313-4; p. 94 below and *Works,* IV, 162; p. 98 below and *Works,* II, 420, 626-7; p. 107 below and *Works,* VI, 549-50; p. 127 below and *Works,* V, 250; pp. 147-8 below and *Works,* II, 630-1, 653. It may also be noted that Thackeray's articles on Bulwer-Lytton, Cooper, Disraeli, and Mrs. Gore give much of the rationale for his burlesques of these authors in "Novels by Eminent Hands."

[7] On such topics, for example, as Ireland and Daniel O'Connell, Regency dandies and George the Fourth, Newman and the Tractarian movement, the Catholic church and asceticism, Young England and Disraeli, the middle ages, *gourmandise,* and eighteenth century society.

[8] In 1899 Marion H. Spielmann edited a volume of *Hitherto Unidentified Contributions of W. M. Thackeray to "Punch."* For the period October, 1848 until 1854, he depended on internal evidence for many of his identifications. When I discovered the editor's day-book for this period, giving the authorship of articles in the magazine, only one of Spielmann's identifications proved erroneous, though I was able to add forty-four additional contributions. Should similar documentation concerning the *Morning Chronicle* appear, the results for Thackeray's bibliography would probably be much the same. See my "Thackeray and 'Punch'," *Times Literary Supplement,* 1 January 1949.

II

If Thackeray hardly rivalled Sainte-Beuve in his stint as the *Morning Chronicle's* reviewer, he yet displayed the same knowledge of books and the world, the same unfailing resourcefulness, and the same ability to make a wide variety of topics humanly interesting that the readers of today find in the articles of Mr. V. S. Pritchett for the *New Statesman* or the contributions of Mr. Edmund Wilson to the *New Yorker*. Thackeray's *Morning Chronicle* papers are not merely the culmination of his work as a periodical critic (a specialty with him since 1837); at their best they also anticipate *The English Humourists* and *The Four Georges.* Thackeray's equipment in these articles includes a penetrating insight into character, an ability to present in a few phrases the whole *ambiance* of a subject, a fine irony playing over the incongruities of life, a keen eye for the devastating anecdote, and a felicity in quotation which makes an asset even of this obligatory part of the Victorian reviewer's task. The result is critical journalism of a high order, which has substantial permanent value.

Among the most interesting of Thackeray's *Morning Chronicle* papers are those dealing with such Victorian classics as Dickens's *Cricket on the Hearth,* Disraeli's *Coningsby* and *Sybil,* Jerrold's *Mrs. Caudle's Curtain Lectures,* and Stanley's *Life of Dr. Arnold.* He is particularly expert in revealing where the appeal of these books lay for himself and his contemporaries, as in the following ironical dirge over Mrs. Caudle:

Though Mrs. Caudle had her faults, perhaps there was no woman who died more universally lamented than she. The want of her weekly discourses was felt all over the kingdom. . . . In *Punch's Almanac* we find Caudle married again. It seems a wrong to the departed woman. We feel personally angry that her memory should be so slighted; but the virtues of the sainted deceased appear more clearly, now that her emancipated husband is indulging in vices which were checked by the anxious prescience of the first and best Mrs. Caudle. She and Mrs. Nickleby ought to take their places among the "Women of England," when Mrs. Ellis brings out a new edition of that work. They are both types of English matrons so excellent that it is hard to say which of the two should have the *pas.* Mrs. Nickleby's maundering and amiable vacuity endear her to all her acquaintance; Mrs. Caudle's admirable dulness, envy, and uncharitableness, her fondness for her mamma, brother, and family, and her jealous regard of her Caudle, make her an object of incessant sympathy with her numerous friends, and they regret, now she is no more, that amiable British matron and beldam.

Here Thackeray was altogether in sympathy with his subject; but even where he has serious reservations about a book, he contrives to praise with infectious enthusiasm the aspects of it that he is able to admire. The chief effect upon him of *The Cricket on the Hearth*, for example, was to make him long for "the artist's early and simple manner." Yet he paid ungrudging tribute to Dickens's pre-eminence as "literary master of ceremonies for Christmas"; and he granted that if one takes the book "in a Christmas point of view . . . it and Dot, and the kettle and Gruff and Tackleton become a sort of half-recognized realities which charm and fascinate you, and over which you may laugh or weep according to your mood."

Even better than these papers, however, are those in which Thackeray resuscitates for a moment a vanished society, or sketches a remarkable character of history. As he reviews biographies of Beau Brummell and David Hume, as he notices Mme. d'Arblay's diary and letters, as Horne's *New Spirit of the Age* recalls to him his boyhood admiration for Hazlitt and *The Spirit of the Age*, his historical imagination awakes; and the past lives again in his mind. Here, for example, is his response to the sixth volume of Mme. d'Arblay's memoirs:

Six lovely princesses wept over her immortal novel of 'Camilla,' read it hastily in their apartments at Windsor, or 'comfortably' together at Weymouth. The august eyes of Queen Charlotte moistened with tears over those dingy and now forgotten pages. The king himself had a copy and read in it, and was good-natured to the hysterically loyal Fanny d'Arblay—always ready to gush with tears at the feet of her royal master—always plunging from the embraces of one soft and kind-hearted princess into the closet and arms of another. Peace to their honest big-wigged shades! There is something queer, pleasant, and affecting in the picture which Fanny d'Arblay draws of this primitive and kindly female family of George III.; of the princesses so simple, so tender, so handsome, blooming in powder and pomatum; of the old Queen herself, that just and spotless, that economical but charitable lady.

But not all of the books that came Thackeray's way were potential classics or dealt with famous figures of the past. Perhaps he shows his greatest ingenuity in making tedious books amusing, in transforming sow's ears into silk purses. In his last complete novel he writes: "And yet egotism is good talk. Even dull autobiographies are pleasant to read. . . . Can't you like a man at whom you laugh a little?"[9] Thackeray could, at any rate.

---

[9] *Works*, XVI, 446-7.

He was fond enough of *originals* to take sincere delight in books that ordinary readers found dull or objectionable. Like Democritus brought back to earth, it was his pleasure to

> See motley life in modern trappings dress'd,
> And feed with varied fools th' eternal jest.

So he remarks of Dr. Carus's *Travels in England*:

There seems something prodigious in the prosiness of the book. The staleness, and dulness of the author's reflections amount almost to a marvel. The gravity and self-contempt with which the Doctor lays down the law—the pomp with which he serves out his small-beer—the happy, blundering skill which leads him to miss the great points and occupy himself laboriously with the small—all these considerations may deter many readers, at first, from a book which appears quite unexampled for drivelling stupidity . . . it is only after study and labour that you penetrate the outer dulness, and see what a magnificent treasure is before you.

A brilliant exercise in irony follows in which Carus's ponderous commonplaces and elephantine pleasantries are neatly displayed for the reader's entertainment. Bulwer-Lytton's *The New Timon*, James Fenimore Cooper's *Ravensnest*, Haydon's *Lectures on Painting*, Horne's *New Spirit of the Age*, Lane's *Life at the Water Cure*, Mohan Lal's *Travels in the Punjab*, Alexis Soyer's *Gastronomic Regenerator*, and Trench's *Royal Palaces* afford Thackeray further "victims to be gently immolated," though he treats none of these quite so severely as he does poor Carus.[10]

III

We have thus far been concerned with noting the interest as criticism of Thackeray's *Morning Chronicle* articles. To the student of his work they have the further value of revealing his developing views as to what fiction ought to be. Nowhere else does he speak so explicitly or at such length on this subject. In a significant series of articles he deals with a growing inclination on the part of such writers as Dickens, Disraeli, Lever, and Mrs. Trollope, to make political, economic, or religious manifestos out of their novels.

---

[10] Horne many years later entered a defense against Thackeray's "critique," which had obviously been written, so he contended, "in a half-cynical, half-rollicking, Royster-Doyster mood." See *Letters of Elizabeth Barrett Browning Addressed to Richard Hengist Horne,* ed. S. R. Townshend Mayer, 2 volumes (London, 1877), II, 274-9.

If we want instruction [he argues] we prefer to take it from fact rather than from fiction. We like to hear sermons from his reverence at church; to get our notions of trade, crime, politics, and other national statistics, from the proper papers and figures; but when suddenly, out of the gilt pages of a pretty picture book, a comic moralist rushes forward, and takes occasion to tell us that society is diseased, the laws unjust, the rich ruthless, the poor martyrs, the world lop sided, and *vice versâ*, persons who wish to lead an easy life are inclined to remonstrate against this literary ambuscadoe.

Indeed, Thackeray continues in a subsequent article,

Morals and manners we believe to be the novelist's best themes; and hence prefer romances which do not treat of algebra, religion, political economy, or any other abstract science.

In illustration of these opinions he proceeds to deride Disraeli's "comic philosophy" and "sentimental politics" in his articles on *Coningsby* and *Sybil*, and to provide a burlesque plot for a proletarian novel in reviewing Lever's *St. Patrick's Eve*.

The dictum that the novelist should never attempt a subject concerning which he is not thoroughly informed implies a realistic aesthetic. And, indeed, fidelity to personal experience in fiction is a first principle with Thackeray. Hence one finds him asserting that the proletarian novel is "a magnificent and untrodden field"; but "to describe it well, a man should be born to it. We want a Boz from among the miners or the manufactories to detail their ways of work and pleasure—to describe their feelings, interests, and lives, public and private." Hence he makes his chief ground of praise for *Mrs. Caudle's Curtain Lectures* that Caudle and his wife "have become real living personages in history, like Queen Elizabeth, or Sancho Panza, or any other past character, who, false or real once, is only imaginary now, and for whose existence we have only the word of a book. And surely to create these realities is the greatest triumph of the fictitious writer." Hence his reservation, already noted, concerning *The Cricket on the Hearth*, that its characters and dialogue "are no more like nature than the talk of Tityrus and Meliboeus are like the real talk of Bumpkin and Hodge over a stile." Hence finally his objection to the fashionable novel, whether written by Disraeli or by Mrs. Gore.

Not an unremarkable characteristic of our society-novelists [he writes] is that ardour of imagination which sets them so often to work in describing grand company for us. They like to disport themselves in inventing fine people, as we to sit in this imaginary society. There is something *naïf* in this credulity on both sides: in these cheap Barmecide entertainments to which author and reader are content to sit down.

"Novels by Eminent Hands" constitutes an extension of the views expressed in these and similar passages, just as *Vanity Fair* is an attempt to show what can be done in fiction if the author does limit himself to the aspects of life that he knows intimately.

Indeed, Thackeray's *Morning Chronicle* articles include many significant anticipations of his later work, forming, as they do, an annotated diary of his reading in the three crucial years before *Vanity Fair* began to appear. We see Thackeray discovering in *Coningsby*, for example, what treasures lay open to the hand of the novelist in the available printed records concerning the third Marquess of Hertford and his circle. Disraeli had made from them a series of "amusing, bitter sketches . . . of which the likenesses were irresistible, and the malice tickled everybody." Might not another novelist use them to even better purpose? It is of absorbing interest to the admirer of *Vanity Fair* to witness emerging from Thackeray's reflections on his reading that profound disgust with the frivolity and corruption of well-to-do England which supplies the unifying theme of his great novel. His brilliant essay on Beau Brummell is informed by the most scathing contempt for fashionable Regency society, the leadership of which was contended for by "the Prince of Wales (august shade of sixteen stone!)," and "young Brummell, the footman's descendant." As between the two antagonists, Thackeray greatly prefers the latter:

All the profligate splendours of Carlton House could not compete with the Beau's small tenement in Chesterfield-street; there was a tawdry magnificence about George IV., which must have been felt to be bad taste if not acknowledged. . . . Brummell overcame him by simplicity, elegance, and neat impudence and presence of mind. There seems to have been a calmness about him which flustered and intolerably annoyed the unwieldy antagonist with whom he contended for the first place in a certain society.

But what a light this struggle throws on high life of that day! "Let us respect the world which elevated to honour this respectable man!" is Thackeray's sardonic valedictory to Brummell; "and not be too hard upon him, because he was heartless, and a swindler, a fool, a glutton, and a liar." Nor did fashionable society of his own time, as depicted in Mrs. Gore's *Sketches of English Character*, offer a worthier picture:

Supposing that Pall-mall were the world, and human life finished with the season, and Heaven were truffled turkies and the Opera, and duty and ambition were bounded in dressing well and getting tickets to Lady Londonderry's dancing teas, Mrs. Gore's 'Sketches of Character' might be a good guide book. And we are wrong in saying it has no moral: the moral is that which very likely the author intended—that entire weariness, contempt, and dislike which the reader must undergo after this introduction to what is called the world. If it be as here represented, the world is the most hollow, heartless, vulgar, brazen world, and those are luckiest who are out of it.

It has been possible to suggest only faintly in this brief survey the interest of Thackeray's *Morning Chronicle* essays. He has his word, and it is usually an epigram, on most of the leading issues of the day. There are delightful glimpses of early Victorian life, as in the account of Christmas preparations that prefaces his review of holiday books. His reports of exhibitions of the Royal Academy and the Water Colour Societies include some brilliantly realized word painting, ranging in subject from Hunt's comic boys and Maclise's costume melodramas to Turner's most daring experiments. These essays were written just as Thackeray attained maturity as a writer; none of them is negligible; and the best display the wonderful fullness, freshness, and gusto that mark the first productions of a master who has ended his apprenticeship. What he says of Hazlitt applies equally to his own articles for this paper:

With partialities and prejudices innumerable, he had a wit so keen, a sensibility so exquisite, an appreciation of humor, or pathos, or even of the greatest art, so lively, quick, and cultivated, that it was always good to know what were the impressions made by books, or men, or pictures on such a mind.

[16 MARCH 1844]

Irland. By J. VENEDEY. 2 vols. [Leipzig, 1844.

We encountered a foreign friend some years since, who was making the tour of Britain. He had seen the sights of England and Scotland—London, of course; Oxford, Birmingham, and our manufacturing towns; the Lakes of Cumberland, too. He had been to Loch Cathrine, and the scenes of Walter Scott. He was going to Ireland. What to do? To see the *grand misère.* He went, and came back not in the least disappointed. He visited Scotland for its romantic recollections and beauty—England for the wonders of its wealth—Ireland for the wonders of its poverty. For poverty and misery have, it seems, their *sublime*, and that sublime is to be found in Ireland. What a flattering homage to England's constitutional rule over a sister country.

We own that we are much inclined to be savage with foreigners who come to spy holes in our coats, and who go to Ireland to pity the natives, and execrate the English. We don't want Mynheers and Jack Sprats to turn their eye-glasses upon our shame, which their observations and twopenny-halfpenny criticisms cannot mend. We would follow Napoleon's counsel, and "wash our dirty clothes *en famille*," nor expose Ireland to the foreigner's gaze, till we can mend her rags, wash her face, put a clean smock upon her, and render her fit to walk arm-in-arm down European streets with John Bull.

Herr Venedey has come to England, and has lived, no doubt, in the solitude of London chop-houses, and Aldelphi lodging *ditto.* He has come from that land of Cockaigne, Paris, in which

1

foreigners take the first bait, and he has come to this busy land
to look upon us Londoners in our daily tread-mill. We have
not said three words to him, but allowed him to *flâner* in the
Haymarket, and twist his mustachios in the pit of a theatre,
whilst bad copies of the worst French plays were represented
before him. Hereat he flies off in dudgeon and *ennui* to old
Ireland, which shakes his hand, welcomes him, feasts him, and
cuts most joyous capers at the avatar of a real German descending
upon the land. Accordingly, all through his book the English
are the dullest, most prosaic, cold hearted, melancholy, me-
chanical, diabolical sort of bodies in existence; whilst brother
Paddy, to the German's eyes, is an angel of goodness, jollity,
virtue, and what not. There may be some truth at the bottom
of all this, but in the book before us it is exaggerated into all the
monstrosity of error.

It is useful, however, that we should know the impression which
the sight and examination of the two countries naturally makes
on an intelligent foreigner. And M. Venedey is intelligent. He
is too warm-hearted, simple—too ready to leap to his conclusions.
A sufferer and an exile from having indulged a generous political
aspiration at sixteen, his sympathy for the Irish was but too
natural. A native of Cologne, under the yoke of Prussian ministers of religion and police, could not but join hands with an Irishman under the yoke of Peel. And he, therefore, makes too little
allowance for the difficulties attending the linking together of
two such unequally advanced countries together; and, instead of
making it a matter of historical research, he treats it as a romance,
personifying England as the villain of the tale, and Ireland as
the heroine and the victim.

We regret this, for M. Venedey's book will go through Germany, where religious difference and sects exist; and his picture
of Protestantism treading Catholics under foot, will cause the
blood to rise, and equanimity and tolerance to disappear in the
heart of many a German Catholic. Raumer and Kohl[1] were
more dispassionate. And yet we should not reproach M. Venedey
from the warmth of feeling which distinguishes him, however
disagreeable to us may be the effects.

---

[1] Friedrich Ludwig Georg von Raumer, *England im Jahre 1835*, 1836-
1842; Johann Georg Kohl, *Reisen in Irland*, 1843.

The first volume of the present publication is a history or historical review of Ireland, of course intended for German readers, to whom, alive as they have become to this religious agitation, it must be most welcome. We are so sick, however, of Irish historical surveys, in which no writer ever keeps possession of his temper or his judgment, that we shall at once pass over this volume. The second volume consists of M. Venedey's personal observations, records of what he has heard, sketches of what he has seen. The account is interesting, simple, and is the only one that brings livelily before one those scenes of which one has hitherto read only in the inflated accounts of party newspapers.

The account of the first *meeting* which M. Venedey attended—that of Athlone—is most graphically written. His journey thither, round by Ballinasloe—his making more friends in ten minutes than he had in England in ten months—his introduction to O'Connell on the platform—the agitator welcoming him with an arch look, when he said he was from Cologne—all is well told, and must prove exceedingly popular in Germany.

We prefer, however, taking, as an extract, the account of the author's personal reception by Mr. O'Connell in Dublin and in the bosom of his family:—

"Peel's speech on Mr. O'Brien's motion has just come to Dublin, the day before I dined with Mr. O'Connell, who that very day had answered it in the Repeal Association. I was bidden to come half an hour before dinner, but Mr. O'Connell, I was told, was reposing. So I gave in my name, and was shown into the drawing-room, where I found Mr. French, O'Connell's eldest daughter, and Mrs. Morgan O'Connell—the former in mourning for the death of her husband: she was pale, but her features, and especially her eyes, were full of life. Mrs. Morgan O'Connell is a fine specimen of Connaught beauty. But I have no right to put down our conversation, nor have I an excuse, in the celebrity of their great relative, to draw the light of publicity upon these ladies. I shall only say that intellect shone forth in one, as much as beauty and cordiality in the other. Daniel O'Connell, jun., soon came: he is a fine young man, who has studied under his father's superintendence; and, lastly, came O'Connell himself and his two eldest sons, Morgan and John, with Mr. Fitzpatrick. O'Connell wore a green coat with a black collar, and over that a blue cloak, which he kept on during dinner time. He begged me to excuse him for not taking it off, having the habit of keeping himself thus wrapped up after he had spoken in public. He kissed his daughter and daughter-in-law, and sat down in the circle. All eyes were of course directed towards him. And, indeed, without either his name or his acts, O'Connell is a man to be of himself the centre of any company. He sat there like a colossus or statue of Jupiter, dominating all. There were the signs of exhaustion on his countenance, but this did not prevent spirit sparkling from his eye, and humour playing round his mouth. Speaking little himself, he encouraged others with cordiality and cheerful smiles. Dinner soon came. O'Connell sat at the head of the table; Mr. Morgan O'Connell at the foot; Mrs. French sat on the right of her father, and Mrs. Morgan on the left; and at either side the guests and other members of the family. Before we sat down, O'Connell said a short grace. It was Friday, and therefore no meat was brought to the table. There was everything else in abundance, the best wine, and the newest fruits. During dinner O'Connell was always the leader of the converse, though he spoke little, and only to his children and his guests, to beg of them to help themselves to such and such a dish, or such and such wine. The greatest silence prevailed during the whole dinner, and, at times, I felt a certain uneasiness seize me, such as I had not for a long time before had, and which brought back to my recollection my days of boyhood. After dessert, O'Connell's grandchildren came in, and I believe, if he had a dozen, that he had sixty of them. They each gave their grandfather a kiss. He then took his daughter by the hand, and held it in his for a short time; he gave the other to his daughter-in-law, and thus sat hand in hand with them. There was something solemn in this, which one would not have expected at such a moment of relaxation. When the dinner was over, O'Connell said grace, and again kissed his grandchildren, and all the ladies then left the room with them. The whole dinner had quite the character of a patriarchal family scene, and inspired me with more and more veneration for the man—a sentiment which increased every day I remained in Ireland. The conversation did not get quite free even after dinner, and I perceived it was necessary for O'Connell to talk himself, in order to get his friends to do the same. None of his sons spoke save young Dan, just returned from travel. I had an opportunity, however, of observing to Mr. O'Connell that in Germany we were unionists, whilst the Irish were separatists. We clamoured for a union, whilst Irish efforts were to dissolve a union. I was then obliged to explain, and to show the difference between Ireland and Germany—Germany having much that Ireland wants, and Ireland possessing much that Germany has not. Germany has provincial institutions—Ireland imperial institutions, which, without the support of provincial ones, are but a misfortune. Ireland might learn much from Germany, would find much to better her condition in England and Ireland. These few remarks gave life to the conversation.

"Tea was served in the drawing-room, whilst O'Connell retired to his study, and did not again appear. This is his daily habit, and shows the patriarchal fear in which he is held by his children and grandchildren. They see him seldom, except working for the good of Ireland; and they are young enough to known him only the Great Man, and the Liberator of Ireland. I heard that O'Connell was the gayest companion in this world, and would amuse a whole company by his spirit, fun, and humour. This can the more easily be believed, as he, being the soul of all, must naturally communicate his feelings to those around him.

"I dined another day with O'Connell. He was quite a different man from when I was there before. At dinner he was quite alive, and did honour to the viands and the wine. The conversation was friendly, and on general topics; but when the ladies and the children left the dining-room, the conversation took a severer turn. The principal topic was repeal, it is a subject ever new and ever interesting in Ireland. Mr. Fitzpatrick, one of the guests, said that sending a petition for repeal to the Parliament in London, was tantamount to a tacit recognition of the supremacy of English and the English Parliament. O'Connell answered that if he could hope to bring on the repeal by such means, he would not prevent that petition from being presented. Right was on the side of Ireland, and power on the side of England; and if Ireland had once the power of ruling itself, a mere matter of form could not stand in its way, nor prejudice its right.

"One of the guests then remarked, how difficult it would be to bring England to a compromise. O'Connell answered, that the emancipation in 1829, even to the last hour of its passing, was so improbable, that nothing in England's conduct to Ireland could be despaired of as improbable.

"He then spoke of his own plans, and said, that the way in which new epochs were founded in history, were in a manner quite new, and without precedent. The Magna Charta had been obtained by unconstitutional means, and so had the foundation of the Orange and Hanoverian dynasties. Such new regulations were themselves a precedent, if they were founded upon necessity and the state of circumstances. John then brought the conversation upon the Dublin press, and I complained that they did not, like the London press, make the affairs peculiar to the country and acts of the national meetings the subject for leading articles. O'Connell agreed that the journals were very unimportant, and that there was only one of the journals which had really well-written articles. I wondered at these complaints, but much more so when I found out that O'Connell, in spite of his power, left the Dublin press to its entire freedom. There was another remark which astonished me much. O'Connell said, that Peel's *do nothing* policy was the very best for him. *All that Peel could do would only do harm to* ENGLAND.

"John O'Connell gave his father a *fête* yesterday, to which I had the honour of an invitation. I rejoice to have had an opportunity of observing Daniel O'Connell in another point of view. The Irish have an admirable custom in summer of entertaining their company, as much as possible, in the open air. They are a poetical people, and feel that nature is required to set off the most splendid feast. John O'Connell had chosen Dalkey Island for that purpose. This island is situated at the southernmost extremity of Dublin Bay; its position is very beautiful, the island itself is a steep rock, upon which only a scanty herbage grows. A Martello tower, a signal house, and the ruins of an old chapel—where in Ireland is there a place without ruins—are the only signs to show that the island is not uninhabited. The tower and signal house are English, but the rock and the ruins are Irish. The weather was not very inviting, and I preferred going by land to the shore opposite Dalkey Island, whilst part of the company, with Mr. O'Connell, were to go in a boat from Kingstown; but the sea-sickness taught them better, and they came to a resolution to give up the island which required so unfriendly a passage. Therefore, when I came to the railway station in Kingstown I learnt from a servant of O'Connell's that the guests who had chosen the road by *terra firma* had changed the plan of campaign, and that we were to assemble at the cottage of Dr. M'Donald.

"We lost nothing by this change. I knew this cottage well; it was one of my favourite resorts. There is a splendid sea view there. In order to reach this cottage one must pass over the cape which separates Dublin Bay from the sea. At the extremity of this point there is a wall which has stone steps leading up to its top. On one side of these steps is a beautiful view of Dalkey Island, Kingstown, and Dublin Bay; and on the other one sees Killiney Bay. Dr. M'Donald's cottage is situated in a position which commands the most beautiful view. In front is the sea stretching in a semi-circle, and beginning almost at our feet; to the right wild and steep rocks, against which the waves dash. Above these are Killiney mountains, which seem to give the hand to the county Wicklow. Three or four chains of mountains, one over the other, and a tongue of land, stretching forth into the sea, like a confused mass of rocks heaped together, surround a quiet, luxuriant, and blossoming valley of several miles extent. I never saw such contrasts of colour so beautifully blended, and if one was transported there on a summer's evening, one would imagine oneself in the genial clime of the south. When I arrived at the rendezvous the company had already assembled. There seemed to be a great dread of sea sickness. The gentlemen read the papers, and the ladies reposed. This cottage was not such a musty, roomless country house as there is generally in Ireland. The table was laid with cold viands, and in a corner there was another table upon which coats, shawls, hats, umbrellas, and parasols were placed. The company consisted of O'Connell's whole family—sons, daughters, brothers-in-law, and grandchildren—Mr. Thomas Steele, Mr. and Mrs. F., Mrs. A., and myself. Mr. F. proposed a walk before dining, and I voted for the proposition. It was adopted by a minority, and they immediately set forth, to my regret. My sense of duty did not permit me to remain, although the majority was more interesting to me than the minority; but at dinner-time we all assembled together again. I think in this world there is nothing so unfortunate as to have a bad stomach. All of our guests—and I think the Irish in general—have no reason to complain in this respect. All O'Connell's friends and kinsmen attacked the bottle with great assiduity, but I was obliged to act teetotaller. Had I dared to place my inclination against my duty I should have fallen; for, without any other merit, it is very hard to be a martyr to abstinence.

"After dinner Tom Steele stood up, and spoke, with comic pathos, a speech which filled me with some anxiety. He said neither more nor less than that we were under a great *delusion*, that we might think we were in a cottage on the mainland, but that in reality and truth, we were, that blessed minute, in the island of Dalkey. Every one laughed, but I was in some perplexity to know what the worthy Tom meant, till a neighbour explained the riddle to me.

"Before the revolution of '98, Dalkey Island was renowned for its king. Once every year all Dublin issued forth to this island to choose a king thereof. The monarch was of the same kind as the jolly king of Yvetot, in France. The deepest drinkers were his first dignitaries. Unhappy Ireland! There came a time when even this innocent joke became a terror to the rulers of Ireland, and means of fun for her sons. It was a national *fête*, and it was quite enough, in order to make it joyous for the patriot, that it should be suspicious to the oppressor. The Irish, who, on Dalkey shore, cried, '*Long live the King of Dalkey!*' filled the Castle with alarm; the celebration was treasonable, and therefore was highly prized. Tom Steele's speech had no other aim than to resuscitate this anniversary, and for this reason he informed us that our *terra firma* cottage was positively on Dalkey Island. All agreed with him; and while the circumstance was explained to me, the election took place. It fell upon Mr. Fitzpatrick, who, on the spot, and without much ceremony, was proclaimed king. All his subjects drank to his health, in answer whereto he spoke a long and beautiful address, just as if he had been born King of Prussia or of France. It was easy to see that kingship was not so awful a burthen, though the bearer strove to make it appear of a certain weight. At last he said, I must name a prime minister to manage affairs of state, and he named Dan O'Connell to the post; we drank approbation and good luck to the choice. O'Connell rose and returned a short speech of thanks, and straight he elevated Tom Steele to the office of Chancellor, he being allowedly most learned in the law. Tom Steele then returned thanks in another speech, and declared his intention to administer law and equity as badly as he possibly could, as was the duty of a legitimate Lord Chancellor. Then O'Connell appointed a court fool, a lord of the bed-chamber, naming for the latter place a young man who spent 18 hours out of the 24 in bed, and who devoted the remaining six to his pipe. I had the honour of being appointed Home Secretary, by right of my being a foreigner; and I declared, in gratitude, my fitness to fill the place, being, in about eight days, to quit the shore of Ireland. The War Minister was a lady, who certainly had a whole park of artillery in her eyes, and another dame was appointed commander-in-chief of the army. The wildest young devil among O'Connell's grandchildren was named master of the ceremonies; and the most taciturn and quiet young man of the company, who had not a word to say, was appointed Speaker of the

House of Commons. But still water runs deep, and the new speaker made a most appropriate speech, being in the following terms, '*Mum, is the word.*' There reigned the most beautiful and indescribable fun and jollity that it is possible to conceive. Man and wife, old and young, grandfather and grandchild, all mingled and played gaily together. It is easy to conceive that the English, who amuse themselves as Froissart says, *moult tristement* could not comprehend this, or render it compatible with the seriousness of life. For an Englishman to see O'Connell at such a moment, would have begotten in him the conclusion, that there was no earnestness in the patriot. A Frenchman might understand this gaiety, or even a German, but an Englishman could only understand it in a comedian; and such is the character which the English bestow upon O'Connell. He has shown himself thus once or twice in London, and this has sufficed to obtain for him such a false and hypocritical character there."

Having indulged in so long an extract, we cannot expatiate much longer on the rest of the work. The following list of the principal chapters will give the best idea of it:—Athlone Meeting; Dundalk ditto; Tara ditto; Dublin, the Repeal Association; the Catholic Clergy; Popular Literature; Father Mathew; the Peasantry; the Anti-Repealers; the North. Nor is M. Venedey all absorbed in Irish party. Thus, in Athlone, though he finds the people tolerant, he finds the priesthood lacking that quality, and he is very indignant at Mr. Murray's being deposed from the office of repeal warden, because he was displeasing to the priest. Had M. Venedey remained longer in Ireland, we should have had more bursts of this kind.

"Everything in Ireland," says he on another occasion, "is half ready and half in its place—house, church, Parliament; aye, even people's stockings."

But we must conclude, strongly recommending Herr Venedey's volumes to whoever is fortunate to lay hold upon them; and we would recommend any one with that intention to be quick; for the Prussian censors have a peculiar grudge to Cologne exiles; and though Leipzig be fortunately out of Prussian beat, still the Berlin police have sufficient influence in Saxony to get the present volumes piled in a mortar, as the Duc de Rovigo, by order of Napoleon, served Madame de Stael's "Corrine."[2]

---

[2] See Lady Blennerhasset, *Frau von Staël: ihre Freunde und ihre Bedeutung in Politik und Literatur,* three volumes (Berlin, 1889), III, 282-3. The book thus dealt with was *De l'Allemagne,* not *Corinne.*

[20 MARCH 1844]

Ireland and its Rulers, since 1829.　Part the first, and Part the
　second.[1]　　　　　　　　　　　　　　　　　　　　　　　[Newby.

The first part of this work has been for some time before the
public, and has reached a second edition.　The appearance of
the second part affords us an opportunity of making a few remarks upon the whole.　It contains much which we admire,
and not a little which we must condemn; but, good or bad, it
is certain to be pretty widely read, for it is very able, very personal,
and very bitter.

The first thing that strikes us is, that while the author is pro-
fessedly and evidently an Irishman, it is impossible to identify
him with any section of Irish party.　His political opinions and
tone form a combination indicative rather of an isolated thinker
than of an active partizan, and yet his narrative of political
struggles is so vivid, and his portraits of individuals so full of
characteristic traits, that we must give him credit, not merely
for keen powers of observation, but for having had peculiar
opportunities of knowing minutely the events of the last twelve
or fourteen years.　His views agree in many respects with those
of the Whig party, and he speaks more highly of the Mulgrave
government than of any previous Irish administration; but how
far he can be considered a Whig partizan may be judged of
from the fact, that while one of the most elaborate parts of his
work is a sarcastic and very unjust depreciation of Mr. Sheil, he
exhausts his ingenuity in finding apologies for Lord Stanley.
O'Connell's career is depicted with considerable power, but his
errors are censured with unsparing severity, and the whole system of repeal agitation and the "Corn Exchangers," who have
carried it on, are treated with contemptuous indignation, as in-
struments by which the *mind* of Ireland has been degraded.

The two volumes before us contain a somewhat irregular history of Irish politics, from the passing of the Catholic Relief
Bill to the time of the Mulgrave government, interspersed with
original observations and sketches of prominent public men.　The
treatment of the whole subject is distinguished by freedom and

---

[1] A work by D. Owen Madden published in 1843-4. Only the first two
of its three parts are here reviewed.

force, both of thought and of style, and we find frequent evidences of a mixture of earnest feeling with philosophical reflectiveness, which is not very common. The characteristic sketches of individuals, though occasionally rather too much spun out, are brilliant and full of point, and are upon the whole the best parts of the work, but the political ideas of the author are also well deserving of attention. His fundamental principle is, that there are, in fact, two *nations* in Ireland, the "upper nation," as he calls it, nearly coinciding with the Protestant population, and the "lower nation," consisting of the Roman Catholics.[2] This distinction has been often insisted upon in one shape or other, but we do not remember to have seen it ever put forth so prominently, or carried out into so many practical conclusions as in the present work. One result is that the author regards the Protestant church of Ireland as an indispensable support of the union. Remove it, he says, and you remove the great motive which attaches the majority of the Protestants to British connection, and you throw them under the influence of feelings of nationality, which would then animate the whole people of Ireland to seek an independent Parliament. A Catholic endowment, therefore, is the means by which he would bring about religious equality and attach the Roman Catholic church to the imperial government. The following are extracts from the chapter on the Church of Ireland, in the second part:—

"The Church is far more dear to that upper nation in Ireland than its sister establishment is to any of the English people. It is connected with all that the Irish upper nation holds most venerable and dear. Whatever of historic pride—whatever of transmitted associations—whatever of inspiring recollections are common to the Irish Protestant, are clustered around the Establishment. . . . At present the Irish Protestants have a great deal of smothered national feeling. They may be distinct from their Catholic countrymen—they are equally so from the natives of England. Their psychology is national, though their politics are imperial. They have more self-control—more self-reliance than their Catholic countrymen; but who that is familiar with their minds but knows that they are full of Irish ardour—of Irish love for whatever is dashing and splendid; and that, in favourable circumstances, they are just the body who, backed by the Catholic multitudes, would achieve a revolution in Ireland, whose vibration would be felt wherever a single

---

[2] It may be surmised that Disraeli found a hint in this distinction for his famous account in *Sybil* of "Two nations . . . The rich and the poor." See below, p. 81.

foundation of British empire has been laid? It would certainly be a most magnificent consummation of Irish history, if that proud and fiery body, the Protestants of Ireland, should, inflamed by a generous nationality—marshal in the ranks of their Catholic countrymen—unfurl the standard of Orange and Green, and, in casting off the shackles of England, display their hereditary valour in fields that would eclipse the glories of Derry and the Boyne. If the Protestants should place themselves at the head of the Catholics, the enthusiasm of the Irish would know no bounds; but it would not escape idly: directed by phlegmatic caution, it would be the impulse to deeds of patriotism and glory. A grand new nation would result from the combination of both, and that lovely island would at length be inhabited by an entire people— rejoicing in their nationality, and aspiring to a place amongst the powers of Europe. . . .

"By the destruction of the Protestant establishment you would unfix a vast amount of that most dangerous and explosive of all political elements—*mind*. Those only who know the state of Ireland can be aware of the number of *minds dangerous to England* that are now quietly muzzled by the Protestant establishment. Three-fourths of the intellect—acquirements—and energy of Trinity College, with all its auxiliary classes are completely imperialized, merely in consequence of the church establishment. The MIND of Ireland has never yet fairly inflamed the brute force of the country. All the movements against England have for the most part been directed by mere agitators, with their half braggadocio style of patriotism—persons often of patriotic sensibilities, but without the head to conceive the methods for regenerating the nation in such a complicated mass of difficulties. Ay! or without the genuine moral power that springs from cool convictions—sceptical intellects devoted to ambitious ends—from acquirements, from educated ability—from judgment quickened by noble ambition—from knowledge inflamed by national passion. What the masses of Ireland want in order to enable them to rock the British power to its very base, is a well-trained corps of noble—gallant—and ambitious minds, filled with exalting ideas gathered from a generous view of things, and disciplined by intellectual pursuits—by philosophical studies—by scientific habits."

The spirited narratives, in the first part of the "Doneraile Conspiracy," and the "Rig of Feargus O'Connor," are curious and valuable illustrations of Irish political life. Of the second part, a large portion is devoted to individual sketches, the principal subjects being Lord Wellesley, Chief Justice Bushe, Baron Smith, Chief Baron Woulfe—all dealt with in a spirit of generous appreciation; and Mr. Sheil, who, on the contrary, is treated in a manner neither generous nor just. As a specimen of the author's power of portrait-painting, we give an extract from his chapter on Lord Normanby's government:—

MADDEN'S *Ireland and its Rulers, since 1829*

A POPULAR LORD-LIEUTENANT.

"First, there was the Earl of Mulgrave, who really seemed to have been specially designed by nature for an Irish lord-lieutenant. In figure—accomplishments—habits—and talents, he was the nearest approximation ever witnessed to the ideal of an Hibernian viceroy. His *personnel* as a lord-lieutenant was perfection itself, and he only wanted two external qualifications for that office, viz.—an illustrious lineage, and a vast estate. But the exalted station made the first defect forgotten, and the absence of splendid wealth, like that of the Bedfords and Northumberlands, rendered his dashing generosity—the gay hospitality—and innumerable acts of kindness, more admirable and loveable in the eyes of his enthusiastic followers. Never surely did any lord-lieutenant exhibit a more amiable, generous, and princely disposition. Without a tenth part of the resources that former viceroys possessed—without the aid of the Irish aristocracy—he, nevertheless, by his tact and skill, contrived to keep up one of the most showy and sparkling vice-royalties that ever gratified the local pride of the Dublin public, and the provincial tastes of the Irish gentry. He was gay, dashing, and brilliant—always setting something on foot to amuse and gratify the public, who were caught, 'at first sight,' by his flashy, and semi-military appearance, as he gracefully curvetted through the streets of the most brilliant provincial city in Europe. He looked, dressed, and acted the part inimitably. He was a super-excellent impersonation of 'his Excellency the Lord-Lieutenant.' And what added to the charm of his appearance and bearing in Irish eyes, was that he really looked and bore himself so like a brilliant and accomplished Irishman. He was not a bluff, red-faced Englishman, or a phlegmatic British Peer, stiff and stubborn as one of his ancestral oak trees. He was full of the vivid and demonstrative character of the Irishman. Fashionable, vivacious, anxious to make all happy, with a relish for pleasure, and a gallant deportment, with a witty head and a generous heart—he was more like a Milesian than a Saxon peer. He possessed great quickness for discerning the manners and habits of the country, and, instead of preserving the *retenue* of May-fair, he adopted something of a demonstrative and familiar deportment. He looked as if he was some Lord Gerald de Normanby, or some Count Phelim O'Mulgrave, or Sir Carny Fitzphipps, that had suddenly started into life from the pages of one of Miss Edgeworth's or Lady Morgan's novels. He possessed the art of returning public salutations to perfection; the move of his hand was quite inimitable; his bow was worthy of Mr. Charles Kemble; his eyes sparkled with true Milesian fire; the graceful fluency of his reply to deputations was worthy of a chastened Irish orator, sparing in smiles, subdued in diction. The temper with which he encountered his Tory opponents was quite Irish; with dauntless gaiety, and sanguine light-heartedness, he made light of opposition; in society he was affable, condescending, as ready to impart as receive pleasure.

"In his politics he acted on the principle that 'Ireland has feelings that must be flattered, and prejudices and habits that to be conquered must be rooted.' His great success, his vast public effort (so far as he was personally concerned) was owing to his wise congeniality with the people and their manners. He made all around him forget that he was an Englishman, and he was looked on as a native 'racy of the soil,' not merely by the populace, but by the gentry of the land."

The character of the late Chief Baron Woulfe appears to be the author's favourite subject; and his delineation of that eminent and excellent person is equally true and beautiful. Mr. Woulfe was a man in whom the most enlightened views were happily combined with integrity, courage, and decision of character; and it was not the least merit of the Mulgrave administration that it appreciated his virtues and abilities, and raised him to a suitable position.

We have not space for further reference to various topics contained in "Ireland and its Rulers," but we may say generally that we remember no recent work on Irish politics written with half so much ability. The wilfulness with which the author launches his sarcasms on all sides, and the dogmatic style in which he is apt to announce his decisions, are sometimes painful, and often provoking enough; but they do not prevent us from recognising a pervading earnestness and honesty of purpose, or from admiring the knowledge of life, penetration, and eloquence which the work displays.

....

[2 APRIL 1844]

A New Spirit of the Age, edited by R. H. HORNE.
[London, Smith and Elder.

There is an easy candour about Mr. Horne which ought to encourage all persons to deal with him with similar sincerity. He appears to us to be generous, honest, in the main good humoured (for in the only instance in which his spleen is shown in the two volumes of the "New Spirit of the Age," it is pardonable, on account of a sort of clumsy sincerity), and he admires rightly, and not mean persons nor qualities. But having awarded the "New Spirit of the Age" praise so far, the critic finds himself at a loss for further subjects of commendation, nay, may feel himself called upon to elevate his voice in tones akin to reproof.

For it is not only necessary that a man should be a perfectly honest and well-meaning individual, but that he should have something novel, or striking, or witty, or profound, to make his works agreeable or useful to the world. Thus, to say that "Shakspeare is a great poet," that "hot roast beef is an excellent food for man, and may be advantageously eaten cold the next day," that "two multiplied by three equals six," that "her Majesty Queen Anne has ceased to exist," is to advance what is perfectly just and reasonable; but other thinkers have attained the same knowledge of facts and history, and coinciding perfectly with every one of these propositions, may not care to have them discussed in print. A number of such undeniable verities are gravely discussed in the two portly volumes, entitled the "New Spirit of the Age." Why the "New Spirit?" Is the work offered as a successor to Hazlitt's book, which bore (without the epithet) the same title? The author of the "Spirit of the Age" was one of the keenest and brightest critics that ever lived. With partialities and prejudices innumerable, he had a wit so keen, a sensibility so exquisite, an appreciation of humour, or pathos, or even of the greatest art, so lively, quick, and cultivated, that it was always good to know what were the impressions made by books, or men, or pictures on such a mind; and that, as there were not probably a dozen men in England with powers so varied, all the rest of the world might be rejoiced to listen to the opinions of this accomplished critic. He was of so different a caste to the people who gave authority in his day—the pompous big-wigs and schoolmen, who never could pardon him his familiarity of manner, so unlike their own—his popular, too popular, habits and sympathies, so much beneath their dignity—his loose disorderly education, gathered here and there at book-stalls or picture galleries, where he laboured a penniless student, in lonely journeys over Europe, tramped on foot (and not made according to the fashion of the regular critics of the day, by the side of a young nobleman in a post-chaise), in every school of knowledge, from St. Peter's at Rome, to St. Giles's in London. In all his modes of life and thought he was so different from the established authorities, with their degrees and white neck-cloths, that they hooted the man down with all the power of their lungs, and disdained to hear truth that came from such a ragged philosopher.

We do not believe that Mr. Horne has inherited any portion

of the stained, travel-worn old mantle which Hazlitt left behind him. He is enveloped in a good stout suit of the undeniable Bow-bell cut; rather more splendid in the way of decoration than is usual out of the district; but it is the wear of an honest, portly, good-humoured man. Under the fine waistcoat there beats a kindly heart, and in the pocket there is a hand that has a warm grasp for a friend, and a welcome twopence for the poor.

To drop this tailor's metaphor (which will not be quarrelled with by those who remember that Mr. Carlyle has written a volume upon it), we will briefly say, that beyond the qualifications of justice and good humour, we cannot see that Mr. Horne has any right to assume the critical office. In the old "Spirit of the Age," you cannot read a page that does not contain something startling, brilliant—some strange paradox, or some bright dazzling truth. Be the opinion right or wrong, the reader's mind is always set a thinking—amazed, if not by the justness of the thoughts, by their novelty and daring. There are no such rays started from the lantern of Horne. There are words—such a cornucopia of them as the world has few examples of; but the thoughts are scarce in the midst of this plentifulness, the opinions for the most part perfectly irreproachable, and the *ennui* caused by their utterance profound.

The "Spirit of the Age" gives us pictures of a considerable number of the foremost literary characters of the day. It is to be followed, should the design of the projectors be fully carried out, "by the political spirit of the age, the scientific spirit of the age, the artistical spirit of the age, and the historical, biographical, and critical spirit of the age," nay, an infantine spirit of the age is also hinted at as a dreadful possibility. The matter is serious, as it will be seen. Only give Mr. Horne encouragement to the task, and he will go and do it. He never doubts about anything. He would write the dancing spirit of the age, or the haberdashing spirit of the age, with as little hesitation; and give you a dissertation upon bombasines, or a disquisition on the true principles of the fandango. In the interest of the nation, people ought to speak, and beg him to be quiet. Now is the time to entreat him to hold his hand; otherwise, all ranks and classes in the empire, from Doctor Wiseman to Fanny Elssler, may find themselves caught, their bodies and souls turned inside out, so to speak, by this frightful observer, and consigned to posterity in red calico.

For the sake of the public, we say, stop; we go down on our knees, like Lord Brougham, and say so.

Mr. Horne has received assistance in his task from "several eminent individuals,"[1] but their names are not [given]; and, as the editor says, with a becoming simplicity, that he deliberated with himself "a good half hour" as to "whether he should try to please everybody," and determined, after the conclusion of that tremendous cogitation, to try and please only one, viz.—himself, he stands the sponsor of the eminent individuals who remain in the shade, and we trust heartily that his satisfaction is complete.

From the tone of the volumes it would seem so. There is not the least pride about the author, who only delivers his opinions for what they will fetch, saying to the public, "Take your change out of that, I believe it to be pure gold;" nor will he be angry, he says, if any sceptic should doubt the authenticity of the bullion. This calm faith is a quality possessed by the very highest souls.

The calm genius glances over the entire field of English literature. From Dr. Pusey to *Punch* nothing escapes the searching inevitable inquiry. He weighs all claims in the great balance of his intelligence, and metes to each his due. Hazlitt used sometimes to be angry; Horne never is. Twice in the course of his lectures he lays "an iron hand," as he calls it (perhaps leaden would have been the better epithet; but Mr. Horne is, as we have said, a judge of his own metal), upon unlucky offenders; but it is in the discharge of his moral duties, and his pleasure, clearly, is, to preach rather than to punish. Indeed, whatever may be thought with regard to the quality of the doctrine, all must agree that the preacher is a kindly soul, and would hurt no man alive.

We cannot invite the reader to discuss all the opinions contained in the "Spirit;" but we may glance at a couple of the most elaborate (though not the best) notices to be found in the volumes, the first of which thus opens with the author's opinions upon—what shall we say?—upon things in general:—

"If an extensive experience and knowledge of the world be certain in most cases to render a man suspicious, full of doubts and incredulities, equally certain is it that with other men such experience and such knowledge exercise this influence at rare intervals only, or in a far less degree; while in some respects the influence even acts in a directly opposite way, and the extraordinary things they have seen or suffered,

[1] Chief among them Elizabeth Barrett.

cause them to be very credulous and of open-armed faith to embrace
strange novelties. They are not startled at the sound of fresh wonders
in the moral or physical world—they laugh at no feasible theory, and
can see truth through the refractions of paradox and contradictory
extremes. They *know* that there are more things in heaven and on the
earth than in 'your philosophy.' They observe the fables and the visions
of one age become the facts and practices of a succeeding age—perhaps
even of a few years after their first announcement, and before the world
has done laughing: they are slow to declare any character or action to
be unnatural, having so often witnessed some of the extreme lights and
shadows which flit upon the outskirts of nature's capacious circle, and
have perhaps themselves been made to feel the bitter reality of various
classes of anomaly previously unaccountable, if not incredible. They
have discovered that in matters of practical conduct a greater blunder
cannot in general be made than to 'judge of others by yourself,' or what
you think, feel, and fancy of yourself. But having found out that the
world is not 'all alike,' though like enough for the charities of real life,
they identify themselves with other individualities, then search within
for every actual and imaginary resemblance to the great majority of
their fellow-creatures, which may give them a more intimate knowledge of
aggregate nature, and thus enlarge the bounds of unexclusive sympathy.

"To men of this genial habit and maturity of mind, if also they have
an observing eye for externals, there is usually a very tardy admission
of the alleged madness of a picture of scenery, or the supposed grossness of a caricature of the human countenance. The traveller and the
voyager, who has, moreover, an eye for art, has often seen enough to
convince him that the genius of Turner and Martin has its foundation
not only in elemental but in actual truth; nor could such an observer
go into any large concourse of people (especially of the poorer classes,
where the unsuppressed character has been suffered to rise completely
to the surface) without seeing several faces, which, by the addition of
the vices of social man, might cause many a dumb animal to feel indignant at the undoubtedly deteriorated resemblance. The curse of evil
circumstances acting upon the 'third and fourth generation,' when added
to the 'sins of the fathers,' can and does turn the lost face of humanity
into something worse than brutish. As with the face, so is it with the
character of mankind; nothing can be too lofty, too noble, too lovely
to be natural; nor can anything be too vicious, too brutalized, too mean,
or too ridiculous. It is observable, however, that there are many degrees and fine shades in these frequent degradations of man to the mere
animal. Occasionally they are no degradation, but rather an advantage,
as a falcon eye, or a lion-brow, will strikingly attest. But more generally
the effect is either gravely humorous, or grotesquely comic; and in these
cases the dumb original is not complimented. For you may see a man
with a bull's forehead and neck, and a mean grovelling countenance
(while that of the bull is physically grand and high purposed), and the
dog, the sheep, the bird, and the ape in all their varieties, are often
seen with such admixtures as are really no advantage. Several times
in an individual's life he may meet in the actual world with most of

the best and worst kind of faces and characters of the world of fiction. It is true that there are not to be found a whole tribe of Quilps and Quasimodos (you would not *wish* it); but once in the life of the student of character he may have a glimpse of just such a creature; and that, methinks, were quite familiar proof enough both for nature and art. Those who have exclusively portrayed the pure ideal in grandeur or beauty, and those also who have exclusively, or chiefly, portrayed monstrosities and absurdities, have been recluse men, who drew with an inward eye, and copied from their imaginations: the men who have given us the largest amount of truth under the greatest variety of forms, have always been those who went abroad into the world in all its ways; and in the works of such men will always be found those touches of nature which can only be copied at first-hand, and the extremes of which originalities are never unnaturally exceeded. There are no caricatures in the portraits of Hogarth, nor are there any in those of Dickens. The most striking thing in both, is their apparently inexhaustible variety and truth of character."

The above sentence may be put down as thus:—Extensive knowledge of the world makes some men incredulous, some men less incredulous, some men exceedingly credulous. These latter, taking experience and history into account, end by being astonished at nothing. They have remarked "the lights and shadows flitting on the outskirts of nature's capacious circle," so as to make themselves aware of "the bitter reality of various classes of anomaly." They then find that they must not judge of others by themselves; they then identify themselves with other individualities, and they then plunge into a process entirely undescribable, in which they search within for an actual and imaginary resemblance to the majority of their fellow-creatures, a more intimate knowledge of aggregate nature, by which "they enlarge the bounds of their sympathy."

If these people have an eye for externals, they will scarce allow that any picture is mad, or the grossness of any caricature; and, as regards the latter, they will see in the poorer classes such faces, resembling animals, as might make the animals themselves ashamed of their human types. In faces, or souls, there is nothing too hideous on the one side, or too pure on the other. (Then follow further illustrations of the fact by which apes, sheep, birds, and high-purposed bulls, are made to be ashamed of their likenesses among men.) All these points are to be observed by the man of genius—Hogarth and Dickens are men of genius—therefore there is no distortion in the works of Hogarth and Dickens.

What does all this mean, letting alone the big words?—letting alone "the lights and shadows flitting on the outskirts of nature's circle," the process of "searching within for imaginary resemblances with mankind," the distinction between "actual and elementary truth," the indignation of the dumb animals, the physical high purpose of the bull's head?—It means, as we take it, that there are amazing varieties in nature; that what seems monstrous and absurd is often natural; that Dickens and Hogarth have observed many of these extremes, and that there are no caricatures in their portraits. After a wind and war of words, exploding incoherently over five pages, you get an assertion that "there are more things in heaven and earth than are dreamed of in our philosophy," an assertion that men are like animals in features, which is of similar novelty, and an assertion that Dickens and Hogarth do not caricature, which any body may believe or disbelieve at pleasure.

Bating the confusion of metaphors, this is all very well meaning; but well meaning is not enough for "The Spirit of the Age." Men cannot go on in this way, unwrapping little stale truths from the midst of such enormous envelopes as these. We have no time for such labour: we have the debates to read, Lord Brougham up every night, the League[2] and Anti-league meetings, and private business to attend to. Ah, Mr. Horne, why did you take Hazlitt's name in vain!

Having brought Mr. Dickens and Hogarth together, "The Spirit of the Age" proceeds to say that both are moral comic artists, and that they are alike; then, to show that they are unlike, or, in other words, that Hogarth is Hogarth after all, and Dickens Dickens, he notices with just approval the kindly spirit which animates both—the peeps of love and sweetness which we have in their darkest scenes. He discovers Mr. Dickens's propensity to animate inanimate objects, and make nature bear witness to the ludicrous or the tragic moral in the author's mind. He shows also Mr. Dickens's manner of writing rhythmical prose, and takes the pains to set out some passages in blank verse, of different metres, for the reader's benefit. Has not every one with a fair share of brains made the same discoveries long ago; and was there a necessity to propound them now, any more

---

[2] The anti-corn law league, whose agitation for free trade in wheat was at this time reaching its height.

than to declare that apple-pie is good, and Queen Elizabeth no more?

The second volume of the series opens with a fine portrait of Mr. Tennyson, and much hearty and just approbation on the writer's part of the merits of that great poet. These just remarks are prefaced by such stuff as this:—

"The poetic fire is one simple and intense element in human nature; it has its source in the divine mysteries of our existence; it developes with the first abstract delight of childhood, the first youthful aspirations towards something beyond our mortal reach; and eventually becomes the master passion of those who are possessed with it in the highest degree, and the most ennobling and refining influence that can be exercised upon the passions of others. At times, and in various degrees, all are open to the influence of the poetic element. Its objects are palpable to the external senses, in proportion as individual perception and sensibility have been habituated to contemplate them with interest and delight; and palpable to the imagination in proportion as an individual possesses this faculty, and has habituated it to ideal subjects and profoundly sympathetic reflections. If there be a third condition of its presence, it must be that of a certain consciousness of dreamy glories in the soul, with vague emotions, aimless impulses, and prophetic sensations, which may be said to tremble on the extreme verge of the fermenting source of that poetic fire, by which the life of humanity is purified and adorned. The first and second of these conditions must be clear to all; the last will not receive so general an admission, and perhaps may not be so intelligible to everybody as could be wished. We thus arrive at the conclusion that the poetic element, though simple and entire, has yet various forms and modifications of development according to individual nature and circumstance, and, therefore, that its loftiest or subtlest manifestations are not equally apparent to the average mass of human intelligence. He, then, who can give a form and expression to these lofty or these subtle manifestations, in a way that shall be the most intelligible to the majority, is he who best accomplishes the mission of a poet."

It is the speech we, however, before quoted, spoken in different words; for our lecturer, before entering on his subject, seems to be partial to prefacing it by a general roar, to call the attention of the audience. But what have we here? "The poetic fire is one simple and intense element of our nature." What does this mean?—this simple and intense element? Suppose he had begun by saying that the poetic genius was a subtle and complex essence distilled from the innumerable conduits which lead from the alembic of the brain? We should have been just as wise, should have had just as much notion of the fluid as of the fire, and the

deductions might have been continued. Some men have more
poetic fire, some less, in some it is strong, in some vague—which
we take to be the meaning of the big words. The assertion which
follows we gladly admit, that Mr. Tennyson is a poet of the
highest class, and one "whose writings may be considered as
peculiarly lucid to all competent understandings that have cultivated a love for poetry." In this pompous way our author will
talk. We do not here quarrel with the sentiment—which is, that
the best judges of poetry think Mr. Tennyson a great poet—but
with the manner of expressing it, the persevering flatulence of
words. Mr. Horne then turns away to speak of Keats. Like
Tennyson, and yet unlike, and, with a true and honest admiration for the genius of both (for, as we have said before, Mr.
Horne's admirations appear to us to be well placed, and his
sympathies generous and noble), he begins to characterize the
poet, and is impelled by his usual *afflatus*. He is tumbling about
among the "essences" and "elements" forthwith. "He has
painted the inner and essential life of the gods;" "his imagination
identified itself with the essences of things;" "his influence has
been spiritual in its ideality;" and, profiting by his example,
"kindred spirits will recognize the voice from other spheres, and
will have their inherent impulses quickened to look into their
own hearts, and to work out the purposes of their souls." As
for Tennyson, "the art *stands* up in his poems self-proclaimed,
and not any mere modification of thought and language, but
the operation of a separate and definite power in the human
faculties." "He has the most wonderful command of language,
without having recourse to exotic terminologies." Certain of
"his heroines are transcendentalisms of the senses, examples of
the Homeric ειδωλα, or rather descendants of the ειδωλα, lovely
underbodies, which no German critic would hesitate to take to his
visionary arms." But we, says the "Spirit of the Age," are such
a people for "beef." . . .

Well, why not? Beef is better than this—beef is better than
wind—better, nay more poetical, than exotic terminologies—the
"underbody" of the sirloin is better than the descendant of the
Greek ειδωλον, whom German philosophers are in the habit of
hugging. Above all, the practisers of βοολατρεια, call their god
by his name of Beef. It would be just as easy as not, to call it
an element or an eon; to call soup an essence, or a round of

beef a circle of the god, or cabbage a green horticultural emana-
tion, which commingled with concoct particles of the animals
which Egyptians worship, which Brahmins adore, and whose form
once Zeus assumed, is denominated in the Anglo-Saxon vocabu-
lary, bubble and squeak; but it is best not to seek after exotic
terminologies, and so the beef-eater says, bubble and squeak at
once. This bull baiting is ungrateful and unnatural. Let not
the noble animal die gored to death, and by a Horne.

For a great deal of benefit has the author of the "Spirit of
the Age" had from the despised quadruped. He is "morally
high-purposed," as he says bullocks are physically. He is never
ungenerous or unmanly; his sympathies are honourable and well
placed; and he tells the truth as far as he knows it. So as he
deals with others ought he to be done by; and as in these volumes
he has not hesitated to lay hold of an amusing poet, and worry
his harmless phantasies as if they were the gravest and deepest
crimes; and as he has taken to himself the title formerly adopted
by the most brilliant of critics, and as he has no business to be
left in possession of that dignity of spirit of the age; and as he
mistakes words for meanings, and can see no further into a millstone than other folk, so let the critic, imitating his words. to the
unlucky wag in question, lay a friendly hand on his shoulder
and say, yawning, "Friend, a great deal too much of this."

....

[4 APRIL 1844]

The Three Kingdoms. By the Vicomte D'ARLINCOURT. 2 vols.
[London. Bentley. 1844.

French writers have certainly the gift of longevity, if not of
immortality. There are a dozen of them who seem to have lived
from all time, or who, like poor Tom Hill,[1] date their nativity
from some unfathomable depth of the last century. There is
Paul de Kock, who has written a novel every year of the past

---

[1] A well-known character of the London literary world, who had died
in 1840 at the age of eighty. Thackeray is supposed to have put him
into chapter thirty of *Pendennis* as Mr. Archer.

hundred, and who is as young and vivacious as the first day—there is Chateaubriand, just as pompous, pretentious, and as admirable a pamphleteer as ever—there is; but why run over the list of the *Academy*. The profession of letters in England seems to be accompanied by a wear and tear of spirit, an exhaustion of the principle of life; for its followers drop off early, and cease to haunt the world as spectres in the vacancy of age. The French materialists must have substituted some more durable machinery, for their very poets thrive on the working, and all find in the pen a philosopher's stone, which excels Dr. Everybody's pills in bestowing health, wealth, and longevity.

We have heard of M. Le Vicomte d'Arlincourt for an incalculable series of years.[2] Somewhere about the year 1818 or 1819, the French were awakened to the discovery that there might be some other work of fiction than Pigault Le Brun's, or Paul de Kock's novels, whose lively, rattling, vulgar and licentious, and therefore very natural characters and dialogues, formed the idea of the times. The courtiers of the restored Bourbons cried fie! upon the vulgarity, if not upon the licentiousness; and up started Monsieur Le Vicomte to tell of sylphs with azure eyes, and romantic heroes to match; which, if he did not find in Newman-street, he had the honour of re-inventing. D'Arlincourt excited stouter minds and quills, who dethroned him after a reign of some four or five years. And we really thought, we had almost said hoped, that M. D'Arlincourt had disappeared, and been buried with the kings and courtiers of the restoration.

Not so. It appears he is alive, and as amiable as ever, and in these pages tunes his old lute to the same tales and strains which succeeded so astoundingly thirty years back. Times and tastes will change, however, though authors may not. And we shall not say a word upon the stories and chapters of fiction dispersed through these volumes. The Vicomte d'Arlincourt has not only outlived his own school at home, but he has outlived a later school with us in England, in which he might have shone. M. d'Arlincourt is a viscount, and, what is better, a gentleman, in all the genuine and sterling qualities, as in some of the absurdities of the term. But, alas! he wants the seasoning which has given

---

[2] See *Letters,* **II,** 737, for Thackeray's account of a meeting with d'Arlincourt in 1851.

such success to the literary viands of the aristocratic school. M. D'Arlincourt wants impertinence. He wants the monkey mischievousness of Puckler Muskau or Custine.[3] He is but polite and good-natured, and consequently insipid. His blandness is his bane, and hangs like a millstone round his two volumes. And yet his want of impertinence ought to endear him to us. How would Puckler Muskau have depicted Englishmen, had he but seen their handy work in the political manipulation of Ireland?

M. D'Arlincourt visits England of course, on his way to Ireland, and made his *entrée* there at a *matinée dansante* given by Lady Chesterfield, where he sees the Duke of Wellington "like an Œdipus or a Belisarius, surrounded with homage and adulation." We imagined Œdipus and Belisarius otherwise surrounded. Thence the vicomte goes to court:—

"The Queen of England has the prettiest little foot in the world, and she dances in the most charming manner; it is said, moreover, that being mistress of every accomplishment, she sings enchantingly. How many crowns at one and the same time are hers!

"In each of the *salons* of the palace a throne and dais were erected; as soon as the youthful sovereign had finished dancing in one apartment, she re-commenced in the next, her arrival in and departure from each room being announced by the national air of 'God save the Queen.' All this gave a new impulse to the *fête*, as from her Majesty's constantly changing her position, each of the ladies seated in the different *salons* had the satisfaction in turns of seeing her pass close to them. What a throng of pretty women!"

Who can explain the following?—

"At Woolwich two cannon-balls are shown, which have been 300 years under water; immediately on their being exposed to the air they broke in pieces, and a soldier, putting one of these pieces in his pocket, had his coat singed by it. Can this be accounted for?"

The viscount then hastens to Ireland, to Lord Donoughmore, to Malahide Castle, and to all the *videnda* in or near Dublin. Father Mathew, the Lover's Leap, fill each their chapter. At the Seven Churches the traveller is fairly bamboozled, and his head turned with cock-and-bull stories called legends. And having learned the art of legend making from the Irish guide at

---

[3] *"The Empire of the Czar; or, Observations, &c. on Russia. By the Marquis of Custline"* is reviewed in the *Morning Chronicle* of 29 January 1844. Since this review antedates Thackeray's firm connection with the paper, I have excluded it from the present volume; but it may well be by him.

Glendalough, whose name he most unfairly suppresses, the author exercises this new science on Swift and Vanessa, whom he treats much as the guide did St. Kevin, Cathleen, and Finmacoul.

The next scene described is the meeting at Tara, and is as follows:—

"The elevated stage erected for O'Connell was on the summit of Tara-hill; the high ground on which it was constructed had been hired for the meeting, at an expense of 200 guineas. Forty bands, each consisting of from fifteen to twenty musicians, were ranged one above the other all up the mountain, and welcomed with flourishes the arrival of the Liberator. O'Connell, in a carriage and six, advanced at this moment, followed in procession by several Roman Catholic bishops and priests, the different corporations with their banners and devices, the members for the county, and an innumerable multitude. He ascended slowly, in the midst of most deafening acclamations, towards the kind of throne on which he was about to sit. The air seemed no longer to support the shouts of transport that rent it. Carriages and four, and other vehicles, covered with flags, were seen above this sea of human waves, perpetually agitated to and fro in a commotion without revolution, and in a hurricane without a storm. O'Connell bowed right and left, with evident emotion. His powerful and sonorous voice addressed here and there a few words of gratitude to the crowd. He arrived at the summit of the hill. There was placed the Stone of Destiny, the sacred stone of the land. Was he about to use the language of a king? No, it was as a prophet that he spoke:—'Irishmen—a little longer, and you will have regained your rights! You will have your parliament in Dublin; you will become a great nation!'

"This was received with frenzied acclamations. O'Connell, pointing with his hand towards Heaven, continued in a solemn tone—

"To day is the 5th of August, the day on which the mother of our Lord was carried in triumph to heaven; like her, and speedily, you also will rise triumphant to freedom. On such an anniversary, the language of imposture and error could not issue from my lips. You shall be free: *God wills it!*

"Thus spoke Peter the Hermit, announcing victory to the Crusaders; he promised the Holy Land, he destroyed the infidels. Alas! the Holy Land is still to be conquered, and the infidels are still to be destroyed!

"Opposite the platform on which O'Connell stood, was the figure of the immortal Ossian dressed in the costume of the earliest ages. The old man, who represented the poet of by-gone days, had his white beard, his brown robe, and his golden harp. His glance was by turns calm and animated; seated, and leaning on the lyre of the bards of Morven, he seemed to invoke for O'Connell the inspirations of glory and liberty. One would have fancied that, rising from the fogs like a true son of Fingal, he said to the people, 'Come forth from the night of the tomb! The palace of lightnings open! Behold the king of meteors!'

D'ARLINCOURT'S *Three Kingdoms*

"I had arrived within a little distance from O'Connell's throne. Mr. Henry Grattan, one of the most popular orators in the country, was suddenly recognised by the multitude; from forty to fifty thousand persons welcomed him by clapping their hands as he passed, and I found myself thus in the centre of a popular ovation. The people would have taken off our horses if there had been room to move, but the carriage was shut in and compressed as if between iron walls. Henry Grattan, standing upright by my side, his head bare, and his eyes filled with tears, greeted the people with voice and gesture. We could not advance a step through the close ranks which were crowded together and all shouting at once, in the midst of which our horses disappeared half stifled. The road, the earth itself was no longer visible. Nothing was to be seen but a mass of heads, which, like living waves, undulated from one horizon to another. Henry Grattan, whose destined post at the meeting was beside the great man of Ireland, took this opportunity of leaping from the carriage, and was borne along by the multitude to the spot where the Liberator awaited him. I found myself obliged to follow him.

"This scene will be ever present to my memory, as one of the most extraordinary I have witnessed in my life. On I went, tossed about for I know not how long on the backs and shoulders, faces and arms of the people, astounded by the clamour that arose from this strange and swelling sea. I understood not, half bewildered as I was, how I could advance on this incomprehensible human shield; but light and air were with me; I towered above both mountains and men. Henry Grattan was there triumphant, and, squeezed, compressed, and fettered as he was, he breathed the atmosphere of liberty. 'Independence, liberty!' This has been the cry of every age: will the dream last for ever?"

Notwithstanding this extraordinary feat of the Frenchman walking on the heads and necks of the Irish, and notwithstanding his subsequent admiration of Mr. O'Connell it is evident that the rude energy of the Liberator frightened the gentle nature of the Vicomte, for the latter declared he had quite enough of it, and made off unceremoniously without his dinner.

In Scotland the writer was far more at home. The lochs, and the now peaceful Highlanders, and Walter Scott, and Queen Mary, were themes and companions far more to his taste than monster meetings and popular orators; and accordingly the vicomte revels through a whole volume in the land of cakes. We cannot follow him there, however, having already said and extracted as much as is fitting from these amiable volumes.

[29 APRIL 1844]

EXHIBITION OF THE SOCIETY OF PAINTERS IN WATER COLOURS.

The private view of this collection took place on Saturday, and assembled, as usual, most of the well-known patrons of this branch of English art—the most national, original, and pleasing form of it which, perhaps, exists in this country. On the day previous his Royal Highness Prince Albert paid his accustomed visit to the exhibition, than which none better merits such high favour; and, without pretending to record the names of the wealthy and celebrated personages who thronged thither on Saturday, it may be mentioned that even the entrance to the exhibition gave an idea of the rank and fashion assembled within it, so filled was Pall-mall with carriages, and so richly and closely lined were the lobbies of the gallery with the most splendid and aristocratic footmen.

There are but three-and-forty artists whose works are shown in this delightful little gallery; but their exhibition is always among the most agreeable which the town affords. Perhaps it is because the painters do not generally attempt what is called the highest species of art, and content themselves with depicting nature as they find her, and trusting to the poetry and charms of the scenes which they copy, rather than to their own powers of invention, and representing ideal beauty. The figure painters of this exhibition are very few in number; one of the best artists in this latter branch we miss—Mr. LEWIS, whose address is given in the catalogue as at Cairo—a long way from Pall-mall. The author of the pictures of *Zumalacarregui* and *Murillo* is greatly missed at this Academy. Is Mehemet Ali a more enlightened patron of art than Mr. LEWIS can find in his own country?

Mr. CATTERMOLE, who used to divide the palm with the former gentleman in these exhibitions, appears this year in great force. His large picture (81) *The Contest for the Bridge*, is perhaps his finest performance; nor do we remember any water-colour piece at all equal to it for force and richness of tone. Parties of Cavaliers and Roundheads are engaged battling for a bridge that crosses a rocky stream dashing through a dark forest, over the trees of which are seen the tall grey towers of a castle. The painting of these trees is remarkably fine; the small figures of the warriors and horsemen engaged glitter brilliantly in the stormy depths of the shadow. The trees look as if they were fighting too, and one may almost fancy one hears the wind roaring among the enormous cracking branches. To be sure the critic might ask of what kind some of these monster trees are, of which the *ingens umbra ramorum*[1] casts such a gloom over the combatants below, and question the correctness of the drawing of some of the horses and riders; but it is the sentiment, colour, and poetry of this fine drawing which should be examined rather than the minute parts of it: and the former can only elicit the highest admiration.

In another large piece, the *Refectory* (135), the artist exhibits the same mastery over his material, and the sober richness of colour for which his works are remarkable. Here, however, the figures are larger, and the faults of drawing more visible. Two smaller drawings, *Rook Shooting* (303), and *A Porch* (150), which appear to be drawn upon a coarse, common, grey paper, are admirable in their way, and perfect curiosities of skill. It seems as if the artist had a sort of pleasure in overcoming manual difficulties, and with the smallest and roughest means producing the most astonishing effects.

Mr. FREDERICK TAYLOR's drawings are not quite so numerous, or of so large a size, as some he has exhibited in former years; but they exhibit all the dexterity of handling which belongs to his rich and flowing pencil, and the charm of his peculiar and delightful colour. *Crossing a Brook* (316) is a little gem of this kind; the pretty group of crossing figures shining upon the dark ground of the picture, as bright and pure as the colours of a prism. A small *Hawking Party* is beautifully airy and sparkling. A piece, the *Interior of a Larder* (257), remarkable for the breadth and skill with which the various living and inanimate objects are painted. But by far the finest piece, to our thinking, is 276, *Houseless Wanderers*, which, besides the mere skill of colourist and draughtsman which this gentleman's pictures always exhibit, has a beauty and dramatic power equal to WILKIE; indeed it is a pity that painters who have this faculty do not employ it more. There surely can be no harm in throwing the charm of subject into a picture as well as that of execution; and excellently as Mr. TAYLOR's still life is painted, we would have preferred a piece of half the size, containing the feeling, pathos, and humour, which the wanderers show.

[1] Virgil, *Georgics*, II, 489.

EXHIBITION OF THE SOCIETY OF PAINTERS IN WATER COLOURS

Along with his curious and admirable fruit, flowers, and birds'-nest pieces (the minute fidelity of which keeps all spectators in wonder), Mr. HUNT always takes care to provide us with some of those deep and interesting dramatic pieces which he has such a genius for inventing. This gentleman may be called the KEELEY of the Fine Arts: his genius having that tragical and awful bent which distinguishes the dreadful representative of *Hasserac*,[2] at present frightening nightly audiences at the Lyceum Theatre. In representing the woes and pleasures of children Mr. HUNT is unrivalled: there is one young gentleman especially, who has served him as a model for many years past, and seems to have attained a certain height, and to have grown no bigger for years past, like TOM THUMB, and in whose fate and disposition every frequenter of the Water-colour Gallery must have got by this time to have a warm interest. We have seen him while being washed—we have seen him in a frantic state of joy while about to attack a mutton pie—and we have beheld him, entirely gorged with that delicacy, sinking back in his chair and slumbering in an almost apoplectic condition of contentment.

On the present occasion the young gentleman figures in a little drama in two acts, and in the catalogue numbered 237, first act, *The Aspirant*. The young gentleman has procured a cigar somewhere, and is puffing it into the face of the spectator with an air of triumphant roguery. In act 2 he appears as "done up." Dead sick, he reclines on a chair, and the fatal cigar lies beside him (quite a curiosity in painting is that cigar), and so wonderful is the fidelity of the sickness represented in the poor wretch's countenance, that one cannot but suspect the artist to have followed the example of the painter of ancient days (who killed a man in order to depict his agonies to the death), and to have made this unlucky lad really sick with a cigar, in order to copy him as a warning for other youth.

The picture of the *Toilet* may be also mentioned. Before the girl (who is having her hair curled with the kitchen tongs), there lies a lump of yellow soap in a saucer, and an exceedingly ancient comb and brush, which are quite frightful for their fidelity.

Mr. OAKLEY's groups, 307, 371, *Young Gipsy Women*, *Gipsies*

---

[2] Presumably Robert Keeley's role in *Open, Sesame,* the afterpiece of the current bill at the Lyceum Theatre, which also included *The Three Wives of Madrid* and *Polkamania* (*Times,* 29 April 1844).

EXHIBITION OF THE SOCIETY OF PAINTERS IN WATER COLOURS

with Cards, are exceedingly clever, and painted with great care, truth, and skill. But they have this fault, that they are exceedingly like the same artist's young gipsy women of last year. They sit there, squarely set out in groups, as if for the express purpose of having their portraits taken; and we confess ourselves to be rather tired of their company. Why should not artists *think* as well as paint? It would be possible without any painful stretch of intellect to devise some subject a little more stirring and novel than this; and we hope next year that Mr. O'AKLEY's skill and talents (his drawing is good, his colouring careful and clear, and his manner of handling shows that he is perfectly well grounded in his art) will exhibit themselves in some more various way.

The *Poacher's Hut* (179), by Mr. ALFRED D. FRIPP, and several more figure-pieces by the same hand, give very great promise. This artist's pictures are not quite complete as yet; but they show great powers and very clever and careful drawing and colouring. Mr. S. W. WRIGHT's *What do you think* (130), and other little drawings, are remarkable for their delicate beauty, as far as the figures go at least. The back-grounds of the drawings, feeble, woolly, and ineffective, are entitled to any thing but praise.

Among the landscapes, *Venice*, from various hands, figures as usual with bright red buildings and ultra-marine skies. Mr. HARDING's pieces have all their accustomed delicacy and skill. Mr. PROUT's *Town Halls* are here, as before, in the ancient and venerable Prout manner. Mr. C. FIELDING's wide landscapes and misty downs and sweeps (flanked by burnt-sienna trees, and wonderful delineations of carts and ploughmen), show all this well-known painter's skill, excellence, and mannerism. Some of Mr. CALLOW's drawings (125), *The Wetterhorn* and (4) the eternal *Dogana of Venice*, are almost very good, but the former picture is placed unluckily near one by Mr. COPLEY FIELDING (126), *View over the Vale of York*, a vast airy landscape, the peculiar excellence of which shows the defect in the clever drawing of the younger painter, [while], with similar ill-fortune, Mr. CALLOW's Venetian piece (of which the buildings are excellent and the sky very skilfully painted) has a sea no more transparent than a faded billiard cloth, and hangs hard by a picture of Mr. BENTLEY, whose drawing and painting of water are quite unrivalled. We have never seen better drawings than those exhibited this year by the last named gentleman. *The Seventy-four off Spithead* (19),

Off Saint Malo (161), and *The Mont St. Michael at early Morning*
(127), are beautiful specimens of this artist, the latter particularly
(which on Saturday was as yet unsold), struck us as the very
best and most brilliant of all.

Mr. G. A. FRIPP, we believe a young exhibitor in this society,
has even more promise than his brother, the figure-painter. Mr.
G. FRIPP's pictures are beautiful, and he takes his place with the
very best of the painters here. Among his drawings may be
particularly mentioned the *Thames at Wargrove*, and *Scene on the
River Wharfe, near Bolton Abbey* (72), of which the general effect
is very fine, and the painting of the trees and the water most
masterly. Some rocks in the *Scene on Loch Maree* (87), by W.
TURNER, will also be admired by the lover of landscape drawing,
as well as other pictures by the same artist. The Rhine scenes
of Mr. FREDERICK NASH, (8), *Braubach*, (5) *Bacharach*, will also
be recognized by most tourists, and admired—not for their dash
and dexterity, the chief quality of many of the drawings of the
exhibition—but for their great fidelity to nature. Some rather
rugged drawings by Mr. BYRNE struck us as possessing excellent
quality; and there are many others worthy of mark, which have
no doubt been passed over in a first visit to the gallery, and were
not seen over the backs of the fashionable crowd who were
assembled to admire them.

[6 MAY 1844]

The Life of George Brummell, Esq. By Captain JESSE.

There is a great deal of pleasant, curious gossip in these careless volumes. The disreputable old ghosts of the close of the last
century are brought up from "limbo," and made to walk the
world again. Fox and Sheridan, the beautiful Georgina of Devonshire, the Prince of Wales (august shade of sixteen stone!), and
numbers more of the fashionable defunct make their appearance
round the revived Brummell, and live in Jesse's volumes one
day more.[1] And the book has a moral with it—the moral of

[1] An adaptation of *The Dunciad*, I, 89-90:
    "Now night descending, the proud scene was o'er,
    But lived in Settle's numbers one day more."

"the Rake's Progress." The great discoverer of starched neck-cloths flourishes in a society of which it may be said that it was worthy of him; is vanquished by common sense, in the stern person of the bailiff; lives on in exile a swindling epicure; and dies a miserable old idiot in the straw of the Bon Sauveur. The story is narrated by a manly, jovial historian, quite alive to the moral of the tale, while he gives its details very agreeably, in the tone of a man to whom the usages of good society are familiar, and who, no doubt, has taken his share of the pleasures of the world which he describes.

As regards the great subject of the memoir personally, the materials from which Captain Jesse has compiled his history of Brummell seem to be not very copious: we had heard of a collection of Brummell-papers in the hands of Mr. Armstrong, one of the last and fastest of the poor man's friends; but these, if they exist, probably remain in that gentleman's possession. Captain Jesse's chief documents are a few letters, written, for the most part, in the latter years of Brummell's life; an album, presented to a young lady, for whom the old Pall-mall Themistocles seems to have felt some natural kindness and affection; and a few stray notices by acquaintances of the dandy in his days of pride. This is not much, but perhaps it is enough about him. There are plenty of materials for judging of what the hero of fashion was made.

It may be consoling to the middle classes to think that the great Brummell, the conqueror of all the aristocratic dandies of his day, nay, the model of dandyhood for all time, was one of them, of the lower order. There is a comfort to consider that his grandfather was a footman—a Treasury lackey, who had a son who rose to be a Treasury clerk, and to enjoy the confidence of great people, and who amassed sixty thousand pounds, a third part of which sum came to George Brummell at his majority. Let men who aspire to the genteel, then, never be discouraged. This footman's grandson was a better gentleman than the Prince of Wales. When he stood in the pit of the opera he called dukes and marquesses, who came cringing to him, as kings used to come to Napoleon. His reign lasted rather longer than that of the latter, and each went into exile within a year of the other.

He must have had a much finer taste than the Prince of Wales, that is quite clear. Every man who saw the King's trinkets, clothes, and snuff-boxes, must remember the savage, gaudy, barbarous love of ornament which distinguished the first gentleman of Europe. It is enough to say for George IV., that he built and ornamented Brighton and Buckingham Palace. It was surely only loyalty, natural ignorance, and that love of the Sovereign which the British aristocracy possesses, that ever could have blinded them to the qualities of the royal leader of ton. Young Brummell, the footman's descendant, engaged and overcame this gigantic power. All the profligate splendours of Carlton House could not compete with the Beau's small tenement in Chesterfield-street; there was a tawdry magnificence about George IV., which must have been felt to be bad taste if not acknowledged. Impartial history will be induced, perhaps, one day to whisper the word "vulgar" as the proper epithet to characterise the great dandy. Brummell overcame him by simplicity, elegance, and neat impudence and presence of mind. There seems to have been a calmness about him which flustered and intolerably annoyed the unwieldy antagonist with whom he contended for the first place in a certain society. That question of "Who's your fat friend?" must have quivered like a poisoned arrow in the flesh of the Prince: how superior it is to all the latter's clumsy attempts at bullying and bravado! Nothing, surely, shows the Regent's unfitness to occupy the great post of first dandy of the empire more than his conduct in his feud with Brummell—his irresolution, his important bluster of ill-will, his miserable endeavour to crush his enemy with attack, which the other repelled in a moment, causing the big adversary to quail, who had thought to browbeat him so easily. Those who are interested in these deep matters of history (and, indeed, they are as important as a quarrel between Noodle and Doodle, or a row between two dancing-masters at a fair), must allow, after studying Captain Jesse's account of the war between the two Georges, that the royal aspirant was totally unfit to lead. The genteel annalist must blush to record the fact, that the Prince Regent actually condescended to apply to be asked to a ball which Brummell gave, and then insulted his entertainer; that afterwards, meeting Brummell at the Opera, the latter "cut" his Royal Highness in a manner so provokingly respectful, that the Prince slunk floundering back from the Beau; that then the terrible title of the "fat friend" was launched against him, and that the Regent had not the courage to annihilate this malefactor or even to forgive him. He had a chance up to the last moment—George IV., on his way to Hanover, saw Brummell starving and swindling at Calais; what a moment for the King to have *réhabilité* himself with the genteel world of Europe! He might have had his great revenge that day by forgiving Brummell; but he had not the heart to do so, and passed on. An ambitious man, who could lose such an opportunity as that of bringing, by a benefit, his enemy mortified to his feet, never deserves to succeed; and accordingly, let history exalt Brummell far above his royal rival.

We have said that Captain Jesse has executed his task in a good humoured, agreeable manner, interspersing his narrative with anecdotes of the people among whom Brummell lived: but perhaps, for a moral purpose, it would have been as well that the narrative of this great man's life had been shortened, not enlivened with gaiety and anecdote, but told with the gravity and simplicity becoming such a theme.

Thus, of the Beau's life at Eton, all that is recorded is the fact that he used to wear breeches and worsted stockings there, and to dine with perfect satisfaction at noon: that he was a favourite with his schoolfellows, and was once seen serenading the daughter of his dame with a hurdy-gurdy—indicating his future humour.

On leaving Eton, he entered the 10th Hussars, which he quitted, having attained the rank of captain, and broken his nose in that eminent corps. He now came to London, the friend of the Prince, and the associate of the greatest and most genteel people.

As for his wit, all his compositions show prodigious pains, but likewise that he was an entire ninny. The worst articles of the worst magazines are not comparable to Brummell's letters for the elaborate vacuity of intellect which they display. This wit immediately placed our young aspirant greatly above all men in the fashionable world, and procured him intense respect and admiration there. He appears to have had even less heart than wit, which likewise contributed to the cordiality of his reception in the world.

This good man (like other sages) has left his maxim or saying behind him. His is *"country washing, clean linen, and plenty of it."* Brummell made this truth his great guiding star through life, and modestly adduced it to account for his successes as a man of fashion, forgetting the other qualities we have just mentioned.

He also invented starched white neckcloths, for which ought not the youth of England of the present day to be thankful to him? This invention (in company with his wit and kindness of heart) served to place him at the topmost height of the genteel world.

Having expended his patrimony, not merely in country washing, but in gambling and other species of debauchery, and having run into debt as far as his tradesmen would possibly allow him, and having failed (although he told lies for the purpose) to get money from his friends, Mr. Brummell quitted the country, and, cheating his creditors, established himself at Calais.

His high qualities had made him so popular, that his friends in London did not here desert him for a while, but supplied this worthy man with continual donations. He would accept these, or anything else that was offered him, especially dinners, which formed the great business of his life; and a story is told of his honesty and enthusiasm in these volumes, which is very moral. One day, walking in Calais with a Marquess, a former friend, Mr. Brummell met a very fat and vulgar individual, who excited my lord's ridicule, and whom Mr. Brummell declared on his honour he did not know. But the fat man, passing the beau with a hideous nod, said *"How do Brum—goose at four"*—which tale shows into what an abject state the beau had fallen, and exhibits his amiable gratitude and manliness of character. It appears that the illustrious exile spent near the half of his day in sleeping, three hours in dressing, four at dinner, at which he consumed daily a bottle of Dorchester ale and one of claret, devoting the rest of his time to writing, reading, and conversation, and the pasting of a great screen, which occupied much of his valuable life.

Having lived many years in this agreeable way, and borrowed money of many tradesmen, Mr. Brummell, for his great deserts, was named consul at Caen, whither he went, and where he likewise contracted debts. He lived as before, with the additions of his consular duties; but, as these were very light, he rendered them still more easy by neglecting them altogether.

He presently lost his consulship. He was then put into prison for debt. There his reason was shaken, and after flickering for a while, was utterly extinguished, and this great man died an idiot in the hospital of the Bon Sauveur, at Caen. Let us respect the world which elevated to honour this respectable man; and not be too hard upon him, because he was heartless, and a swindler, a fool, a glutton, and a liar.

The following are the personal descriptions which Mr. Jesse gives of the great man:—

"BRUMMELL'S PERSON.

"His face was rather long, and complexion fair; his whiskers inclined to sandy, and hair light brown. His features were neither plain nor handsome; but his head was well-shaped, the forehead being unusually high; showing, according to phrenological development, more of the mental than the animal passions—the bump of self-esteem was very prominent. His countenance indicated that he possessed considerable intelligence, and his mouth betrayed a strong disposition to indulge in sarcastic humour; this was predominant in every feature, the nose excepted, the natural regularity of which, though it had been broken by a fall from his charger, preserved his countenance from degenerating into comicality. His eyebrows were equally expressive with his mouth, and while the latter was giving utterance to something very good-humoured or polite, the former, and the eyes themselves, which were grey and full of oddity, could assume an expression that made the sincerity of his words very doubtful.

"This flexibility of feature enabled Brummell to give additional point to his humorous or satirical remarks; his whole physiognomy giving the idea, that, had he devoted himself to dramatic composition, he would have written in a tone far more resembling that of the *School for Scandal* than the *Gamester*, or any plot developing reflection and deep feeling. His voice was very pleasing."

"BRUMMELL'S NECKCLOTH.

"Brummell was one of the first who revived and improved the taste for dress; and his great innovation was effected upon neckcloths: they were then worn without stiffening of any kind, and bagged out in front, rucking up to the chin in a roll; to remedy this obvious awkwardness and inconvenience, he used to have his slightly starched; and a reasoning mind must allow, that there is not much to object to in this reform.

"He did not, however, like the dandies, test their fitness for use, by trying if he could raise three parts of their length by one corner without their bending; yet it appears, that if the cravat was not properly tied at the first effort, or inspiring impulse, it was always rejected. His valet was coming down stairs one day with a quantity of tumbled neck-cloths under his arm, and being interrogated on the subject, solemnly replied, 'Oh, they are *our* failures.' Practice like this of course made him perfect; and his tie soon became a model that was imitated, but never equalled.

"The method by which this most important result was attained, was communicated to me by a friend of his, who had frequently been an eye-witness of the amusing operation.

"The collar, which was always fixed to his shirt, was so large that, before being folded down, it completely hid his head and face; and the white neckcloth was at least a foot in height. The first *coup d'archet* was made with the shirt collar, which he folded down to its proper size; and Brummell then standing before the glass, with his chin poked up to the ceiling, by the gentle and gradual declension of the lower jaw, creased the cravat to reasonable dimensions, the form of each succeeding crease being perfected with the shirt which he had just discarded.

"His morning dress was similar to that of every other gentleman— Hessians and pantaloons, or top boots and buckskins, with a blue coat, and a light or buff-coloured waistcoat; of course fitting to admiration on the best figure in England. His dress of an evening was a blue coat and white waistcoat, black pantaloons which buttoned tight to the ankle, striped silk stockings, and opera hat; in fact, he was always carefully dressed, but never the slave of fashion."

BRUMMELL'S TAILOR.

"Brummell's tailors were Schweitzer and Davidson, in Cork-street, Weston, and a German of the name Meyer, who lived in Conduit-street. The Stultzes and Nugees, &c., did, I believe, exist in those days; but they were not then held in the same estimation as their more fortunate brethren of the shears. Schweitzer and Meyer worked for the Prince; and the latter had a page's livery, and on great occasions superintended the adornment of his Royal Highness's person. The trouser, which opens at the bottom of the leg, and was closed by buttons and loops, was invented either by Meyer or Brummell—the beau, at any rate, was the first who wore them, and they immediately became quite the fashion, and continued so for some years.

"A good humoured baronet, and brother Etonian of his, who followed him at a humble distance in his dress, told me that he went to Schweitzer's one morning to get properly rigged out, and that while this talented purveyor of habiliments was measuring him, he asked him what cloth he recommended? 'Why, sir,' said the *artiste*, 'the Prince wears superfine, and Mr. Brummell the Bath coating; but it is immaterial which you choose. Sir John, you must be right; suppose, sir, we say Bath coating—I think Mr. Brummell has a trifle the preference.'

"Brummell's good taste in dress was not his least recommendation in the eyes of the Prince of Wales, by whom his advice on this important subject was constantly sought, and, for a long time, studiously followed. Mr. Thomas Raikes says, in his 'France,' that his Royal Highness would go of a morning to Chesterfield-street to watch the progress of his friend's toilet, and remain till so late an hour that he sometimes sent away his horses, and insisted on Brummell's giving him a quiet dinner, which generally ended in a deep potation."

BRUMMELL IN EXILE.

"Though I have spoken of Brummell's style of dress in his early life, I shall again briefly describe it here as it came under my own observation. He stood to his Whig colours to the last. His dress on the evening in question consisted of a blue coat with a velvet collar, and the consular button, a buff waistcoat, black trowsers, and boots. It is difficult to imagine what could have reconciled him to adopt the two latter innovations upon evening costume, unless it were the usual apology for such degeneracy in modern taste, the altered proportions of his legs. Without entering into a description of the exact number of wrinkles in his white neckcloth, I shall merely say that his tie was unexceptionable, and that his *blanchisseuse* had evidently done her very best in the "getting up," as these good bodies term it. I may here observe that I never heard the Beau accused, as I have some *lions*, of having a tin case with a Bramah lock to keep his neckcloths in, folded, and free from the unhallowed touch of others, though he always gave careful instructions to his washerwoman how she was to fold them; and his valet assured me at Boulogne, with becoming earnestness, that he never had a failure, —he always succeeded in his tie. They were, however, subjected to the strictest inspection, and a speck on one of them, however minute, was the warrant for its return to the soapsuds.

"The only articles of jewellery that I observed about him were a plain ring, and a massive chain of Venetian ducat gold, which served as a guard to his watch, and was evidently as much for use as ornament. Only two links of it were to be seen, those that passed from the buttons of his waistcoat to the pocket. The chain was peculiar, and was of the same pattern as those suspended in *terrorem* outside the principal entrance to Newgate. The ring was dug up on the field of the cloth of gold by a labourer, who sold it to Brummell when he was at Calais. An opera hat and gloves, that were held in his hand, completed an attire which, being remarkably quiet, could never have attracted attention on any other person. His *mise* was peculiar, only for its extreme neatness, and wholly at variance with an opinion that I have already mentioned as very prevalent among those who were not personally acquainted with him, that he owed his reputation to his tailor, or to an exaggerated style of dress."

Nor has any satirist in the world invented an account more dreadful than the following one of the ruling passion strong still in the mind of the poor idiot:—

"It would be painful as well as tedious to detail all the different stages of mental decay through which this unfortunate man passed, before he became hopelessly imbecile. One of the most singular eccentricities that he exhibited was the following:—On certain nights some strange fancy would seize him, that it was necessary he should give a party, and he accordingly invited many of the distinguished persons with whom he had been intimate in former days, though some of them were already numbered with the dead.

"On these gala evenings, he desired his attendant to arrange his apartment, set out a whist-table, and light the *bougies* (he burnt only tallow at the time), and at eight o'clock this man, to whom he had already given his instructions, opened wide the door of his sitting-room, and announced the 'Duchess of Devonshire.' At the sound of her grace's well-remembered name, the Beau, instantly rising from his chair, would advance towards the door, and greet the cold air from the stair-case, as if it had been the beautiful Georgiana herself. If the dust of that fair creature could have stood reanimate in all her loveliness before him, she would not have thought his bow less graceful than it had been thirty-five years before; for, despite poor Brummell's mean habiliments and uncleanly person, the supposed visitor was received with all his former courtly ease of manner, and the earnestness that the pleasure of such an honour might be supposed to excite. 'Ah! my dear Duchess,' faltered the beau, 'how rejoiced I am to see you; so very amiable of you at this short notice! Pray bury yourself in this arm-chair; do you know it was a gift to me from the Duchess of York, who was a very kind friend of mine; but, poor thing, you know she is now no more.' Here the eyes of the old man would fill with the tears of idiotcy, and, sinking into the fauteuil himself, he would sit for some time looking vacantly at the fire, until Lord Alvanley, Worcester, or any other old friend he chose to name, was announced, when he again rose to receive them, and went through a similar pantomime. At ten, his attendant announced the carriages, and this farce was at an end."

. . . .

[13 MAY 1844]

Coningsby; or, the New Generation.

We may augur for this book a very extensive popularity. It is quite as curious as it is clever. It is the fashionable novel, pushed, we do really believe, to its extremest verge, beyond which all is naught. It is a glorification of dandyism, far beyond all other glories which dandyism has attained. Dandies are here made to regenerate the world—to heal the wounds of the wretched body politic—to infuse new blood into torpid old institutions—to rec-oncile the ancient world to the modern—to solve the doubts and perplexities which at present confound us—and to introduce the supreme truth to the people, as theatre managers do the sovereign to the play, smiling, and in silk stockings, and with a pair of wax candles.

It is impossible to help admiring the intenseness of the Dis-raelite-*ego*. He fancies a thing to the utmost. Those who recol-lect the prodigious novel of "The Young Duke," will remember, when Mr. Disraeli had a mind to be fashionable, to what a pitch of fashion he could raise himself: he out-duked all the dukes in the land—he invented splendours which Stafford House never can hope to equal—he dreamed better dreams than Alnaschar[1] himself; and, as in the before-named work he fancied himself fashionable, in this he fancies himself young. In the first volume we have the biography of a fifth-form boy at Eton, and astonishingly young does our author make himself. He becomes entirely and utterly rejuvenescent; his soul wears a jacket and a turned-down collar; it eats lollypops at school, and sweetly submits to kneel down and undergo the ceremonies which were performed in Dr. Keate's private room. Who knows but we may have Mr. Disraeli flinging his imagination into a bib and tucker next, and writing his autobiography before he was weaned?

The strong faith of the writer influences his reader very considerably, and the latter can't help fancying (we speak for ourselves), after perusing the volumes, that he too is a regenerator of the world, and that he has we don't know how many thousands a year. That he is a man of the utmost fashion, is a matter of course. Our novelist will allow the work of reform to be done by no vulgar hands, and will introduce us to none but the very best company. [Hence] his "Duchess, and a glass of Malvoisie," "Beau, what will the duke, your father, say?" and so on. Not an unremarkable characteristic of our society-novelists is that ardour of imagination which sets them so often to work in describing grand company for us. They like to disport themselves in inventing fine people, as we to sit in this imaginary society. There is something *naïf* in this credulity on both sides: in these cheap Barmecide entertainments, to which author and reader are content to sit down. Mr. Disraeli is the most splendid of all feast-givers in this way—there is no end to the sumptuous hospitality of his imagination.

To return to his novel of "Coningsby." It is a dandy-social, dandy-political, dandy-religious novel. Fancy a prostrate world kissing the feet of a reformer—in patent blacking; fancy a prophet delivering heavenly messages—with his hair in papers, and the reader will have our notion of the effect of the book. The dandyism, moreover, is intense, but not real; not English, that is. It is vastly too ornamental, energetic, and tawdry for our quiet

---

[1] The story of Alnaschar in *The Arabian Nights* was a favorite with Thackeray. See *Letters*, I, 297.

habits. The author's coxcombry is splendid, gold-land, refulgent, like that of Murat rather than that of Brummell. But in taking leave to rank Mr. Disraeli among the coxcombs, we should do him an injustice were we to omit saying that there are coxcombs for whom we have a very high respect, and that we believe this gentleman to be not only a dandy but a man of genius.

This superb coxcombry the author of "Coningsby" brings to bear upon a great number of very rare faculties and powers of mind. He has admirable humour, and scorn for *many* things which are base, not for all; and, in the midst of his satire, coxcombry intervenes, and one is irresistibly led to satirize the satirizer. He writes for a page or two in passages of the most admirable and pure English, thoughts finely poetical, fresh, startling, or ingenious; but one may be pretty sure of not being able to turn half-a-dozen leaves without coming upon something outrageous. Never was a moralist who laid himself more open to censure, a philosopher more personally weak, or a dandy and teacher of *ton* whose own manner was more curiously and frequently offensive. Politically, "Coningsby" is an exposure and attack of Whigs and Conservatives. Of Whigs much, but of Conservatives more. The author exposes the cant and folly of the name, and the lies of the practice. He lays bare dirty motives and intrigues, laughs with a great deal of just ridicule at a number of the doctrines they have sworn to stand by and fled from; calls upon the elders of the Conservative party to accept the Reform Bill and the new institutions consequent upon it; but calling in vain, and seeing how powerless the old party are to avert from the menaced country the dangers of anarchy, poverty, revolution, hanging over it—intimates that YOUNG ENGLAND is likely to save us from these evils; and in a parable, or three-volumed prophecy, as it were, typifies the restorer of the monarchy. Who can it be? Not Mr. Disraeli himself; he declines the office of regenerator, as we shall see presently. Not Mr. Peter Borthwick;[2] he is rather old for "us youth," and, besides, not of high lineage enough. Not Lord John Manners; that young nobleman's character is drawn in these volumes as the pious and chivalrous aide-de-camp[3] of the great Reformer. Can it be the noble marquess, member for Woodstock? He is the youngest

[2] Borthwick, editor of the *Morning Post* and M. P. for Evesham, was born in 1804.

[3] I.e., Henry Sidney.

England, barely two-and-twenty; a great qualification, according
both to Mr. Disraeli and a contemporary critic in the *Times*,
who enumerated, with much satisfaction, on Saturday, the deeds
which had been done by very young men—Cortes, Don John of
Austria, Napoleon, and our own Wellington. What process
Young England is to adopt, is no more told us than who the
regenerating hero himself is to be. But it is hinted that the
country is to be restored, by restoring faith among us: organizing
revenue, stopping a good deal of the authority of the House of
Commons, and strengthening considerably the monarchy. Perhaps in a second edition we shall be told what faith, among all
those which obtain in Ireland, in Scotland, in Oxford, in Exeter-
hall, is to be the means of uniting the people of the English
islands; how "reverence," if dead, is to be brought to life again,
and on what objects it is to be directed; but, meanwhile, it is good
at least to find gentlemen sitting with the present government
acknowledging the cant of its professions, the entire uncertainty
of its aims, the hollowness of its views, and for the imminent
convulsions of the country its utter inadequacy to provide.

Numerous disquisitions find place in the volumes regarding
various political fallacies. Many of them are well and ingeniously
argued—the hits at both parties are severe and just, the evils are
shown well enough; but it is only when the Young Englander
comes to legislate for them that his reasoning becomes altogether
unsatisfactory. If we might venture to suppose that Mr. Disraeli
had borrowed his ideas from any one, we should say that the
"Hero Worship" of Mr. Carlyle had been carefully read by him.
Young England, too, is pining, it appears, for the restoration of
the heroic sentiment, and the appearance of the heroic man.

The story upon which all these questions of politics and philosophy are made to hang, is a very simple one. Coningsby is the
grandson of the most wealthy, clever, and dissolute marquess in
his Majesty's dominions. The marquess had disinherited the
boy's father (his second son) for marrying against his will: but
adopts the young Coningsby—is struck by his cleverness, manliness, and candour; sends him to Eton (where he passes nearly
a volume); then to Cambridge; proposes to leave him the bulk
of his unentailed property, and to make a great man of him.
But all these plans of aggrandisement Coningsby destroys by
boldly asserting his Young English opinions—the marquess cuts

off the lad with a miserable ten thousand pounds, and death
cuts off the marquess surrounded by his mistresses, and in the
midst of a glass of champagne. How in spite of these ill chances
Coningsby prospers; how the natural daughter to whom my lord
leaves all his property dies, bequeathing it to the young gentleman
whom she loved in secret; how he in his turn marries the young
person on whom his affections were fixed—are matters which
can be understood by every novel reader who is aware how
generous authors commonly are to the heroes of their romances.

The character of the marquess[4] is evidently drawn from that of
the late Marquess of Hertford. Other contemporary personages
are brought upon the scene with similar unscrupulousness. There
is the Duke of Beaumanoir, and his family, and house—if Beaumanoir does not mean Belvoir,[5] our experience of the fashionable
world may be set down as nought: there is Lord Eskdale, whose
original may be seen any day at the Post-office, or the French
Play;[6] there is Sidonia, who, if we mistake not, is no other than
our author, Mr. Benjamin Disraeli himself; finally, there is Rigby,
the old Tory hack. Who can this amiable statesman be?[7] Let
the reader judge from the following portrait of him:—

"Mr. Rigby was a member for one of Lord Monmouth's boroughs.
He was the manager of Lord Monmouth's parliamentary influence, and
the auditor of his vast estates. He was more; he was Lord Monmouth's
companion when in England, his correspondent when abroad—hardly
his counsellor, for Lord Monmouth never required advice; but Mr.
Rigby could instruct him in matters of detail, which Mr. Rigby made
amusing. Rigby was not a professional man; indeed, his origin, education, early pursuits, and studies were equally obscure; but he had contrived in good time to squeeze himself into Parliament, by means which
no one could ever comprehend, and then set up to be a perfect man of
business. The world took him at his word, for he was bold, acute, and
voluble; with no thought, but a good deal of desultory information;
and though destitute of all imagination and noble sentiment, was
blessed with a vigorous, mendacious fancy, fruitful in small expedients,
and never happier than when devising shifts for great men's scrapes.

"They say that all of us have one chance in this life, and so it was
with Rigby. After a struggle of many years, after a long series of the

[4] I.e., Lord Monmouth.
[5] Belvoir was the seat of Charles Cecil John Manners, sixth Duke of
Rutland.
[6] I.e., William Lowther, second Earl of Lonsdale, who was Postmaster
General in Peel's cabinet.
[7] Disraeli drew Rigby from the writer and politician John Wilson
Croker, one of the pillars of the *Quarterly Review*.

usual alternatives of small successes and small failures, after a few
cleverish speeches and a good many cleverish pamphlets, with a considerable reputation indeed for pasquinades, most of which he never
wrote, and articles in reviews to which it was whispered he had contributed, Rigby, who had already intrigued himself into a subordinate
office, met with Lord Monmouth.

"He was just the animal that Lord Monmouth wanted, for Lord
Monmouth always looked upon human nature with the callous eye of
a jockey. He surveyed Rigby, and he determined to buy him. He
bought him; with his clear head, his indefatigable industry, his audacious
tongue, and his ready and unscrupulous pen; with all his dates, all his
lampoons; all his private memoirs, and all his political intrigues. It
was a good purchase. Rigby became a great personage, and Lord
Monmouth's man.

*   *   *   *   *

"Mr. Rigby had a classical retreat, which he esteemed a Tusculum.
There, surrounded by his busts and books, he wrote his lampoons and
articles, massacred a she liberal (it was thought that no one could lash
a woman like Rigby), cut up a rising genius whose politics were different
from his own, or scarified some unhappy wretch who had brought his
claims before Parliament, proving by garbled extracts from official
correspondence that no one could refer to, that the malcontent, instead
of being a victim, was on the contrary a defaulter. Tadpole and Taper
would back Rigby for a 'slashing reply' against the field. Here too, at
the end of a busy week, he found it occasionally convenient to entertain
a clever friend or two of equivocal reputation, with whom he had become acquainted in former days of equal brotherhood. No one was
more faithful to his early friends than Mr. Rigby; particularly if they
could write a squib."

It is certain that Mr. Disraeli, by painting this neat portrait,
has gained for himself a friend for life. Let us look out with meek
patience for the reply to his pretty piece of biography in the
next number of the *Rigby Review*. The next extract which we
shall give describes the magnificent Sidonia—

"Coningsby had never met or read of any one like this chance companion. His sentences were so short, his language so racy, his voice
rang so clear, his elocution was so complete. On all subjects his mind
seemed to be so instructed and his opinions formed. He flung out a
result in a few words; he solved with a phrase some deep problem that
men muse over for years. He said many things that were strange, yet
they immediately appeared to be true. Then, without the slightest
air of pretension or parade, he seemed to know everybody as well as
every thing. Monarchs, statesmen, authors, adventurers of all descriptions and of all climes—if their names occurred in the conversation,
he described them in an epigrammatic sentence, or revealed their precise
position, character, calibre, by a curt dramatic trait. All this, too,

without any excitement of manner; on the contrary, with repose amount-
ing almost to nonchalance. If his address had a fault in it, it was rather
a deficiency of earnestness. A slight spirit of mockery played over his
speech even when you deemed him most serious; you were startled by
his sudden transitions from profound thought to poignant sarcasm. A
very singular freedom from passion and prejudice on every topic on
which they treated might be some compensation for this want of earnestness; perhaps was its consequence. Certainly it was difficult to ascertain
his precise opinions on many subjects, though his manner was frank
even to abandonment. And yet throughout his whole conversation,
not a stroke of egotism, not a word, not a circumstance, escaped him
by which you could judge of his position or purposes in life. As little
did he seem to care to discover those of his companion. He did not by
any means monopolize the conversation. Far from it; he continually
asked questions, and while he received answers, or had engaged his
fellow traveller in any exposition of his opinions or feelings, he listened
with a serious and fixed attention, looking Coningsby in the face with
a steadfast glance.

" 'I perceive,' said Coningsby, pursuing a train of thought which the
other had indicated, 'that you have great confidence in the influence
of individual character. I have also some confused persuasions of that
kind. But it is not the spirit of the age.'

" 'The age does not believe in great men, because it does not possess
any,' replied the stranger. 'The spirit of the age is the very thing that
a great man changes.'

" 'But does he not rather avail himself of it?' inquired Coningsby.

" 'Parvenus do;' rejoined his companion, 'but not prophets, great
legislators, great conquerors. They destroy and they create.'

" 'But are these times for great legislators and great conquerors?'
urged Coningsby.

" 'When were they more wanted?' asked the stranger. 'From the
throne to the hovel all call for a guide. You give monarchs constitutions to teach them sovereignty, and nations Sunday-schools to inspire
them with faith.'

" 'But what is an individual,' exclaimed Coningsby, 'against a vast
public opinion?'

" 'Divine,' said the stranger. 'God made man in his own image;
but the public is made by newspapers, members of parliament, excise
officers, poor law guardians. Would Philip have succeeded, if Epami-
nondas had not been slain? And if Philip had not succeeded? Would
Prussia have existed had Frederick not been born? And if Frederick
had not been born? What would have been the fate of the Stuarts if
Prince Henry had not died, and Charles I., as was intended, had been
Archbishop of Canterbury?'

" 'But when men are young, they want experience,' said Coningsby;
'and when they have gained experience, they want energy.'

" 'Great men never want experience,' said the stranger.

" 'But everybody says that experience—'

" 'Is the best thing in the world—a treasure for you, for me, for millions. But for a creative mind, less than nothing. Almost everything that is great has been done by youth.' "

The magnificent Sidonia proceeds to form a catalogue of youthful prodigies who have made their mark in history. "Youth is a blunder," says he, "manhood a struggle, old age a regret." "Do not imagine," he adds, "that I hold that youth is genius— all that I say is, that genius, when young, is divine;" and then follow the instances, Pascal, Pitt, Grotius, Cortes, Maurice of Saxe, and the like. "But it is useless," as he says, "to multiply examples. The history of heroes is the history of youth." This speech has a marvellous effect on the youthful Coningsby, who exclaims naturally—

" 'Ah! I should like to be a great man.'

" 'The stranger threw at him a scrutinising glance. His countenance was serious. He said in a voice of almost solemn melody:

" 'Nurture your mind with great thoughts. To believe in the heroic makes heroes.'

" 'You seem to me a hero,' said Coningsby, in a tone of real feeling, which, half ashamed of his emotion, he tried to turn into playfulness.

" 'I am, and must ever be,' said the stranger, 'but a dreamer of dreams.' Then going towards the window and changing into a familiar tone, as if to divert the conversation, he added, 'What a delicious afternoon! I look forward to my ride with delight. You rest here?'

" 'No; I go on to Nottingham, where I shall sleep.'

" 'And I in the opposite direction.' And he rang the bell and ordered his horses.

" 'I long to see your mare again,' said Coningsby. 'She seemed to me so beautiful.'

" 'She is not only of pure race,' said the stranger, 'but of the highest and rarest breed of Arabia. Her name is 'the Daughter of the Star.' She is a foal of that famous mare which belonged to the Prince of Wahabees; and to possess which, I believe was one of the principal causes of war between that tribe and the Egyptians. The Pacha of Egypt gave her to me, and I would not change her for her statue in pure gold, even carved by Lysippus. Come round to the stable and see her.'

"They went out together. It was a soft sunny afternoon; the air fresh from the rain, but mild and exhilarating.

"The groom brought forth the mare. 'The Daughter of the Star' stood before Coningsby with her sinewy shape of matchless symmetry; her burnished skin, black mane, legs like those of an antelope, her little ears, dark speaking eye, and tail worthy of a Pacha. And who was her master, and whither was she about to take him?

"Coningsby was so naturally well-bred, that we may be sure it was not curiosity; no, it was a finer feeling that made him hesitate and think a little, and then say:

" 'I am sorry to part.'

" 'I also,' said the stranger. 'But life is constant separation.'

" 'I hope we may meet again,' said Coningsby.

" 'If our acquaintance be worth preserving,' said the stranger, 'you may be sure it will not be lost.'

" 'But mine is not worth preserving,' said Coningsby earnestly. 'It is yours that is the treasure. You teach me things of which I have long mused.'

"The stranger took the bridle of the 'Daughter of the Star,' and turning round with a faint smile, extended his hand to his companion.

" 'Your mind at least is nurtured with great thoughts,' said Coningsby, 'your actions should be heroic.'

" 'Action is not for me;' said the stranger, '*I am of that faith that the Apostles professed before they followed their Master.*' "

Our author utters some prodigious apologies in other parts of his volumes for "the Mosaic Arabs," as he calls his race—shows that the "Caucasian races" are indestructible; and brings forward some singular statements regarding their present position, not a little curious, if authentic.

MOSAIC STATESMEN AND WARRIORS.

" '*The fact is you cannot destroy a pure race of the Caucasian organization.* It is a physiological fact; a simple law of nature, which has baffled Egyptian and Assyrian Kings, Roman Emperors, and Christian Inquisitors. No penal laws, no physical tortures, can effect that a superior race should be absorbed in an inferior, or be destroyed by it. The mixed persecuting races disappear, the pure persecuted race remains. And, at this moment, in spite of centuries, of tens of centuries, of degradation, the Jewish mind exercises a vast influence on the affairs of Europe. I speak not of their laws, which you still obey; of their literature, with which your minds are saturated; but of the living Hebrew intellect.

" 'You never observe a great intellectual movement in Europe in which the Jews do not greatly participate. The first Jesuits were Jews: that mysterious Russian diplomacy which so alarms Western Europe, is organized and principally carried on by Jews; that mighty revolution which is at this moment preparing in Germany, and which will be in fact a second and greater Reformation, and of which so little is as yet known in England, is entirely developing itself under the auspices of Jews, who almost monopolize the professorial chairs of Germany. Neander, the founder of spiritual Christianity, and who is regius professor of divinity in the University of Berlin, is a Jew. Benary, equally famous, and in the same university, is a Jew. Wehl, the Arabic professor of Heidelberg, is a Jew. Years ago, when I was in Palestine, I met a German student who was accumulating materials for the History of

Christianity, and studying the genius of the place; a modest and learned man. It was Wehl; then unknown, since become the first Arabic scholar of the day, and the author of the life of Mahomet. But for the German professors of this race, their name is Legion. I think there are more than ten in Berlin alone.

" 'I told you just now that I was going up to town to-morrow, because I always made it a rule to interpose when affairs of state were on the carpet. Otherwise, I never interfere. I hear of peace and war in the newspapers, but I am never alarmed, except when I am informed that the sovereigns want treasure; then I know that monarchs are serious.

" 'A few years back we were applied to by Russia. Now there has been no friendship between the court of St. Petersburg and my family. It has Dutch connections which have generally supplied it, and our representations in favour of the Polish Hebrews, a numerous race, but the most suffering and degraded of all the tribes, has not been very agreeable to the Czar. However, circumstances drew to an approximation between the Romanoffs and the Sidonias. I resolved to go myself to St. Petersburg. I had on my arrival an interview with the Russian Minister of Finance, Count Cancrin; I beheld the son of a Lithuanian Jew. The loan was connected with the affairs of Spain; I resolved on repairing to Spain from Russia. I travelled without intermission. I had an audience immediately on my arrival with the Spanish minister, Senor Mendizabel; I beheld one like myself the son of a Nuevo Christiano, a Jew of Arragon. In consequence of what transpired at Madrid, I went straight to Paris to consult the president of the French council; I beheld the son of a French Jew, a hero, an imperial marshal, and very properly so, for who should be military heroes if not those who worship the Lord of Hosts.'

" 'And is Soult a Hebrew?'

" 'Yes; and several of the French Marshals, and the most famous— Massena, for example; his real name was Manasseh: but to my anecdote. The consequence of our consultations was, that some Northern power should be applied to in a friendly and mediative capacity. We fixed on Prussia, and the president of the council made an application to the Prussian minister, who attended a few days after our conference. Count Arnim entered the cabinet, and I beheld a Prussian Jew. So you see, my dear Coningsby, that the world is governed by very different personages to what is imagined by those who are not behind the scenes.'

" 'You startle, and deeply interest me.'

" 'You must study physiology, my dear child. Pure races of Caucasus may be persecuted, but they cannot be despised except by the brutal ignorance of some mongrel breed, that brandishes faggots and howls exterminations, but is itself exterminated without persecutions by that irresistible law of nature which is fatal to curs.' "

This is a hit at somebody, doubtless, who has offended our Caucasian. We should like to know the names of the "several French marshals" besides Soult and Massena. Napoleon was previously disposed of: he, too, was "an Arab," perhaps "a

Mosaic Arab." Caucasism seems to be a *sine qua non* with Mr. Disraeli. "But I come also from Caucasus," hints simple Coningsby. Verily (replies the man of the mountain), and thank your Creator for being such—*your race is sufficiently pure.* The question henceforth, then, regarding a man must be, is he a Caucasian? If not, woe be to him. But we have not done with the Mosaic Caucasians; and, indeed, in the midst of his extravagance, can heartily admire the chivalrous energy of this champion of a persecuted people:—

MOSAIC MUSICIANS.

"Great poets require a public; we have been content with the immortal melodies that we sung more than two thousand years ago by the waters of Babylon and wept. They record our triumphs; they solace our affliction. Great orators are the creatures of popular assemblies; we were permitted only by stealth to meet even in our temples. And as for great writers, the catalogue is not blank. What are all the school-men, Aquinas himself, to Maimonides; and as for modern philosophy, all springs from Spinoza.

"But the passionate and creative genius that is the nearest link to divinity, and which no human tyranny can destroy, though it can divert it; that should have stirred the hearts of nations by its inspired sympathy, or governed senates by its burning eloquence, has found a medium for its expression, to which, in spite of your prejudices and your evil passions, you have been obliged to bow. The ear, the voice, the fancy teeming with combinations, the imagination fervent with picture and emotion, that came from Caucasus, and which we have preserved unpolluted, have endowed us with almost the exclusive privilege of MUSIC, that science of harmonious sounds which the ancients recognized as most divine, and deified in the person of their most beautiful creation. I speak not of the past, though were I to enter into the history of the lords of melody, you would find it the annals of Hebrew genius. But at this moment even, musical Europe is ours. There is not a company of singers—not an orchestra in a single capital—that are not crowded with our children under the feigned name which they adopt to conciliate the dark aversion which your posterity will some day disclaim with shame and disgust. Almost every great composer, skilled musician, almost every great voice that ravishes you with its transporting strains, spring from our tribes. The catalogue is too vast to enumerate—too illustrious to dwell for a moment on secondary names, however eminent. Enough for us that the three great creative minds to whose exquisite inventions all nations at this moment yield—Rossini, Meyerbeer, Mendelssohn— are of Hebrew race; and little do your men of fashion, your "muscadins" of Paris and your dandies of London, as they thrill into raptures at the notes of a Pasta or a Grisi, little do they suspect that they are offering their homage to the sweet singers of Israel!"

We had marked out many more passages for extract—many especially relating to the ways of treasury hacks and Parliament men, which are described with excellent humour and satire. "I like your high-flyers," says Tadpole to Taper (both of these heroes are small officials, hoping only for small places); "it is your plodders I detest, wearing old hats and high-lows, speaking in committee, *and thinking they are men of business: d—n them.*" There is wonderful truth in this sketch of certain mongrel Caucasians, who hang about all governments. The definition of the present government is similarly excellent. We beg all readers to admire Mr. Disraeli's account of

THE GREAT CONSERVATIVE CAUSE.

" 'By Jove,' said the panting Buckhurst, throwing himself on the sofa, 'it was well done; never was anything better done. An immense triumph! The greatest triumph the Conservative cause has had. And yet,' he added, laughing, 'if any fellow were to ask me what the Conservative cause was, I am sure I should not know what to say.'

" 'Why it is the cause of our glorious institutions,' said Coningsby. 'A crown robbed of its prerogatives; a church controlled by a commission; and an aristocracy that does not lead.'

" 'Under whose genial influence, the order of the peasantry, 'a country's pride,' has vanished from the face of the land,' said Henry Sydney, 'and is succeeded by a race of serfs, who are called labourers, and who burn ricks.'

" 'Under which,' continued Coningsby, 'the Crown has become a cipher, the church a sect, the nobility drones, and the people drudges.'

" 'It is the great constitutional cause,' said Lord Vere, 'that refuses everything to opposition; yields everything to agitation: conservative in Parliament, destructive out of doors; that has no objection to any change, provided only it be effected by unauthorized means.'

" 'The first public association of men,' said Coningsby, 'who have worked for an avowed end, without enunciating a single principle.'

" 'And who have established political infidelity throughout the land,' said Lord Henry.

" 'By Jove,' said Buckhurst, 'what infernal fools we have made ourselves this last week!' "

We wish Sir Robert Peel joy of his Young England friends; and, admiring fully the vivid correctness of Mr. Disraeli's description of this great Conservative party, which conserves nothing, which proposes nothing, which resists nothing, which believes nothing: admire still more his conclusion, that out of this nothing a something is to be created, round which England is contentedly to rally, and that we are one day to re-organize faith and reverence round this wretched, tottering, mouldy, clumsy, old idol.

[3 JUNE 1844]

Stanley's Life of Dr. Arnold.

The columns of a newspaper are ill-suited to the examination of such a work as this. We can do little more than recommend the serious reader to study it, and record briefly the feelings of admiration and affectionate reverence which the perusal of the life and letters of Dr. Arnold have awakened. They describe a character the most noble and the most wise—the most just, manly, benevolent, and thoughtful. If learning and wisdom, justice and love ever belonged to a man, Arnold had them. His scholars must think of him as the disciples of Socrates did of their master, or the American soldiers of Washington. There is something heroic in the qualities of the man; his lofty simplicity, his burning love of truth, his great heart so full of love and power. Nor should a journal professing Liberal opinions forget to mention, that they have such an authority as Arnold's on their side; and that they were advocated by one of the most learned and pious and wise men the country has ever seen. Scholars, who will read this biography on account of the reputation which the subject of the memoir has obtained throughout Europe, will see in the midst of his learned labours what a hearty citizen he was; how this scholar and theologian, with Christian truth as the centre round which the whole of his noble life turned, advanced his political belief as an article and consequence of his Christian faith—that he deduced charity, freedom, equality of Christian worship, not merely from his philosophic reading, but from his Scripture studies, upon which foundations his opinions rose. That they should have subjected him to much obloquy in his time, who can wonder? The matter of surprise and sorrow with us is not that the priest-party should have cried him down, but that the then Liberal government of this country, which had the power to show its sense of the merits of its servants, by placing them in positions of honour and eminence, should have neglected or been afraid to place Arnold among the heads of the church of which he was an ornament. Not for his sake, but for that of the Church of England, he ought to have died a bishop.

As it is, and while the Newmanite party are recording the miracles of St. Stephen Harding, his mortifications and flagellations, and how the ghosts of defunct Cistercians came to him from the dead, and asked his blessing; and how the faithful were healed by the miraculous "fontanel of oil" which oozed from the tomb of St. Walberga, the Saxon virgin;[1] those readers who desire to find in the biographies of pious and good Englishmen, not canting wonders, nor foolish encomiums of impossible asceticism, but honest lessons of faith and practice, and examples of noble charity, humility, and virtue, will not fail to profit by the account of Arnold's life, which appears to have been one of the best, most useful, and purest that ever was led by an English devine. And it is his public character and services, as well as his private life, which endear him to us, and make us proud that our country should have produced him.

In the history of his life there is, as may be supposed, nothing remarkable. It is the account of a man of great parts and noble heart, doing his duty. He has no special manifestations of Heaven, like those of which we are so often made to read in the biographies of both the Newman and the Whitefield schools, only, indeed, that special gift of Providence which endows some favoured beings with a greater aptitude for all sorts of good than is accorded to most human hearts, and which gives them the best gifts of intellect and industry, justice, and a love for all holy things, and which sets such persons apart for weaker men to reverence, and to endeavour to follow at a distance, however humble. Any criticism upon such a life can be but an encomium; nor perhaps can the reader understand the warmth with which such a book must be spoken of, until he himself has perused it. We hope it may be read extensively; it is one of the most grateful duties of a public journal, to be able to point out to its readers how they may acquire so much benefit to themselves, and we recommend to them "Arnold's Life and Letters" as a source from which they can gain the best and highest instruction.

Every man whose own school-days are not very distant, and who can remember that strange ordeal of his early life—the foolish old-world superstitions which obtained in the public

---

[1] These miracles are recorded in the first two parts of *The Cistercian Saints of England,* edited by John Henry Newman in 1844. The sanction that Newman thus lent to the legends concerning the "unguentiferous" Walburga was long held against him; indeed, Kingsley made it part of his indictment in "What, Then, Does Dr. Newman Mean?" twenty years later. See *Newman's Apologia Pro Vita Sua,* ed. Wilfrid Ward (London, 1913), pp. 39-44.

school; the wretched portion of letters meted out to him there—the misery, vice, and folly, which were taught along with the small share of Greek and Latin imparted to him—the ten years wasted in the pursuit of a couple of languages which not one lad in a hundred mastered—the total ignorance upon all other matters of learning, which was almost enjoined by the public school system—will be apt to think, as we imagine, "Why had I not Arnold for a master?" and by such the long chapter in the first volume about Rugby School (over which Dr. Arnold presided, and which he rendered one of the most celebrated educational institutions in the country) will be read with great interest. The account of his treatment of his younger pupils especially is very affecting—of his affectionate earnestness to bring them to religion—of his delicacy on the point of honour—of his high-minded regard and warm sympathy with the successes of his scholars in college and after-life. He was more "Conservative" in his school management than in any other part of his public career, and we might wish that his Liberalism had interfered here a little more. Fagging can no more be good for a boy than for a negro; if the baculine law is necessary, it surely might be restricted to the masters, and not administered by the active cudgels of the sixth form. But Arnold was one of those who had been himself so successful in school and college life, that he took, as we think, too favourable a view of both. From his earliest childhood he showed wonderful powers and memory, great aptitude for learning and fondness for it; hence a natural liking for the institutions to which he was himself so well adapted. But we question whether the unlucky majority would coincide with him: the hopelessly dull agree in the propriety of fagging and flogging, the timid and weak admit the beauties of bullying, all which laws of the schoolboy code Doctor Arnold was disposed to maintain; and as he writes in one of his letters, in a moment of impatience, against the Whig government, "If such a thing is not right, why is it done?" we may say likewise, if tyranny is not right in men, how is it right in boys; and what boyish custom or expediency can excuse it?

We must content ourselves with giving a few extracts from his life and opinions, once more cordially inviting the reader to read and re-read them all.

STANLEY's *Life of Dr. Arnold*

THE POLITICS OF CHRISTIANITY.

"Popular principles and democracy (when he used these words in a good sense) were not the opposition to an hereditary monarchy or peerage, which he always valued as precious elements of national life, but were inseparably blended with his strong belief in the injustice and want of sympathy generally shown by the higher to the lower orders,— a belief which he often declared had been first brought home to him, when, after having as a young man at Oxford held the opposite view, he first began seriously to study the language used with regard to it by St. James and the Old Testament Prophets. Liberal principles were not merely the expression of his adherence to a Whig ministry, but of his belief in the constant necessity of applying those principles of advance and reform, which, in their most perfect development, he conceived to be identical with Christianity itself; which, even in their lower exemplifications, he maintained to have been, by the very constitution of human society, the representatives of the cause of wisdom and goodness, in every age of the world except before the Fall of man from Paradise, and more especially since the Christian revelation had furnished a standard of moral excellence so far above the actual institutions of mankind, with principles of moral duty, which no intermixture of races or change of national customs could possibly endanger."

THE TORIES AND THE CATHOLIC CLAIMS.

"As to the principles in the pamphlet, it is a matter of unfeigned astonishment to me, that any man calling himself a Christian should think them bad, or should not recognise in them the very principles of Christianity itself. If my principles are bad, I only wish that those who think them so would state their own in opposition to them. It is all very well to call certain principles mischievous and democratical; but I believe very few of those, who do so call them, would be able to bear the monstrous nature of their own, if they were obliged fully to develope them. I mean, that they would then be seen to involve what in their daily language about things of common life their very holders laugh at as absurdity and mischief. For instance, about continual reforms, or the wisdom of our ancestors—I have heard Tories laugh at the farmers in their parish, for opposing the mending of the roads, because, as they said, what had been good enough for their fathers was good enough for them; and yet these farmers were not an atom more silly than the people who laughed at them, but only more consistent. And so the arrogance of tone in the pamphlet, I do not consider it to be arrogance to assume that I know more of a particular subject, which I have studied eagerly from a child, than those do who notoriously do not study it at all. The very men who think it hard to be taxed with ignorance of modern history, and of the laws and literature of foreign nations, are men who, till this question came on, never pretended to know anything about them; and, in the case of the Evangelicals, professed to shun such studies as profane. I should consider no man arrogant who, if I were to talk about some mathematical or scientific question which he had studied habitually, and on which all scientific men were agreed, should tell me that I did not and could not understand the subject, because I had never liked mathematics, and had never pretended to work at them. Those only who have studied history with that fondness that I have done all my life can fully appreciate the pain which it gives me to see the most mischievous principles supported, as they have been on this question, with an ignorance truly audacious. I will only instance Mr. C.'s appeal to English history in proof that God's judgments will visit us if we grant any favour to the Catholics." . . .

THE CHURCH, AND WHAT IT SHOULD BE.

"Our church now has a strict bond in matters of opinion, and none at all in matters of practice; which seems to me a double error. The Apostles began with the most general of all bonds in point of opinion— the simple confession that Jesus was the Son of God—not that they meant to rest there; but that, if you organize and improve the church morally, you will improve its tone theoretically; till you get an agreement in what is essential Christian principle, and a perfect tolerance of differences in unessential opinions. But now, the true and grand idea of a church, that is, a society for the purpose of making men like Christ—earth like heaven—the kingdoms of the world the kingdom of Christ—is all lost; and men look upon it as 'an institution for religious instruction and religious worship,' thus robbing it of its life and universality, making it an affair of clergy, not of people—of preaching and ceremonies, not of living—of Sundays and synagogues, instead of one of all days and all places, houses, streets, towns, and country. I believe that the government are well disposed, and I wish, at any rate, to try them. I know at least what I mean myself, and have a definite object before me, which, if I cannot reach, I would at least come as near to it as I can."

. . . .

[2 AUGUST 1844]

Historic Fancies. By the Hon. GEORGE SIDNEY SMYTHE, M.P. One vol.   [Colburn, 1844.

"Young England" is gradually manifesting its spirit and its outline to the world, through the medium of the press; gradually, say we, and somewhat mysteriously too, for it cannot be pretended that hitherto we have had any very definite revelations as to the character and mission of this new political creation. Nevertheless, progress it has made, and though, as yet, without very obvious results, it has certainly not been without method. The Tractarians led the way to give a religious sanctity to the enterprise; and in order at once to engage the sympathies of the masses (we must use the new-coined word),[1] the spirit of Christian charity was made to go rather ostentatiously hand in hand with Christian doctrine for the sufferings of the poor, who always have suffered since the world began, were now bewailed as they never had been, by the rich and lordly—the selfish vices of the wealthy confessed and rebuked by men from amongst its own very ranks. Above all, a vague alarm for the consequences of these things was sedulously expressed; gloomy prospects painted of the future; whilst, by way of contrast, bright and tantalizing visions were conjured up of the state of society in some indefinitely "by-gone days," when the rich cared for the poor, and fed them with all good things of this earth, the poor doing light and cheerful service in return, and all men lived in the fear of God, and in charity and love with one another. To heighten the effect of this comfortable picture, something yet was added by the skilful hand of this moral magician—the sports and pastimes of the good ancient days were invoked upon the tapis after the roast beef and ale of Old England had been disposed of, and so the best wish that could be offered to man was in imagination realized—plenty waited on appetite, health and contentment on both!

All this was very subtle, but, to our minds, very unsatisfactory. It is not enough to disturb men's minds, and make them more unhappy than they really would be if left alone, by telling them how happy they might be if something—something as yet undefined—were done for them. "What is that something?" impatiently demand a myriad of voices; "and who is to give it us?" "What is that something that you drive at?" inquire somewhat perplexed men in power. But two questions at once is too much for any one to answer;—what that something is which is to be the *panacea* for all evils "New England" will not tell; but who is to supply it, or rather, who shall *not* supply it, that he does not long hesitate to answer. After one or two dark mutterings and significant hints, the secret is avowed. Whatever it be that is to bless and make happy the people of this suffering land, it shall

---

[1] The N. E. D. cites an example of "masses" in the sense of populace or lower orders as early as 1837, but the document in which it occurs was not printed until 1857.

not be administered by the great ones now in power: for their sins of no-principle they shall be denied the blessing of doing good. Blessing and good shall yet be done, but it shall be after their day; it shall be done when "Young England" is grown to man's estate, and the present worn out actors have quitted the stage which they have too long disgraced. Such is the denunciation at first vaguely put forth by "Young England" against the "Conservative" party, whom he taunts with having nothing to conserve, not merely of their own, but of any body else's. They have no honour, no principles.

So were they denounced the other day by Coningsby, the Jeremiah of the clubs; and bitterly did he scoff at every man of them as he pointed to the sword of destruction which was suspended above their heads. But still no hint was given of who were to supply their places, nor of what sort of principles were to rule the destinies of man, after their no-principle reign was over; or, if anything was hinted, it was so loosely and so vaguely, that it will probably not be understood till the prophecy is fulfilled.

In this state of things, we confess, that from the first moment of its announcement we looked forward with considerable interest to the production of the present volume, coming as it does from the pen of a young patrician—himself not the least accomplished nor least daring member of the "New Generation."

"Historic Fancies! in one volume," following up an historic novel in three volumes—fact after fiction! It struck us that this one volume would prove an important and intelligible step in the great change now preparing for us. We fancied, and not unseasonably we think, that one of the mystic leaders of the "New Generation" having heretofore spoken as it were in parables, his brother and successor would, in taking up a theme of a more historic character, so treat it as to render it the means of shadowing forth more clearly the precepts which these parables implied; and, however we might be predisposed or not to acquiesce in the precepts so to be evolved, we certainly did anticipate much intellectual exercise and excitement from their investigation. We instinctively ran over in our minds the principal salient periods in history, which—most dramatic in themselves—have been of most notable influence upon posterity, the early acts as it were of the great drama of the world, of which the succeeding scenes are yet passing before us. We reverted to the establishment of the Christian religion, the disruption of ancient empires, and the origin and growth of modern nations, the progress of civil liberties in such and such states, the growth of despotisms in others; we thought of the cause of the people, and state of the people in all; or, to speak more within bounds, we thought of the revival of letters and the arts, which led to the destruction of the modern empire of the Popes; the new sympathies and connections of nations, instead of provinces, which ensued; the splendid rise of the monarchy upon the ruins of the aristocracy in France under her Sullys and Richelieus and Mazarins; in England the growth of an oligarchy upon the abasement of the monarchy; the brief and splendid era of Spain and the Ottoman empire; the effect of tyranny all over the world, in scattering mankind and his arts, leading to colonization; the effect of all this upon the quantity, quality, and distribution of national wealth; and, finally, what is yet wanted to remedy the evils attendant upon this vital question: in fact, a thousand matters of pregnant importance, upon which, without at all going deeply into the dogmas of politics and political economy, a young man of sound principles, of generous impulses, and of independent feeling, might indulge in "fancies" by the hour; fancies which could not but prove of interest to those who, having only studied history and facts in the beaten track, have been hitherto too apt to apply the principles of the old world to the altered phases of the new.

This was expecting a good deal, perhaps. "Blessed is he who expecteth nothing!" he shall not be disappointed. It seems that we were too sanguine in our estimation of the importance of the work which Mr. Smythe had proposed to himself. "Young England" is not so far advanced in the race as we had imagined. To use a sporting phrase, which is now all the order of the day with our legislators, the colt has not yet been broken in; he has not been backed; the saddle-mark is not upon him; and he sports and scampers at random over the open fields and downs, showing good promise of speed, and a fine temper, but little aware of the hard training which he must undergo before he will be up to the mark to compete for the Queen's Plate, and that most valuable handicap, the Downing-street Stakes!

To drop horse-racing metaphors, however, and buckle to in earnest. There is much good sense and good feeling amongst

these "fancies," much well-written prose, and more really beautiful poetry; but they all want connection and purpose, at least
any that we can clearly discover. The author himself, in his
preface, states that "*they are full, he fears, of incoherences of expression
and inconsistencies of sentiment.*" And what more fatal defect, we
would ask, could an historical essayist confess to? Yet, in the
very next sentence (as if to give immediate confirmation of the
preceding one), he goes on to say—"*But they are not without some
unity in their system, nor a sustained purpose in their design.*" This is
a paradox which we will leave to be adjusted between the public
and the author, professing that we do not as yet understand it.

One only principle, or rather we should say, one only sentiment, we perceive pervading very uniformly the whole of these
desultory sketches—a sentiment highly creditable to the author
as a man, though, taken in its full extent, not a very safe one
for a statesman. This sentiment, we should observe, we had
attributed to our author from the whole tenor of his writing, long
before we lighted on it, formally enunciated by an amiable
apparition in a fanciful sketch, at the end of the volume, entitled
"Toleration." It is this:—"*Ever think good of others*—ever wish
good for others—ever do good to others." And again—"*Truth
is not mine, but multiform,* and benevolence is the disciple of truth."
Now all this is very plausible—very good-natured, perhaps; but
at the same time liable to lead to much error. If we "ever think
good of others," we must sometimes think good of those who do
not deserve it, and thus confound the good with the bad; we
shall want that rule of appreciation of the conduct of others,
without which we cannot pursue a straight and useful line of
conduct ourselves. Similarly erroneous is the proposition that
"truth is multiform," at least if the author intends it as we understand it. We cannot admit, for instance, that in any given case
there can be more than one true answer, one true course to adopt.
But Mr. Smythe illustrates these doctrines with an allegory,
which we cannot help thinking the bench of bishops would pro-
nounce the extreme of heterodoxy. He is accosted in a dream
by the Spirit of Toleration:—

"I looked up and beheld a maiden of singular loveliness. Her eyes
were very large, and full of fire. Her dark hair seemed still darker in
its contrast to her fair, pale forehead, and the small diamond crescent
which glittered above it. She beckoned me to follow her. I arose and
obeyed, in silent admiration and astonishment. Her robe of loose green

concealed her shape, but I could ever and anon perceive her small white feet, shining like glowworms before me. She stopped at the portal of the palace. I would fain have addressed her, but she at once hushed and silenced me. 'Stranger,' she said, and her voice was full of quiet and melodious meaning, 'speak not, think on as thou hast thought. Ever think good of others, ever wish good for others, ever do good for others.' She took my hand in one of hers as she spoke, while with the other she pressed against the gate. It flew open at her touch, and discovered what seemed an endless corridor of marble. At first I could distinguish nothing but a long, broad line of light; but, as I advanced, I could see that on either side of the vast hall were ranged golden thrones, and upon them were seated the Mighty Warriors and Rulers of the Faithful.

"But the maiden passed on swiftly and regardless of them all, till we had arrived nearly at the extreme end of the hall. And here methought I saw direct before me, a throne far loftier than any one of those I had seen before, with many steps up to it, and a canopy all inlaid, and heavy with precious stones above. And, beyond this again, a golden staircase arose, and it appeared to extend high upwards afar beyond the reach of mortal sight. And, as I drew nearer to the throne, methought it was the Great Prophet himself who sat thereon. And when we reached the lowest step, the maiden bowed down her head upon it, with folded arms and humble attitude. But, lest I should be thought to kneel and worship, I crossed myself in sign of my own Western Faith, and stood upright before the Prophet. And he came down the steps, and looked earnestly into my face, and smiled kindly. And he said, "Thy heart has been stirred within thee, at the glories of Islam. Doubt not. Truth is not mine only, but multiform. And Benevolence is the discipline of Truth." With these words, he raised me up to the very foot of the throne, and bade me look around me. *And I saw not one throne, but many thrones: not one corridor, but many corridors, and they all ended at the foot of the illimitable golden staircase.*"

Reader, mark the words in italics, in connection with the whole passage. If we mistake not, it means that all religions lead equally to the one end—an opinion for which "Young England" would have been burned at the stake, if he had lived in "the good old times" which he is so fond of dwelling upon; and which is now considered damnable by all proper men. But we must not enter upon polemics.

We must admit, by the way, that all the above passage *seems* to embody something like a principle, but then it is a principle that has no practical application, or one which "Young England" himself, if in power, would die rather than see brought into operation. So, also, is another sentiment which we see embodied in repeated passages here and there, but which, being also as constantly met by a countervailing sentiment, cannot be spoken of as a principle. We allude to what he says of the aristocracy of France, and of aristocracies in general. "It is clear," says he, "to the most superficial observer, who looks back at this distance of time upon scenes of such extravagance (he speaks of the period just preceding the French revolution), that no country could long support two such burthens as an absolute and profligate King, and an *insolent and tyrannical aristocracy.*" Again:— "It was not the poor and persecuted who were the instigators and leaders of the great Revolution;" no, it was the nobles, and he runs over many of their names, adding, "*but why eliminate names from the list, when the whole catalogue is so black with treachery?* Why dwell upon a stray passage, when the whole story of aristocratic ingratitude is so notorious?" Again:—"*The whole history of the Revolution,* from its alpha to its omega, from its first thought to its last deed, from Voltaire to Talleyrand, *is written in the perfidy of nobles.*" And then, a little further on, he enunciates this bold and stunning proposition: "Why deplore (query, for "deplore" read *condemn?*) the excesses of an oppressed population? It is the tendency of misery to brutalize. Why regret (query again, *denounce!*) the perfidy of nobles? *It is the tendency of prosperity to harden.* Thus education and pursuits alike prepare and exact the condition which is essential to their existence. *It is the very nature of an aristocracy to be sycophantic during the stability of monarchy, and perfidious during its decline. Woe to the sovereign who confided in—woe to the people who submitted to them.*"

All this is not very flattering, nor very promising, though we are afraid it is too true. "Truth is multiform," however, according to Mr. Smythe, and therefore, after having kicked *Milord Français* down stairs, he runs after him and picks him up, begs him not to take it personal, and after going over all the history of his misfortunes, after gently hinting the subsequent perfidies by which some of his family had lately sought to mend their broken fortunes, he concludes by assuring him that he has the highest esteem, respect, and regard for him and all his relations.

"But I am already more than presumptuous in attempting to praise or to blame contemporaries. It is not given to a foreigner to discriminate between the nice shades of party difference, or even to adjudge between those nobles who affect the Orleans Tuileries, or those who prefer the workshops of the people.* *It is sufficient that his own admiration is dis-*

* "The Monarchy of the Middle Classes."

interested and sincere. He has ventured to pay to the aristocracy of France a homage full of regret for the past, full of solicitude for the future. It is offered in their misfortune and decline. His praise, however valueless, is not for the powerful; his song, however humble, not for the prosperous. And, *in his augury of a fairer fortune, he hazards no political opinion if he has been unable to separate their destinies from those Elder Bourbons,* with whom all their renown, their virtues, their defects, and, it may be, their hopes, are connected."

Why here is flat treason against common sense, at least, if not against the Bourbons. Mr. Smythe first vituperates the nobles of France, and imputes to their perfidy and crimes the ruin of the house of Bourbon, then commiserates with their misfortunes, which they suffered jointly with that dynasty, and hints that *they* owe those misfortunes to *their* association with that royal house; in fact, the very converse of all he had said just previously.

But enough of principles; and, principles apart, there is much to interest and amuse in these sketches. For the most part they are brief, and strictly "fanciful," having little or no foundation in absolute recorded incidents, and, with one exception, illustrating no great historical period. That exception is the period of the French Revolution, which occupies continuously one hundred and eighty out of the three hundred and eighty-six pages of which the volume consists. The manner in which all this matter is introduced, by the way, is odd enough. Mr. Smythe writes two poems, entitled "The Loyalist of the Vendée," and "The Jacobin of Paris," the former of forty-eight the latter of seventy-six lines, and appended to them as it were in the capacity of notes to the text, we have elaborate and well-written memoirs of Larochejaquelein on the one hand, and of Mirabeau, Dumouriez, Hoche, Marat, Louvet, St. Just, Robespierre, and, in short, of all the principal leaders of the Revolution. In treating these subjects, he certainly acts up to his doctrine of "Ever think good of others;" for the portraitures are decidedly lenient, not to say flattering. Both St. Just and Robespierre, in particular, he courageously defends from the opprobrium with which they have so generally been treated, and which more justly attached to some of their fellows. After comparing St. Just with our Akenside, the poet, as far as temperament and prevailing sentiment go, he concludes with the following brilliant passage:

"Akenside's plebeian origin, his love of contradiction, his enmity to all things established, would have thrown him forward into ranks, more advanced, and opinions more austere. He would have attached himself as closely, as did St. Just, to Robespierre. He would have rushed into his closet, as eagerly, with some new paradox to be asserted, or some received and old one to be crushed. He would have found a fitter audience in the Jacobins, than in the Squires of Northamptonshire, for his clamours for Equality. He would have quoted not Hobbes and Shaftesbury, but Spinosa and Rousseau. He would have dogmatised, with as persevering an acuteness. He would have adopted, in extenuation of his systematic cruelties, an apology like that of St. Just. 'The fire of Liberty has refined us, as it chases the scum from the vessel to purify the metal that remains.' But if Akenside was a more admirable poet than St. Just, if the Pleasures of Imagination are a more successful poem than Organt, he had not enough of character or resolution to become a statesman of his height and proportions. He would have been as ruthless, but not so disinterested; his list of proscriptions would have been as long, but his capacity was unequal to plan, enact, execute, the measures which made the Revolution. And of the greatest among these, St. Just was the originating power; the report against the King, that against the Girondists, and that against the respective friends and followers of Danton and Hébert.

"It is by such comparisons that we shall best appreciate the Greatness of St. Just. He was a Poet Republican. He was of that temper, which in its fairest uses, may form a Great man, and in its worst abuses can never form a mean man. He was exalted by that spirit of Liberty, which at its highest may make almost a prophet, and at its lowest, almost an assassin—which glorifies even into a Milton, and degrades even into an Alibaud. But nothing of self advancement or self-interest, nothing of a stunted morality, nothing of small delinquencies, belong to characters like these. They are capable of great virtues or great crimes. And, if St. Just had lived, he would have disdained the mimetic grandeurs of an Imperial Dignitary, even with the bribe of such enormous appointments as a Vice Grand Elector. But with his ancient companion-in-arms and comrade, Hoche, with whom he must soon have been reconciled, he would have rendered France as great, and yet more formidable, than she became under the empire. And they would have given to her, in their own lives, a renown which would have been only less glorious, and far more pure, than that which now attaches to the idea of Napoleon."

In his summary of the character of Robespierre, we have the following remarkable observation:—

"He conquered the Constituent, he dictated to the Legislative, he intimidated the Convention. He effected this by a strong sense, and rigid performance of duties (while all around him were moved by interest or impulse), which, however little they can meet with English sympathy, it would be difficult to condemn by any standard of mere morality. He was not to be seduced from his object by any bribe, intrigue, or fascination. He pursued his public course with a straightforward and unswerving onwardness of purpose. His private life was, to the last, pure and irreproachable. Poor, he lived within his income; he was scrupulous in little matters, careful in his dress, regular in his habits, laborious in his industry, attached to every decency and all respectabilities. He had lived thirty-two years when the Constituent was dissolved; and if there were few who, at that time, thought him a great man, there were none who did not call him a sincere and a good man. The general opinion was, that he was an obstinate, and what we call a *crotchetty*, philanthropist. But subtle and keen observers, like Siéyès or Talleyrand, in all probability foresaw that his opinions were so fanatical in their excess that they might well plunge him into any other. He belonged to that worst species of monsters, what the elder Scaliger once eulogistically termed the *monstrum sine vitio*. He derived a sort of indemnity for his barbarities in the excellence of his morals and the austerity of his character. By nature he was averse from cruelty. He wrote a pamphlet against the punishment of death; he introduced a bill against it. His timid and narrow bigotry was revolted at the large and broad traditions of the feudal age. It would be absurd to account for the inconsistency between his early life and the Reign of Terror, by attributing the first to hypocrisy. An hypocrisy of thirty-two years duration becomes a principle which no man would do ill in adopting. The reason of Robespierre's cruelty is to be found in the intensity of his self-esteem. He was the very incarnation of the letter I; but it was not a genuine and certain faith, as with an Englishman; it was rather a wayward, suspicious, fretful egotism—a faint and wavering shadow of Rousseau's own uncertain and sensitive idiosyncracy. It was to this— the fanciful demon which possessed him—that he sacrificed his hecatomb of victims."

The sting, however, is in the tail; and in this one little bit we have the only manifesto which the present volume contains against the "Conservative" incapables of the present age:—

"The judgment upon Robespierre of such men, who had studied his character, will hardly be disputed. The moral his life presents to inferior understandings is the same which we were taught in England by Mr. Pitt's immediate successors. It is a public evil when clerks become ministers, and statists statesmen, when small men inherit from the great. Mediocrity with the inspirations of genius; Robespierre enforcing the visions of Rousseau—a mortal in the chariot of the sun—and the world was nearly plunged into darkness, and civilization retarded in her onward and radiant career!"

We must now close this volume, from which, if the reader do not derive any very important truths of principle, he cannot fail of deriving much entertainment.

[27 MARCH 1845]

Egypt Under Mehemet Ali. By Prince PUCKLER MUSKAU.
[Colburn, London.

There are two grand categories into which the crowd of modern
"posters of the sea and land"[1] naturally divide themselves—the
travellers and the tourists. A hundred years ago a man might
have built up a very respectable traveller's reputation within the
confines of Europe; he might have mounted into the honour over
the Alps or the Pyrenees. But now the case is different: Europe
is abandoned to the mere tourists—the diminutives of travellers;
and we hardly think of giving a wanderer credit for belonging to
the latter class until he has, at least, passed a fashionable season
at Timbuctoo—aired himself on a peak of the Himmalehs, or done
honour to a buffalo-hump dinner amid the Rocky Mountains!

The famous land of Egypt, too, is, in this point of view, becoming quite European. A fortnight's pleasant voyaging may
waft us from the Thames to the Nile—from our green English
fields and woods to the deserts and palm trees of the country of
the Pyramids. A widely different place, indeed, is the Egypt
of the present day from the savage land it was when Bruce
pushed his way up the Nile, and Belzoni groped amid the recesses
of the Catacombs. Mehemet Ali is making the Arabs civilized
whether they will or no. Steamers are frightening the crocodiles
of the old Nile. Every autumn, crowds of English, French, and
German ramblers swarm in the busy streets of Cairo, and people
again the once solitary ruins of Thebes. We have heard of a
pic-nic on the top of the Great Pyramid, and one of the advertise-
ments of the enterprising Mr. Waghorn soothed the doubts of
would-be pilgrims to the East, by the pleasant tidings that plenty
of soda water would be found in the Desert![2]

We hardly know, however,—taking the scene of his exploits
and the character of the man—whether Prince Puckler Muskau
should be treated as one of the travellers, or one of the tourists.
He certainly pushed his way further up the country than most
of his here to-day there tomorrow brethren; attaining—now, by
means of boating it on the Nile, again, by the help of an easy-

---

[1] *Macbeth,* I, iii, 33.
[2] Thomas Waghorn, who pioneered the overland route to India, had
recently described its attractions in a series of pamphlets.

going dromedary—to the capital of Soudan, the territory bordering upon Abyssinia. The prince is altogether a pleasant travelling companion—a little conceited, a little egotistical, a little too fond of keeping the reader continually in mind that he is a prince, and has a suite, and travels with Mehemet Ali— but he is also intelligent, persevering and energetic. He has a keen scent after antiquities—clambers among ruins, measures sphinxes' noses, and gets half choked in groping into the dusty recesses of tombs; and then emerging, lays down the law solemnly touching the uses to which the Pharaohs and their contemporaries intended these structures to be put; gleaning wonderful theories of old Egyptian manners and customs from unintelligible hieroglyphics and mutilated sculptures, and, after the fashion of antiquaries in general, treating with high disrespect every body's theories but his own. But the Prince is not merely content with trying to recall what Egypt was, he is diligent in his researches into, and sensible in his remarks upon the resources now beginning to develope themselves in that country. He narrates several interesting interviews he had with Mehemet Ali upon the subject of the government and the prospects of Egypt. For the acuteness of intellect, and the strength of mind of that extraordinary man, he entertains a most deservedly high admiration. He was favoured with rare opportunities of judging of them, and it is but just to say that he well availed himself of them. His book, then, is altogether a pleasant melange of speculations on what probably was the past, and on what probably will be the future state of Egypt. He gives us both antiquities and statistics; add to this that he gossips agreeably of the thousand and one little incidents of travel which he encountered—that he sketches with spirit and effect the scenes he saw and the people he met with, and that he now and then in a very free and easy way halts in his onward progress to administer a belabouring to some hapless critic who may have attacked one of his former works, or to instruct us with a gastronomic lecture—for the prince has very sensible notions of *gourmandise*—imagine a writer with all these characteristics, and it is scarcely possible but that the book he produces will be pleasant light reading, its faults comparatively venial, its good points really good and salient.

Of the present state of Egypt, the work, which has been some years written, cannot be expected to give a very exact account.

There are, however, many points which the lapse of a short time do not render less interesting or important. With respect to the much talked of Fellah population of Egypt, the Prince says,

"Having still a little spare time, we proceeded to the railway, which had been lately constructed for the purpose of conveying stones to the buildings which were in the course of erection along the shore. Here we found a great number of Fellahs, men, women, and children, at work. The viceroy had just increased the wages of all employed on the public works half a piastre per diem.

"As most of the accounts of Egypt which have fallen into my hands are filled with the most dismal lamentations of the misery of this unhappy class, I was not a little surprised at finding, for the most part, vigorous, healthy, and cheerful-looking men, who performed their work amid song and jest, were most indulgently treated by their overseers, and seemed only in joke when they solicited us to give them a bakshish, an odious habit which prevails in other countries as well as here. They were ragged enough, to be sure, and barely clad; but where do we find it otherwise in the East, nay, even in Greece? The climate requires so little, and order and cleanliness are certainly not indigenous in these parts. I have since paid much attention to this subject, and am fully persuaded that the Fellahs of Egypt are infinitely better off than many of their class in Europe. Take, for instance, the Irish peasants, who are subjects of the most enlightened government in the civilised world, or take the poor weavers in Vogtland, of whom I read only this very day, in the newspapers, in the year 1843, that the utmost which they can earn is twopence a-day; and that when potatoes, their only staple article of food, fails, they are ready to perish with famine; hence I maintain, that these Fellahs, though unquestionably exposed to much harsh and arbitrary treatment, are nevertheless in a situation which might excite the envy of many of our countrypeople."

His account of the labouring population generally in Egypt is as favourable. Several chapters are devoted to the fleet and the arsenals the Pacha has established, and to the schools he has set on foot.

After proceeding up the Nile to Cairo, the prince is honoured with an interview with Mehemet himself:—

"His highness received me in one of the lower apartments of the palace, which was filled with a respectful crowd of his courtiers and officers of state. When I had made my way through the midst of them, I saw the viceroy standing on the platform, before his ottoman, with only Artim Bey, his dragoman, at his side. My surprise was great, for, judging by the bust which I had seen at Alexandria, and some portraits which are considered as likenesses, I had pictured to myself an austere, nay, harsh-looking man, in a splendid oriental dress, with features very closely resembling those of Oliver Cromwell. Instead of this there stood before me a friendly little old man, whose vigorous, well-proportioned frame was set off by nothing but a freshness of complexion, and a cleanliness, which might almost be called coquettish, but whose features were equally expressive of calm dignity and benevolent good-nature, and who, though his sparkling eagle eyes seemed to penetrate my inmost thoughts, yet the grace of his smile and the affability of his manner inspired me with involuntary partiality, without the slightest tincture of timidity. He was dressed in a plain brown pelisse, with the white trimming of which, his venerable beard of the same colour was singularly blended; on his head he wore a simple red tarbush, without any shawl or jewels to ornament it; he had no rings on his fingers, nor, what is so usual in the East, did he hold a valuable rosary in his hand, which, by the bye, is in general so beautifully shaped, that a lady might envy it.

"I afterwards found that my first impression of this great man was perfectly in unison with the behaviour of his courtiers, who, though full of respect, are very familiar and easy in their intercourse with him; and, while he treats individuals with a nicety of distinction, he always manifests urbanity to all around him. Nothing is more easy than to obtain an audience of the viceroy; it is impossible for any governor to be more accessible, or to adopt fewer measures for his personal security than Mehemet Ali, who fearlessly exposes himself every day to the attacks of any fanatic who might aim at his life."

The conversations which the illustrious traveller had with the Pacha develope to a remarkable degree the far-seeing and comprehensive character of the Pacha's mind—the intuitive sagacity and energy with which he pursues his objects—and the honesty of purpose with which he labours in his great work of the civilization of Egypt.

After passing some time in antiquarian researches in Thebes, the prince proceeded up the Nile. We have a vivid description of the passage of the Cataracts, and a series of entertaining sketches of the villages and antiquities all along the banks. In the course of his progress an eclipse of the moon gives occasion to the enunciation of the following piece of African astronomical lore. The *savant* is Faki of Dongola:—

" 'Only the ignorant people,' said he, 'believe that it is a dragon which endeavours to swallow the moon. The moon is a living being as well as we, but a very exalted potentate in the kingdom of heaven, which is governed by God exactly in the same manner as the earth is by the Sultan. When, therefore, one of the governors there does not do his duty, the Lord of Heaven, like the Sultan here, has his head cut off, or sends him the bow-string. Now, it is evident that the moon had incurred such a punishment, and therefore when his countenance began to be darkened, we fired lustily and uttered tones of lamentation, to testify our desire to help him, and our compassion for his situation, for he might still obtain pardon; but as we soon observed that there was no more grace for him, and that he at length totally vanished, we set up a louder noise, mingled with demonstrations of joy, in order to recommend ourselves as much as possible to the new moon; which, accordingly, scarcely two hours after the execution of the last, appeared in more splendour than its predecessor had ever done.' We see that the people of rank here understand as well as ourselves what is beseeming a good courtier—'*Le roi est mort! Vive le roi!*' "

With the following sketch of dromedary-riding we close these volumes, leaving the prince near Mandarah on the blue Nile, and recommending his book to the attention of all who relish a pleasant, familiar, sketchy description of Egypt and the Egyptians:—

"It was the first time in my life that I had mounted a dromedary. I must observe, by the way (for what is quite common and well-known here, is not always so among us) that what is here called a dromedary, is not a different animal from the camel, but identically the same beast with one hunch; and the difference between a dromedary and a camel is like that between an elegant saddle-horse and a clumsy cart-horse. It is not by any means difficult to mount them, because the animals are accustomed to kneel down when they are saddled, while one of the forelegs is bound fast with the long bridle, and the leather holds it by the head to prevent its rising too rapidly, by which the rider might easily be thrown upon the sand. These singular animals have three joints in their hind legs, and require three movements to rise as well as to lie down; this action always appears very violent to the unpractised rider, who must be exceedingly careful to bend forwards and backwards with precision, or he will inevitably lose his balance, of which we had more than one diverting instance among our party.

"The pace of the dromedary in walking is very inconvenient, jerking, jolting backwards and forwards; but he is generally made to go at a pretty quick pace, which gives the rider much the same sensation as what we call the short jog trot of a very hard trotting horse. Hence riding in this manner six or seven miles, and often longer without intermission, is very fatiguing, but for a short distance it is not by any means disagreeable, and the uniform, continued shaking is certainly advantageous both to the health and appetite. The seat itself on the wooden frame of the saddle, round the high pummel of which the rider must lay his legs crossways, is likewise not a little inconvenient to a European till he has become accustomed to it. It is therefore advisable for every one coming hither in his boat, so to arrange matters that the first stages of his journey may be very short, in order to wean himself after the long repose which makes a voyage, on the Nile at least, on account of this want of exercise, a truly indolent life.

"The dromedary, when going as slowly as possible, travels nearly five miles an hour; in its quick trot, twice or thrice as much, and continues at this rate for ten or twelve hours without resting. Mehemet Ali once accomplished the journey from Suez to Cairo, a distance of one hundred and fifteen miles, on his dromedary, in twelve hours, in order to prevent a conspiracy of the Mamelukes, and his sais, holding on by the tail of the animal and running on foot, reached Cairo at the same time. Sonnini affirms that the Nedshi dromedary can travel a hundred leagues in twenty-four hours; but it strikes me that this must certainly be an exaggeration.

"Both dromedaries and camels are ill-tempered and disagreeable animals: I never mounted mine but it testified its displeasure by a snarling noise, and sometimes even by an attempt to bite me. Yet when once set a-going, I found it, like its leader, to be always docile and tractable, and a slight touch with a kurbatsh on its long neck was sufficient to excite it to the most rapid trot. The bit of the bridle is not in the animal's mouth, but it is drawn through one nostril, and there fastened by a wooden peg. When the rider wishes to dismount, he must make a kind of hoarse groan, which it is extremely difficult to imitate, on hearing which the dromedary immediately lies down. No sign is necessary to make it rise again, for it invariably does so of its own accord as soon as ever the rider is mounted and has taken the bridle into his hand."

....

[3 APRIL 1845]

LEVER'S ST. PATRICK'S EVE—COMIC POLITICS,

Since the days of Æsop, comic philosophy has not been cultivated so much as at present. The chief of our pleasant writers—Mr. Jerrold, Mr. Dickens, Mr. Lever—are assiduously following this branch of writing; and the first-named jocular sage, whose apologues adorned our spelling-books in youth, was not more careful to append a wholesome piece of instruction to his fable than our modern teachers now are to give their volumes a moral ballast. To some readers—callous, perhaps, or indifferent to virtue or to sermons—this morality is occasionally too obtrusive. Such sceptics will cry out—We are children no longer; we no longer want to be told that the fable of the dog in the manger is a satire against greediness and envy; or that the wolf and the lamb are types of Polk gobbling up a meek Aberdeen,[1] or innocence being devoured by oppression. These truths have been learned by us already. If we want instruction, we prefer to take it from fact rather than from fiction. We like to hear sermons from his reverence at church; to get our notions of trade, crime, politics, and other national statistics, from the proper papers and figures; but when suddenly, out of the gilt pages of a pretty picture book, a comic moralist rushes forward, and takes occasion to tell us that society is diseased, the laws unjust, the rich ruthless, the poor martyrs, the world lop-sided, and *vice versâ*, persons who wish to lead an easy life are inclined to remonstrate against this literary ambuscadoe. You may be very right, the remonstrant would say, and I am sure are very hearty and honest, but as these questions you propound here comprehend the whole scheme of politics and morals, with a very great deal of religion, I am, I confess, not prepared at the present moment to enter into them. Without wishing to be uncomplimentary, I have very shrewd doubts as to your competency to instruct upon all these points; at all events, I would much rather hear you on your own ground—amusing by means of amiable fiction, and instructing by kindly satire, being careful to avoid the discussion of abstract principles, beyond those of the common ethical science which forms a branch of all poets and novelists' business—but, above all, eschewing questions of politics and political economy, as too deep, I will not say for your comprehension, but for your readers'; and never, from their nature, properly to be discussed in any, the most gilded, story-book. Let us remember, too, how loosely some of our sentimental writers have held to political creeds:—thus, we all know that the great philosopher, Mrs. Trollope, who, by means of a novel in shilling numbers,[2] determined to write down the poor-laws, somewhere towards the end of her story came to a hitch in her argument, and fairly broke down with a confession that facts had come to light, subsequent

[1] The Earl of Aberdeen, Foreign Secretary in Peel's cabinet, had replied in a reasonable and conciliatory fashion to the belligerent remarks about the northwestern boundary of the United States made by President Polk in his inaugural address of 5 March 1845. During the following year a treaty was concluded settling the Oregon problem to the satisfaction of both nations.

[2] *Jessie Phillips: a Tale of the New Poor Law,* which appeared in eleven shilling parts between 31 December 1842 and 30 November 1843.

to the commencement of her story, which had greatly altered her opinions regarding the law; and so the law was saved for that time. Thus, too, we know that the famous author of "Coningsby," before he propounded the famous New England philosophy, had preached many other respectable doctrines, viz., the Peel doctrines, the Hume doctrines, &c.: all this Sir Robert Peel himself took the pains to explain to the House of Commons the other night, when the great philosopher alluded to called the right honourable baronet an organised hypocrite.[3]

The moral of this is (for we wish to show that newspaper critics can make morals as well as successful novelists) that as a Trollope and a Disraeli, persons of a fiery and poetical imagination, have gone astray when treading the crabbed labyrinths of political controversy; and not only gone astray, but, as it were, tripped, stumbled, broken their noses, and scratched themselves in an entirely ludicrous and undignified manner; other imaginative writers should take warning by the fate of these illustrious victims, nor venture into quagmires where they may flounder beyond their depth.

It is but fair to say that the above moral dissertation has been occasioned, not by Mr. Lever's moral story alone, but by other moral tales of other moral writers of great wit and merit, who have adopted the didactic tone. Mr. Lever is by far the most gentle of the comic satirists: he is not only gentle and kindly in his appreciation of the poor man, but kindly and gentle in regard to the rich, whom certain of Mr. Lever's brother moralists belabour so hardly; and if occasion is here taken of one of his stories to enter a protest against sentimental politics altogether, it is .not because this author is more sinful on this score than any other, but because the practice amongst novelists is prodigiously on the increase, and can tend, as we fancy, to little good. You cannot have a question fairly debated in this way. You can't allow an author to invent incidents, motives, and characters, in order that he may attack them subsequently. How many Puseyite novels, Evangelical novels, Roman Catholic novels have we had, and how absurd and unsatisfactory are they.

---

[3] When Disraeli made the celebrated accusation that "a Conservative Government is an organized hypocrisy" in his speech of 17 March 1845, Peel replied by outlining the inconsistencies of Disraeli's political career (William Flavelle Monypenny, *The Life of Benjamin Disraeli, Earl of Beaconsfield,* three volumes, New York, 1913-4, II, 320-2).

Monsieur Eugène Sue, for instance, has lately set all France against the Jesuits, because he has chosen to invent a story in which two or three most monstrous scoundrels, belonging to that order, are made to swindle and otherwise oppress several personages, equally imaginary, of the most interesting virtue and beauty. The Jesuits are, no doubt, bad enough: but they are not to be exterminated on account of M. Sue's *Rodin*. The landlords may be wickedly to blame; the monsters get two per cent. for their land; they roll about in carriages, do nothing, and drink champagne; while the poor labourer remains at home and works and starves;—but we had better have some other opinion than that of the novelist to decide upon the dispute between them. He can exaggerate the indolence and luxury of the one, or the miseries and privations of the other, as his fancy leads him. In the days of Marmontel and Florian it was the fashion to depict shepherds and shepherdesses in pink ribbons and laced petticoats, piping to their flocks all day, and dancing and serenading all night; in our time writers give a very different view of the peasant. Crime, poverty, death, pursue him: the gamekeeper shoots him or banishes him from his home and little ones; the agent grinds him down; the callous landlord pockets the rent which has been squeezed out of the vitals of his victim, and goes home and drinks a cool bottle of claret after church. Much of this may be true as regards the luckless peasant of the present time—but what remedy or contrast has the political novelist to propose? An outcry against the landlords. His easy philosophy has led him no farther. Has any sentimental writer organised any feasible scheme for bettering the poor? Has any one of them, after weeping over poor Jack, and turning my lord to ridicule, devised anything for the substantial benefit of the former. At the conclusion of these tales, when the poor hero or heroine has been bullied enough—when poor Jack has been put off the murder he was meditating, or poor Polly has been rescued from the town on which she was about to go—there somehow arrives a misty reconciliation between the poor and the rich; a prophecy is uttered of better times for the one, and better manners in the other; presages are made of happy life, happy marriage and children, happy beef and pudding for all time to come; and the characters make their bow, grinning, in a group, as they do at the end of a drama when the curtain falls, and the blue fire blazes behind the scenes. This is not the way in which men seriously engaged and interested in the awful question between rich and poor meet and grapple with it. When Cobden thunders against the landlords, he flings figures and facts into their faces, as missiles with which he assails them; he offers, as he believes, a better law than their's as a substitute for that which they uphold. When Sir Robert Peel resists or denies or takes up the standard which he has planted, and runs away, it is because he has cogent prudential reasons for his conduct of the day. But on one side and the other it is a serious contest which is taking place in the press and Parliament over the "Condition of England question."[4] The novelist as it appears to us, ought to be a noncombatant. But if he persists in taking a side, don't let him go into the contest unarmed; let him do something more effectual than call the enemy names. The cause of either party in this great quarrel requires a stronger championship than this, and merits a more earnest warfare.

We have said that the landlords in Ireland are by no means maltreated by Mr. Lever; indeed his remedy for the national evils is of the mildest sort and such as could not possibly do harm to that or any other afflicted country. The persons who, it is proposed, shall administer the prescribed remedies, viz., the absentees, who are called upon to return to Tipperary and elsewhere, might not at first relish the being brought so near the patient; but for the sick man himself, there can be no doubt that the application of a landlord would not injure him, any more than that of a leech in a case of apoplexy, or of a teaspoon full of milk and water in a fever. That the medicine would be sufficiently powerful is another question. It has been proposed by many persons: by Miss Edgeworth, by Mr. Carleton, and others, as well as Mr. Lever; but we fancy it would not answer onehundredth part of the purpose for which it is intended; besides that, the landlords obstinately decline being put forward for the experiment.

The aim of our author's book is, he says, to show that absentees should return; that "prosperity has as many duties as adversity has sorrows; and that those to whom Providence has accorded many blessings are but the stewards of heaven's bounty to the poor."

---

[4] The title of chapter one of Carlyle's *Chartism* (1840).

As a general proposition none can be more amiable and undeniable than this; but we deny that Mr. Lever has worked it
well, or has so constructed his story as especially to illustrate
this simple moral. His purpose is very good, but his end, when
he defines it, is frequently entirely preposterous. For instance,
in the following passage, the author pleads eloquently against
absenteeism:—

"Alas! no; Mr. Leslie, when not abroad, lived in England. Of his
Irish estates he knew nothing, save through the half-yearly accounts of
his agent. He was conscious of excellent intentions; he was a kind,
even a benevolent man; and, in the society of his set, remarkable for
more than ordinary sympathies with the poor. To have ventured on
any reflection on a landlord before him, would have been deemed a
downright absurdity.

"He was a living refutation of all such calumnies; yet how was it
that, in the district he owned, the misery of the people was a thing to
shudder at? That there were hovels excavated in the bogs, within
which human beings lingered on between life and death, their existence
like some terrible passage in a dream? That beneath these frail roofs
famine and fever dwelt, until suffering, and starvation itself, had ceased
to prey upon minds on which no ray of hope ever shone? Simply, he
did not know of these things; he saw them not; he never heard of them.
He was aware that seasons of unusual distress occurred, and that a
more than ordinary degree of want was experienced by a failure of
the potato-crop; but on these occasions he read his name, with a subscription of a hundred pounds annexed, and was not that a receipt in
full for all the claims of conscience? He ran his eyes over a list in which
royal and princely titles figured, and he expressed himself grateful for
so much sympathy with Ireland! But did he ask himself the question
whether, if he had resided among his people, such necessities for alms-
giving had ever arisen? Did he inquire how far his own desertion of
his tenantry—his ignorance of their state—his indifference to their condition—had fostered these growing evils? Could he acquit himself of
the guilt of deriving all the appliances of his ease and enjoyment from
those whose struggles to supply them were made under the pressure
of disease and hunger?"

This is strong enough as against the landlord, but is not the
following a little too strong in favour of the tenant?—

"Had the landlord been a resident on his property—acquainting himself daily and hourly with the condition of his tenants—holding up
examples for their imitation—rewarding the deserving—discountenanc-
ing the unworthy—extending the benefits of education among the
young—and fostering habits of order and good conduct among all,
Owen would have striven among the first for a place of credit and honour,
and speedily have distinguished himself above his equals. But alas! no."

Surely it is somewhat ultra-sentimental to set up victims of this sort. In Mr. Lever's story, the hero (a tenant) in the first place gets a farm *for nothing*. He does not better himself; but takes to drink and idleness, and the landlord is rebuked because he is not there to be kind and didactic to him, and teach him how he should go.

In the second part of the story the tenant is turned out of his farm, drinks worse than ever, and finally agrees to *murder* the landlord's agent; but before this crime is committed the landlord returns, the tenant marries the young person to whom he is attached, all parties are reconciled, and all live happily ever after.

Now, have we not a right to protest against morals of this kind, and to put in a word for the landlord, just for novelty's sake? A man gets a farm for nothing (a gentleman surely cannot well let his ground for *less*), and who but the landlord is blamed because his idle tenant does not prosper? The tenant determines on murdering the agent, and the argument is, "Poor fellow! why was not the landlord there to teach him better?" Writers who mount the bench as judges in the great philanthropic suit now pending, have surely no right to deliver such preposterous sentences as these. Here we have an Irish judge convicting the landlords of "*guilt*, in deriving all the appliances of his ease and enjoyment from those whose struggles to supply them were made under the pressure of disease and hunger." Why not hunger? Without hunger there would be no work. We have just seen Mr. Lever's peasant, idling and drinking when he got his farm for nothing, and when he is to pay his landlord, the latter is straightway brought in *guilty*. What a verdict is this! All property may similarly be declared iniquitous, and all capital criminal. Let fundholders and manufacturers look out—Judge Jerrold will show them no favour, Chief Baron Boz has charged dead against them, and so we see it has been ruled in Ireland by the chief authority of the literary bench.

A friend who comes in, and has read both "Saint Patrick's Eve" and the above observations, declares that the story has nothing to do with politics; that no critic has a right to judge it in a political sense; and that it is to be tested by its descriptive, its humorous, its pathetic, or romantic merits.

If such be the case (and we have our doubts), a great deal may be said in praise, and a little in blame of Mr. Lever's new story. In the first place, the writing is often exceedingly careless. The printer or some one else has somehow left out a verb in the very first sentence, by which the whole fabric falls to pieces; and the stops are so wofully disarranged in page 2, as to cause the greatest confusion. Periods are violently torn asunder. Accusatives are wrenched from their guardian verbs, which are left atrociously mangled. A regard for that mother whom the critic and the novelist ought to revere equally, the venerable English grammar, binds us to protest against this careless treatment of her. In regard of the merits, the narrative has the animated, rapid, easy style which is the charm of the author's writing, the kindly and affectionate humour (which appears in this volume to greater advantage, because it is not *over laughed* by the boisterous jocularity which we find in some of his other works), and the gay and brilliant manner of depicting figure and landscape, which distinguishes Mr. Lever's dexterous and facile hand. Parts of the tale are told with exceeding pathos and sweetness; and he who begins must needs go through it, with interest and with unabated pleasure. Great praise must also be bestowed upon the charming, faithful, and picturesque designs with which Mr. Brown has illustrated this brilliant little volume.

....

[13 MAY 1845]

Sybil. By Mr. DISRAELI, M.P.

It will not be the fault of the romantic writers of the present day if the public don't perceive that the times are out of joint, and want setting right very sadly. A few weeks since we had occasion to speak of Mr. Jerrold and Mr. Dickens as social regenerators. Since then Mrs. Norton's eloquent voice has been lifted up, and the "Child of the Islands" has accommodated the new doctrine to the Spenserian stanza; finally comes Mr. Disraeli, to discourse once more upon the world problem, in a three-volume parable, such as becomes a philosopher of his eastern origin.

We stand already committed as to our idea of the tendency and province of the novel. Morals and manners we believe to be the novelist's best themes; and hence prefer romances which do not treat of algebra, religion, political economy, or other abstract science. We doubt the fitness of the occasion, and often (it must be confessed) the competency of the teacher. If Professor Airy, having particular astronomical discoveries to communicate, should bring them forward through Mr. Colburn's duodecimo medium, with, let us say, Newton for a hero—(the apple tumbling on the sleeping philosopher's nose might be made a thrilling incident of romance; and the well-known young lady, with whose finger he stopped his tobacco pipe, might die as a consumptive heroine, victim of indifference and blighted passion)—if the professor, lecturing to a class, should so mingle astronomy and sentiment together, it is needless to say his pupils would not have a very high respect for him; and as they would have a right to doubt and grumble, because upon a matter of astronomy their professor introduced a novel, so, conversely, have novel readers good cause to complain, if their teacher, in an affair of romance, think fit to inflict upon them a great quantity of more or less wholesome philosophy.

It was not from the latter, with all respect be it spoken, that the great success of "Coningsby" arose—not from the Caucasian theory, and discovery of the Venetian origin of the English constitution—but from those amusing bitter sketches of Tadpole, Rigby, Monmouth, and the rest, of which the likenesses were irresistible, and the malice tickled everybody. There is no master in this style of delineation, since Swift's day, more dexterous and faithful than Mr. Disraeli. His various portraits of Peel, as exhibited to the Premier's own face on three or four occasions in Parliament lately,[1] are as savagely ludicrous as the Dean's Duchess of Marlborough. H.B. misses the Premier often,[2] but B. never does, and hits him off in a hundred postures of humbug with admirable grotesque humour and fidelity. What were those keys to "Coningsby" with which certain publishers undertook to furnish simple people in the country, at the rate of "a

---

[1] In his speeches of 20 and 28 February, 17 March, and 11 April 1845 (quoted by Monypenny, *Disraeli*, II, 312, 314-5, 320-1, 327-8). The sketch of the Duchess of Marlborough to which Thackeray alludes is presumably that in *The History of the Four Last Years of the Queen, Prose Works of Jonathan, Swift,* ed. Herbert Davis (Oxford, 1939 following), VII, 8.

[2] Disraeli was a frequent subject in the political cartoons of John Doyle ("H. B.").

shilling including the postage stamp?" They were not, we take
it, keys to the before named Caucasian or Venetian theories, or
to the Young England mystery (which, Heaven knows, wants a
key as much as any problem hitherto unexplained in this world);
but such a key as you buy at Epsom of the running horses, with
the names, weights, and colours of the riders.

Now, we cordially regret to say that there is very little per-
sonality in "Sybil," very little pleasant caricaturing, or laughable
malice, or Gillray grotesqueness; but there is more Venetian
theory, more high flown Young England mystery; much apolo-
gising for the exiled Stuart family; much satire against the "great
English families of the Reformation," and some cruel hard hitting
at the "Stadhouder of Holland" and "the Dutch system of
finance." The author's politics are aristocratic and democratic.
In his aristocratic moods he rallies round the Throne; he denounces the great Whig families that have bullied the sacred
Sovereign; he yearns towards the people, and blesses them with
an unction as affecting as Elliston's, who burst into tears while
performing the part of George IV. at Drury-lane; and he calls
upon us for sympathy for Queen Anne, and for detestation of
the inglorious, impious, and immoral memory of poor dear
William III.! Amen. But her Majesty Queen Anne is dead.
William III. is an old cock to shy at. How much better sport
it is to put up Rigby or Peel! If Aristophanes had fired into
Cadmus, or denounced Hercules as a humbug, his audience
would not have relished his jokes as they did. Nor can our public
be expected to applaud very heartily satire upon subjects so very
profound and recondite as Mr. Disraeli handles. Talk of a key
to "Coningsby"!—as a key to "Sybil," booksellers should send
down to their country correspondents a history of the Reformation, the Revolution, and of parties since the advent of the house
of Hanover—a digest of the social, political, and commercial life
of the Normans and Anglo-Saxons—a history of agriculture,
manufactures, banking and credit—the works of Burke and
Bolingbroke, which in "Sybil" are much discussed; and *then* the
reader would be competent to judge this wonderful author; and
then, surely, to form theories for himself, after mastering such a
political encyclopædia. Unabashed on most occasions as he is,
before themes like these even the newspaper critic must shrink
in despair. The mere reading requisite would take ten years,

and then where will "Sybil" be? Where (alas!) is Queen Anne? Where is that Dutch potentate whose financial system Mr. Disraeli falls foul of? These sybilline leaves may have disappeared by that time as completely as the mysterious copyright of the "Lady of Cumæ."[3]

Our lover of the monarchy, and derider of the great Revolution families, is, however, ardent in good wishes for the people; and a main part of his novel is devoted to speculations upon their future, and descriptions of their present, condition. He has drawn some startling pictures of the latter. His account of a colony of agricultural labourers, starving and rotting under a great landlord, expelled from their holdings on the land they cultivate, to diminish his lordship's poor-rates, living at a distance from their labour, and dying of want in the horrible colony which they are forced to inhabit, is, perhaps, the best part of his volumes: it is written with honesty, truth, and hearty sympathy. His aim would appear to be to take a glance at the whole cycle of labour: from the agricultural he takes us to the manufacturing and the mining districts. Here, as we fancy, his descriptions fail; not from want of sympathy, but from want of experience and familiarity with the subject. A man who was really familiar with the mill and the mine might now, we should think, awaken great public attention as a novelist. It is a magnificent and untrodden field (for Mrs. Trollope's Factory story was wretched caricaturing, and Mr. Disraeli appears on the ground rather as an amateur): to describe it well, a man should be born to it. We want a Boz' from among the miners or the manufactories to detail their ways of work and pleasure— to describe their feelings, interests, and lives, public and private. Mr. Disraeli has done well to point to this mystery. Incomplete as we fancy his descriptions to be, yet they must turn the attention of his very many readers to a subject so full of novelty and wonderment. They may send travellers, in quest of sensations, to Wales or Lancashire this summer, in place of the Alps or Baden. They are not good, as we fancy, but they can do good; they are written with genuine feeling, and are worth all the fantastic Venetian and Dutch theories, to our mind. The book is

[3] According to legend the books of prophecy purchased by Tarquinius Superbus from the Cumaean Sibyl were destroyed during the burning of the Capitol in 83 B. C.

called "Sybil; or, the Two Nations." It is thus the author describes them in his bold, startling, Oriental way:—

THE POOR.

" 'This is a new reign,' said Egremont, 'perhaps it is a new era.'

" 'I think so,' said the younger stranger.

" 'I hope so,' said the elder one.

" 'Well, society may be in its infancy,' said Egremont, slightly smiling; 'but, say what you like, our Queen reigns over the greatest nation that ever existed.'

" 'Which nation?' asked the younger stranger, 'for she reigns over two.'

"The stranger paused; Egremont was silent, but looked inquiringly.

" 'Yes,' resumed the younger stranger after a monent's interval. 'Two nations; between whom there is no intercourse and no sympathy; who are as ignorant of each other's habits, thoughts, and feelings, as if they were dwellers in different zones, or inhabitants of different planets; who are formed by a different breeding, are fed by a different food, are ordered by different manners, and are not governed by the same laws.'

" 'You speak of ——' said Egremont hesitatingly.

" 'The rich and the poor.' "[4]

If this book can have made any members of the one nation think of the other, it is something to have done; to our idea Mr. Disraeli never said truer words than that the one nation does not know what the other does, and that it is time they should be acquainted. They must soon, he says, in a striking passage at the close of the first volume:—

" 'I will frankly own to you, I never had much faith in any of these proposals or proposers; but they were a change, and that is something. But I have been persuaded of late that there is something going on in this country of more efficacy; a remedial power, as I believe, and irresistible; but whether remedial or not, at any rate a power that will mar all or cure all. You apprehend me? I speak of the annual arrival of more than 300,000 strangers in this island. How will you feed them? How will you clothe them? How will you house them? They have given up butcher's meat; must they give up bread? And as for raiment and shelter, the rags of the kingdom are exhausted, and your sinks and cellars already swarm like rabbit warrens.'

" ' 'Tis an awful consideration,' said Egremont musing.

" 'Awful,' said Gerard; ' 'tis the most solemn thing since the deluge. What kingdom can stand against it? Why go to your history—you're a scholar,—and see the fall of the great Roman empire—what was that? Every now and then, there came two or three hundred thousand strangers out of the forests and crossed the mountains and rivers. They come to

---

[4] See above, p. 10.

us every year and in greater numbers. What are your invasions of the barbarous nations, your Goths and Visigoths, your Lombards and Huns, to our population returns?' ''

The novel in alternate chapters takes us from one to the other nation—from the orgies of the Crockford dandies to the amusements of the poor workmen of the mills—from the cabals of parliamentary parties, whose rogueries are admirably satirized, to the Chartists and their conspiracies, and their impracticable selfishness, of which he is an equally bitter castigator. A love story (parts of which are charmingly told) is made to connect the two nations together. Sybil, a young person of "supernatural beauty," is the daughter of a pattern Chartist—a bland Anglo-Saxon, of six feet two, who follows the old faith and struggles for the ancient freedom of his race. Of the other nation is Egremont, a dandy aristocrat of not over good blood—[some three or four centuries, or so; his family is living upon the spoils of holy monasteries, ravished from God and the people by Henry VIII.]—but being of a kindly disposition, and enamoured of Sybil, he learns to look with more favour upon the class to which she belongs, and to see the cruel wrongs under which they labour. They love through three volumes. Sybil (through the medium of Lord John Russell!) is rescued from gaol and trial for Chartism; and turning out to be one of the old, old nobility[5] of all, a baroness of forty thousand pounds a year, she marries Egremont; and these two, doubtless, typify the union of the people and the nobles.

Round these main characters, and to support this queer plot, are grouped hundreds of subordinate personages, some of whom, especially those of the higher sort, are described we think with extraordinary skill. A couple of *statesmanesses*; Captain Grouse, my lord's toady; the listless dandies ("I rather like bad wine," says one, for instance, "one gets so bored with good wine"); the Treasury underlings (and a great chief of theirs, who is introduced once and by the way)—seem to us to be most brilliantly hit off, more so than the plebeian likenesses, the men and women of the mines and the factories, and the terrible chieftain of the Hell-cats, who figure on the other side of the story, and with

---

[5] An echo of the following couplet in "England's Trust" by Lord John Manners:

"Let wealth and commerce, laws and learning die,
But leave us still our old nobility!"

whose features the writer is not sufficiently familiar to be able to sketch them off with the ease that is requisite in the novelist.

We quote some passages from the aristocratic sketches, containing admirable observation and satire:—

THE BULWARKS OF BRITAIN.

" 'In spite of the ministers, and in spite of the peers, had the poor king lived, we should at least have had the badge,' added Sir Vavasour mournfully.

" 'The badge!'

" 'It would have satisfied Sir Grosvenor le Draughte,' said Sir Vavasour; 'and he had a strong party with him; he was for compromise, but d— him, his father was only an accoucheur.'

" 'And you wanted more?' inquired Egremont, with a demure look.

" 'All, or nothing,' said Sir Vavasour; 'principle is ever my motto— no expediency. I made a speech to the order at the Clarendon; there were four hundred of us; the feeling was very strong.'

" 'A powerful party,' said Egremont.

" 'And a military order, sir, if properly understood. What could stand against us? The Reform Bill could never have passed if the baronets had been organized.'

" 'I have no doubt you could bring us in now,' said Egremont.

" 'That is exactly what I told Sir Robert. I want him to be brought in by his own order. It would be a grand thing.'

" 'There is nothing like *esprit de corps*,' said Egremont.

" 'And such a body!' exclaimed Sir Vavasour, with animation. 'Picture us for a moment, to yourself, going down in procession to Westminster, for example, to hold a chapter. Five or six hundred baronets in dark green costume—the appropriate dress of *equites aurati*; each, not only with his badge, but with his collar of SS; belted and scarfed; his star glittering; his pennon flying; his hat white with a plume of white feathers; of course the sword and the gilt spurs. In our hand, the thumb-ring and signet not forgotten, we hold our coronet to two balls!'

"Egremont stared with irrepressible astonishment at the excited being, who unconsciously pressed his companion's arm, as he drew this rapid sketch of the glories so unconstitutionally withheld from him.

" 'A magnificent spectacle!' said Egremont.

" 'Evidently the body destined to save this country,' eagerly continued Sir Vavasour. 'Blending all sympathies: the crown of which they are the peculiar champions; the nobles of whom they are the popular branch; the people who recognize in them their natural leaders. But the picture is not complete. We should be accompanied by an equal number of gallant knights, our elder sons, who, the moment they come of age, have the right to claim knighthood of their sovereign; while their mothers and wives, no longer degraded to the nomenclature of a sheriff's lady, but resuming their legal or analogical dignities, and styled the 'honourable baronetess,' with her coronet and robe, or the 'honourable knightess,' with her golden collar of SS, and chaplet or cap of dignity, may either accompany the procession, or ranged in galleries in a becoming situation, reign influence from above.'

" 'I am all for their going in the procession,' said Egremont.

" 'The point is not so clear,' said Sir Vavasour solemnly; 'and, indeed, although we have been firm in defining our rightful claims in our petitions, as for 'honorary epithets, secondary titles, personal decorations, and augmented heraldic bearings,' I am not clear if the government evinced a disposition for a liberal settlement of the question, I would not urge a too stringent adherence to every point. For instance, I am prepared myself, great as would be the sacrifice, even to renounce the claim of secondary titles for our eldest sons, if, for instance, they would secure us our coronet.'

" 'Fie, fie, Sir Vavasour,' said Egremont very seriously, 'remember principle: no expediency, no compromise.'

" 'You are right,' said the baronet, colouring a little; 'and do you know, Mr. Egremont, you are the only individual I have yet met out of the order who has taken a sensible view of this great question, which, after all, is the question of the day.' "

CLUB LIFE.

"This club was Hatton's only relaxation. He had never entered society; and now his habits were so formed, the effort would have been a painful one; though with a first-rate reputation in his calling, and supposed to be rich, the openings were numerous to a familiar intercourse with those middle-aged nameless gentlemen of easy circumstances who haunt clubs, and dine a great deal at each other's houses and chambers; men who travel regularly a little, and gossip regularly a great deal; who lead a sort of facile, slipshod existence, doing nothing, yet mightily interested in what others do; great critics of little things; profuse in minor luxuries, and inclined to the respectable practice of a decorous profligacy; peering through the window of a club-house as if they were discovering a planet; and usually much excited about things with which they have no concern, and personages who never heard of them."

A PALL-MALL PHILOSOPHER.

"Lord Loraine, a mild, middle-aged, lounging, languid man, who passed his life in crossing from Brookes' to Boodle's and from Boodle's to Brookes', and testing the comparative intelligence of these two celebrated bodies; himself gifted with no ordinary abilities, cultivated with no ordinary care, but the victim of sauntering, his sultana queen, as it was, according to Lord Halifax, of the second Charles Stuart."

The account of the gentleman in Downing-street, and his instructions to Mr. Hoaxem how to receive deputations, is a great picture of a great statesman, which will make Sir Robert Peel laugh quite as cheerfully as he did at some of the pleasantries of the member for Shrewsbury. Here are sketches of a different class:—

POOR MEN'S POST OBITS.

" 'I will have the five shillings, or I will have as good,' said Mrs. Mullins.

" 'Hush, hush, neighbour; now, I'll tell you—you shall have it; but yet a little time. This is great tommy-day, and settles our reckoning for five weeks; but my man may have a draw after to-morrow, and he shall draw five shillings, and give you half.'

" 'And the other half?' said Mrs. Mullins.

" 'Ah! the other half,' said Liza Gray, with a sigh. 'Well, then—we shall have a death in our family soon—this poor babe can't struggle on much longer; it belongs to two burial clubs—that will be three pounds from each, and after the drink and the funeral, there will be enough to pay all our debts and put us all square.' "

MISS JULIA'S POLITICS.

" 'I will never marry any one who is not for the five points,' said Caroline.

" 'I should be ashamed to marry any man who had not the suffrage,' said Harriet.

" 'He is no better than a slave,' said Julia.

"The widow shook her head. 'I don't like these politics,' said the good woman, 'they bayn't in a manner business for our sex.'

" 'And I should like to know why?' said Julia. 'Ayn't we as much concerned in the cause of good government as the men? And don't we understand as much about it? I am sure the Dandy never does anything without consulting me.'

" 'It's fine news for a summer day,' said Caroline, 'to say we can't understand politics with a Queen on the throne.'

" 'She has got her ministers to tell her what to do,' said Mrs. Carey, taking a pinch of snuff. 'Poor innocent young creature, it often makes my heart ache to think how she is beset.'

" 'Over the left,' said Julia. 'If the ministers try to come into her bed-chamber, she knows how to turn them to the right about.'

" 'And as for that,' said Harriet, 'why are we not to interfere with politics as much as the swell ladies in London?'

" 'Don't you remember, too, at the last election here,' said Caroline, 'how the fine ladies from the Castle came and canvassed for Colonel Rosemary?'

" 'Ah!' said Julia, 'I must say I wish the colonel had beat that horrid Muddlefist. If we can't have our own man, I am all for the nobs against the middle class.' "

Perhaps the author's own present politics are something like those of Miss Julia, and he has too strong a leaning for "the nobs against the middle class." Those who desire to know what his opinions are, and how the member for Shrewsbury has always been consistent, are referred to the last pages of "Sybil," where these points are mysteriously set forth.

They don't concern the present notice, which regards the novel of Sybil, from which we should have been glad to see a number of disquisitions, religious, retrospective, and prophetic, omitted. If a man professes to write a book "in a light and un-pretending form," as our author does, why introduce into it subjects both heavy and pretentious? We have a novel, and poor Lord John Russell brought in to get the heroine out of a scrape—a novel in which the Queen is brought to rescue us from "Saxon thraldom"—in which the extinct worship of the Catholic saints is regretted (with an enthusiasm which may be quite sincere, but which is as out of place here, as an Ave Mary would be in a comedy), and in which Charles the First's murder by the middle classes is introduced to account for the present misery of the poor. Charles the First's head![6] Mr. Gunter might just as well serve it up in sugar on a supper-table between a Charlotte Russe and a trifle.

[6] We know that Dickens followed Thackeray's work for the *Morning Chronicle* with interest (*Letters,* ed. Walter Dexter, three volumes, London, 1938, I, 730). It is possible that this passage suggested to him Mr. Dick's famous fixation in *David Copperfield.*

....

[24 DECEMBER 1845]

CHRISTMAS BOOKS.—*No.* 1.

The Cricket on the Hearth. By C. DICKENS.

Anybody who walked the streets yesterday, on one of the finest and most cheerful days of London weather, could not but re-mark what an hilarious air the town wore—how jolly and rosy people's faces looked in the foggy sunshine—how wonderfully pink and happy the little boys' countenances were who are come home for the holidays—and observe many other pleasant Christmas phenomena. To see the butchers' and poulterers' shops was quite a pleasure—the most obese geese, turkeys, and gigantic pantomime joints of beef hung in those hospitable warehouses under the mistletoe boughs—reasoning with yourself, you asked why should those comestibles be fatter now at Christmas than at any other time? Fortnum and Mason's, in Piccadilly, is

always a beautiful and astonishing shop, filled with the gor-
mandizing treasures of the whole world. Yesterday it was a
perfect fairy-palace, and Prince Prettyman Paradise of bonbons,
and French plums, and barley-sugar. Many, many young persons will be ill to-morrow morning, if half of those sweetmeats
sold yesterday are devoured to-day.

All these places and persons, after the present blithsome season
is over, relapse into the sober courses of every-day life—the
bonbons are eaten up and disappear—the geese shrink to their
natural size—the mutton relapses into its ordinary cut—care and
the quarter's bills cloud over the jolly faces of the fathers, and
the pink countenances of the little boys, home for the holidays,
grow thoughtful as the day advances when the Rev. Mr. Swishtail and assistants are expecting the return of "their young
friends" to Bircham Wood Academy.[1]

It is not the sweet and other meat providers only who produce
extra jovialities in compliment to the season; the theatres break
out into pantomimes; the booksellers' windows glitter with gilt
picture-books; and more charming to some well-regulated minds
even than the Fortnum and Mason sugar-candy elysium, are Mr.
Nickisson's library tables in Regent-street, blazing with a hundred
new Christmas volumes, in beautiful bindings, with beautiful
pictures—Peter Parley and Felix Summerly,[2] Pictures and Poems,[3]
and the Etching Club, and the Rose Garden of Persia, and the
Baroness Calabrella, who all come after their kind, and present
a pretty offering to Christmas.

But for three years past the great monopoliser has been Mr.
DICKENS. He has been elected as chief literary master of the
ceremonies for Christmas. It is he who best understands the
kindness and joviality and withal the pathos of the season. Many
thousand copies of the "Cricket on the Hearth" have been sold,
and it is not a week old. You hear talk of it in every company.
What a good fellow Peerybingle is! What a wonderful discovery

---

[1] Flogging, the peculiar institution of English schools, was a frequent
subject for joking with Thackeray; compare, for example, his titles,
"Miss Tickletoby's History of England" and Dr. Birch and his Young
Friends. Dr. Swishtail turns up in "The Fatal Boots," "The Ravenswing,"
and Vanity Fair.

[2] Samuel Griswold Goodrich and Henry Cole, the two principal writers
of children's books at this time.

[3] Thackeray reviewed this work in "About a Christmas Book," Fraser's
Magazine, December, 1845 (Works, VI, 538-47).

Miss Slowboy is (as great as the marchioness herself)! What a darling Dot is! and so forth. Going into the city on Tuesday, the writer of this beheld a bookseller's boy with a bag of "Crickets" over his shoulder, standing stock-still by the Royal Exchange, and reading one, *sub Jove*. On the very same day at dinner everybody had read it; everybody was talking about it; and the very clergyman who said grace confessed that he had been whimpering over it all the morning. He didn't know why, he could not point to any special passage, but the general effect of the writing was of this heart-stirring, kindly character.

To detail the plot of a book which everybody has read by this time, is useless; and having been undeniably charmed and affected by it, as everybody has who has read it, now the critic has to ask, is it a good book which so excites you and all the public with emotion? To us it appears it is a good *Christmas* book, illuminated with extra gas, crammed with extra bonbons, French plums and sweetnesses, like a certain Piccadilly palace before-mentioned.

To our fancy, the dialogue and characters of the "Cricket on the Hearth" are no more like nature than the talk of Tityrus and Melibœus[4] is like the real talk of Bumpkin and Hodge over a stile, or than Florian's pastoral *petits maîtres*, in red heels and powder, are like French peasants, with wooden shoes and a pitchfork, or than Pierrot and Carlotta in a ballet, smiling charmingly, jumping and dancing astonishingly, amidst wreaths of calico roses and fragrant pasteboard bouquets, are like a real spotless nymph, fresh from Ida, and a young demigod lately descended from Olympus. This story is no more a real story than Peerybingle is a real name. It is like one—made, as the calico-roses before-mentioned, much redder and bigger than the common plant. The "Cricket on the Hearth" has the effect of a beautiful theatrical piece: It interests you as such—charms you with its grace, picturesqueness, and variety—tickles you with its admirable grotesque; but you cannot help seeing that Carlotta is not a goddess (dancing as she does divinely), and that that is rouge, not blushes, on her cheeks.

We fancy that we see throughout the aim of the author—to startle, to keep on amusing his reader; to ply him with brisk

---

[4] Idealized shepherds in Virgil's first *Eclogue*.

sentences, rapid conceits, dazzling pictures, adroit interchanges of pathos and extravaganza. The "comic business" begins with the very first sentence:—

"Kettle began it! Don't tell me what Mrs. Peerybingle said. I know better. Mrs. Peerybingle may leave it on record to the end of time that she couldn't say which of them began it; but I say the kettle did. I ought to know, I hope? The kettle began it, full five minutes by the little waxy-faced Dutch clock in the corner before the cricket uttered a chirp.

"As if the clock hadn't finished striking, and the convulsive little hay-maker at the top of it, jerking away right and left with a scythe in front of a Moorish palace, hadn't mowed down half an acre of imaginary grass before the cricket joined in at all!

"Why, I am not naturally positive. Every one knows that. I wouldn't set my own opinion against the opinion of Mrs. Peerybingle, unless I were quite sure, on any account whatever. Nothing should induce me. But this is a question of fact. And the fact is, that the Kettle began it, at least five minutes before the Cricket gave any sign of being in existence. Contradict me; and I'll say ten.

"Let me narrate exactly how it happened. I should have proceeded to do so in my very first word, but for this plain consideration—if I am to tell a story I must begin at the beginning; and how is it possible to begin at the beginning, without beginning at the Kettle?

"It appeared as if there were a sort of match, or trial of skill, you must understand, between the Kettle and the Cricket. And this is what led to it, and how it came about.

"Mrs. Peerybingle going out into the raw twilight, and clicking over the wet stones in a pair of pattens that worked innumerable rough impressions of the first proposition in Euclid all about the yard—Mrs. Peerybingle filled the Kettle at the water butt. Presently returning, less the pattens: and a good deal less, for they were tall, and Mrs. Peerybingle was but short: she set the Kettle on the fire. In doing which she lost her temper, or mislaid it for an instant; for the water, being uncomfortably cold, and in that slippy, slushy, sleety sort of state wherein it seems to penetrate through every kind of substance, patten rings included—had laid hold of Mrs. Peerybingle's toes, and even splashed her legs. And when we rather plume ourselves (with reason too) upon our legs, and keep ourselves particularly neat in point of stockings, we find this, for the moment, hard to bear.

"Besides, the Kettle was aggravating and obstinate. It wouldn't allow itself to be adjusted on the top bar; it wouldn't hear of accommodating itself kindly to the knobs of coal; it would lean forward with a drunken air, and dribble, a very idiot of a Kettle, on the hearth. It was quarrel-some, and hissed and spluttered morosely at the fire. To sum up all, the lid, resisting Mrs. Peerybingle's fingers, first of all turned topsy-turvy, and then, with an ingenious pertinacity deserving of a better cause, dived sideways in down to the very bottom of the Kettle. And the hull of the Royal George has never made half the monstrous resistance to coming out of the water, which the lid of that Kettle employed against Mrs. Peerybingle, before she got it up again.

"It looked sullen and pig-headed enough, even then; carrying its handle with an air of defiance, and cocking its spout pertly and mockingly at Mrs. Peerybingle, as if it said, 'I won't boil. Nothing shall induce me!'

"But Mrs. Peerybingle, with restored good humour, dusted her chubby little hands against each other, and sat down before the Kettle: laughing. Meantime, the jolly blaze uprose and fell, flashing and gleaming on the little haymaker at the top of the Dutch clock, until one might have thought he stood stock still before the Moorish Palace, and nothing was in motion but the flame.

"He was on the move, however; and had his spasms, two to the second, all right and regular. But his sufferings when the clock was going to strike, were frightful to behold; and when a cuckoo looked out of a trap-door in the palace, and gave note six times, it shook him, each time, like spectral voice—or like a something wiry, plucking at his legs."

Is this like nature, or like the brilliant ballet-pantomime to which we have compared it? All the properties on the little stage waken into ludicrous life as they will in the pantomime tomorrow night. The kettle has his passions and jocularity— "leans forward as if drunk," "dribbles like an idiot," is "pig-headed," and "cocks its spout pertly," and so forth. The lid is pertinacious and obstinate; the little haymaker convulsive and spasmodic. So the whole scene is made to distort itself into caricature. The author writes with determined jocularity. Extra jokes there are, we believe, adapted for Christmas. In quieter days, and out of the holiday hubbub, so thoughtful, delicate, and acute a painter of nature as Mr. Dickens will hardly paint so coarsely.

But reconcile yourself to this tone. Believe that the book is a Christmas frolic—that the author is at high jinks with that half-million of the public which regards him and sympathises with him (and indeed he has such a kindly, friendly hold upon every one of us as perhaps no writer ever had before)—and the reader, somewhat confounded by the brusque hilarity of "chirp the first," finds nothing discordant in chirp the second, and is quite willing to join in the general revel at chirp the third. The little plot, so charmingly unnatural, of Peerybingle's jealousy for Dot, his wife, and that "brown sailor fellow," who comes back from "the golden Americas" disguised with a sketching stool and a white wig; Caleb Plummer, the penniless toy-maker, whose whole life has been a benevolent humbug, wherein he has endeavoured to make his sightless daughter imagine that she and he were the most happy and comfortable of human beings;—her blind infatuation for Gruff and Tackleton, the grotesque monster or ogre of the piece;—all these impossibilities, at which one might cavil at any other time but Christmas, become perfectly comprehensible now, and the absurdities pleasant, almost credible. Have you not sympathised with the distresses of many princesses described by Mother Bunch?—given a certain credence to dwarfs and ogres, singing trees, and conversational animals? Take the Cricket in a Christmas point of view, and it and Dot, and the kettle and Gruff and Tackleton become a sort of half-recognised realities which charm and fascinate you, and over which you may laugh or weep according to your mood. Admit this, and Dot, the carrier's wife, may talk like Clarissa; and Peerybingle be as delicate and sensitive as Lord Orville;[5] the blind girl may pine away in mute adoration for Gruff and Tackleton; the haymaker on the clock have convulsions, the "staunch cricket of the hearth and loyal household fairies" may arise and warn and whisper. As a Christmas pageant which you witness in the armchair—your private box by the fireside—the piece is excellent, incomparably brilliant, and dexterous. It opens with broad pantomime, but the interest deepens as it proceeds. The little rural scenery is delightfully painted. Each pretty, pleasant, impossible character has his *entrée* and his *pas*. The music is gay or plaintive, always fresh and agreeable. The piece ends with a grand *pas d'ensemble*, where the whole *dramatis personæ* figure high and low, toe and heel, to a full orchestral crash, and a brilliant illumination of blue and pink fire. If we think that nature and quiet are still better, it is because Mr. Dickens, with other great English humorists have used us to them, O, for the artist's early and simple manner!

There are here, however, many brilliant examples of it, and of those touches of nature for which Mr. Dickens's hand is unrivalled. Certain characters are revealed to him, and described as no other person describes them. Witness Mrs. Fielding and Miss Slowboy, in the present book, who having been once

---

[5] In Richardson's *Clarissa Harlowe* and Fanny Burney's *Evelina*.

introduced to the reader can never be forgotten by him, and remain to be admired and laughed at for ever.

"She was of a spare and straight shape, this young lady, insomuch that her garments appeared to be in constant danger of sliding off those sharp pegs, her shoulders, on which they were loosely hung. Her costume was remarkable for the partial development on all possible occasions of some flannel vestment of a singular structure; also for affording glimpses, in the region of the back, of a corset, or pair of stays, in colour a dead-green. Being always in a state of gaping admiration at everything, and absorbed, besides, in the perpetual contemplation of her mistress's perfections and the baby's, Miss Slowboy, in her little errors of judgment, may be said to have done equal honour to her head and to her heart; and though these did less honour to the baby's head, which they were the occasional means of bringing into contact with deal doors, dressers, stair-rails, bedposts, and other foreign substances, still they were the honest results of Tilly Slowboy's constant astonishment at finding herself so kindly treated, and installed in such a comfortable home. For the maternal and paternal Slowboy were alike unknown to Fame, and Tilly had been bred by public charity, a foundling; which word, though only differing from fondling by one vowel's length, is very different in meaning, and expresses quite another thing."

What can be finer than Miss Slowboy's conduct when at the end of the work everybody is made happy; and "she crying copiously for joy, and wishing to include her young charge in the general interchange of congratulations, handed round the baby to everybody in succession, *as if it was something to drink*."

The woman and the mother-in-law are likewise perfectly depicted in the following portrait:—

"Then, there was a great expedition set on foot to go and find out Mrs. Fielding; and to be dismally penitent to that excellent gentlewoman; and to bring her back, by force if needful, to be happy and forgiving. And when the expedition first discovered her, she would listen to no terms at all, but said, an unspeakable number of times, that ever she should have lived to see the day! and couldn't be got to say anything else, except "Now carry me to the grave;" which seemed absurd, on account of her not being dead, or anything at all like it. After a time, she lapsed into a state of dreadful calmness, and observed, that when that unfortunate train of circumstances had occurred in the indigo trade, she had foreseen that she would be exposed, during her whole life, to every species of insult and contumely; and that she was glad to find it was the case; and begged they wouldn't trouble themselves about her—for what was she? oh, dear! a nobody!—but would forget that such a being lived and would take their course in life without her. From this bitterly sarcastic mood, she passed into an angry one, in which she gave vent to the remarkable expression that the worm would turn if trodden on; and after that, she yielded to a soft regret, and said, if they had only given her their confidence, what might she not have had it in her power to suggest! Taking advantage of this crisis in her feelings, the expedition embraced her; and she very soon had her gloves on, and was on her way to John Peerybingle's in a state of unimpeachable gentility; with a paper parcel at her side containing a cap of state, almost as tall, and quite as stiff, as a mitre."

The mother-in-law, her cap, and Miss Slowboy are wonderfully drawn, too, by Mr. Leech; and there is a drawing of his at page 120 which, rude in execution as it is, is yet admirable for pathos and nature.

As for the title and frontispiece of the volume designed by Mr. Maclise, it may be said that English artists have very seldom surpassed them for grace and fancy, and the engraving of the frontispiece, especially, is one of the most brilliant specimens of the art which has appeared in the very best school of it.

....

[26 DECEMBER 1845]

CHRISTMAS BOOKS—No. 2.

Mrs. Caudle's Curtain Lectures. By DOUGLAS JERROLD.
[Published at the *Punch* office.

The Fairy Ring. By JOHN EDWARD TAYLOR, with illustrations by R. DOYLE. [Murray.

The first of these is a book not for Christmas only, but good for the rest of the year. Though Mrs. Caudle had her faults, perhaps there was no woman who died more universally lamented than she. The want of her weekly discourse was felt all over the kingdom. The Caudle Papers, collected in a volume, are still more pleasant and profitable to read, than when they appeared dispersed through the pages of *Punch.* They form a body of conjugal morality. Swift's Directions to Servants were not more awful lessons for the kitchen and pantry in the last century, than the Caudle Lectures for the parlours of the present age; and, indeed, if one may be permitted to speculate upon the chances of future reputation for works of humour, we should say that this little book is as likely to last as any other that has been produced in modern days. It is quite as keen as the satirical book of the Dean before alluded to, contains wit and scarcasm quite as brilliant, and gives (in caricature) the most queer, minute, and amusing picture of English middle-class life.

In *Punch's Almanac* we find Caudle married again. It seems a wrong to the departed woman. We feel personally angry that her memory should be so slighted: but the virtues of the sainted deceased appear more clearly, now that her emancipated husband is indulging in vices which were checked by the anxious prescience of the first and best Mrs. Caudle. She and Mrs. Nickleby ought to take their places among the "Women of England," when Mrs. Ellis brings out a new edition of that work. They are both types of English matrons so excellent, that it is hard to say which of the two should have the *pas*. Mrs. Nickleby's maundering and amiable vacuity endear her to all her acquaintance; Mrs. Caudle's admirable dulness, envy, and uncharitableness, her fondness for her mamma, brother, and family, and her jealous regard of her Caudle, make her an object of incessant sympathy with her numerous friends, and they regret, now she is no more, that amiable British matron and beldam.

Almost all the events and perplexities of Cockney domestic economy pass before her. Her husband is a citizen[1] (she herself, indeed, is not unlike the faint sketch we possess of the late Mrs. Gilpin); and a foreigner, or a student in the twentieth century, may get out of her lectures as accurate pictures of London life as we can out of the pictures of Hogarth. Caudle's friends, and habits, and predilections; his cozy evenings with the Skylarks— his attachment to punch—his struggles for a latch-key—his natural and manly hatred for cold mutton—the manner in which the odious habit of smoking grows upon him and masters him, are here exposed with the most frightful distinctness. There must be thousands of Caudles in this town who drank punch and annoyed their wives with tobacco-smoke last night. The couple have become real living personages in history, like Queen Elizabeth, or Sancho Panza, or Parson Adams, or any other past character, who, false or real once, is only imaginary now, and for whose existence we have only the word of a book. And surely to create these realities is the greatest triumph of a fictitious

---

[1] Cowper's familiar poem begins:

"John Gilpin was a citizen."

writer—a serious or humorous *poet*. Mr. Dickens has created a whole gallery of these: our quarrel with his last book, and with Dot and Peerybingle, is because we don't *believe* in them.

This credibility of Mr. and Mrs. Caudle is a greater charm than the wit and humour with which their lives are recorded. These come next, and in them the author was never wanting. You come perpetually upon turns of expression the most ingenious, thoughts and sarcasms the most novel, curious, and laughter-provoking. These sparkling, odd, sudden quips and fancies surprise you everywhere amidst the Caudle dialogues. For instance—"No, we women don't get together and pick our husbands to pieces, just as sometimes mischievous little girls rip up dolls." This is a sentiment against the tattling of women, supposed to be echoed by Mrs. Caudle from the mouth of the sleepy old misogynist at her side—a simile as malicious and ingenious as any in Sheridan. Mrs. Caudle, desirous of the country, proposes Clapham to her husband—"*the retired whole-sales don't visit the retired retails at Clapham,*" says the retail trader, declining. Caudle reads: "If it isn't insulting a wife to bring a book to bed, I don't know what wedlock is. But you shan't read, Caudle, no you shan't; not while I've strength to put out a candle." How different are each of these means of exciting laughter—the point of the first, the broad sarcasm of the second, the jovial mischievous grotesque of the third sentence. What wonderful pictures of family miseries are these:—

A FRIEND AT SUPPER.

"It's all very well for you, Mr. Caudle, to bring people home—but I wish you'd think first what's for supper. That beautiful leg of pork would have served for our dinner tomorrow, and now it's all gone. *I* can't keep the house upon the money, and I won't pretend to do it, if you bring a mob of people every night to clear the cupboard.

"I wonder who'll be so ready to give you a supper when you want one; for want one you will, unless you change your plans. Don't tell me! I know I'm right. You'll first be eaten up, and then you'll be laughed at. I know the world. No, indeed, Mr. Caudle, I don't think ill of everybody; don't say that. But I can't see a leg of pork eaten up in that way, without asking myself what it's all to end in if such things go on? And then he must have pickles, too! Couldn't be content with my cabbage—no, Mr. Caudle, I won't let you go to sleep. It's very well for you to say let you go to sleep, after you've kept me awake till this time. *Why did I keep awake?* How do you suppose I could go to sleep, when I knew that man was below drinking up your substance in brandy-and-water? for he couldn't be content upon decent, wholesome gin. Upon my word you ought to be a rich man, Mr. Caudle. You have such very fine friends. I wonder who gives you brandy when you go out!

"No, indeed, he couldn't be content with my pickled cabbage—and I should like to know who makes better—but he must have walnuts. And you, too, like a fool—now don't think to stop me, Mr. Caudle; a poor woman may be trampled to death, and never say a word—you, too, like a fool—I wonder who'd do it for you—to insist upon the girl going out for pickled walnuts. And in such a night too! With snow upon the ground. Yes; you're a man of fine feelings, you are, Mr. Caudle; but the world doesn't know you as I know you—fine feelings, indeed! to send the poor girl out, when I told you and your friend, too—a pretty brute he is, I'm sure—that the poor girl had got a cold and chilblains on her toes. But I know what will be the end of that; she'll be laid up, and we shall have a nice doctor's bill. And you'll pay it, I can tell you—for *I* won't."

WASHING AT HOME.

"A pretty temper you come to bed in, Mr. Caudle, I can see! Oh, don't deny it—I think I ought to know by this time. But it's always the way! whenever I get up a few things, the house can hardly hold you! Nobody cries out more about clean linen than you do—and nobody leads a poor woman so miserable a life when she tries to make her husband comfortable. Yes, Mr. Caudle—comfortable! You needn't keep chewing the word, as if you couldn't swallow it. *Was there ever such a woman?* No, Caudle, I hope not: I should hope no other wife was ever put upon as I am! It's all very well for you. I can't have a little wash at home like anybody else, but you must go about the house swearing to yourself, and looking at your wife as if she was your bitterest enemy. But I suppose you'd rather we didn't wash at all. Yes, then you'd be happy! To be sure you would—you'd like to have all the children in their dirt, like potatoes; anything, so that it didn't disturb you. I wish you'd had a wife who'd never washed—*she'd* have suited you, she would. Yes, a fine lady, who'd have let your children go that you might scraped 'em. She'd have been much better cared for than I am. I only wish I could let all of you go without clean linen at all—yes, all of you. I wish I could! And if I wasn't a slave to my family, unlike anybody else, I should.

"No, Mr. Caudle; the house isn't tossed about in water as if it was Noah's ark! And you ought to be ashamed of yourself to talk of Noah's ark in that loose manner. I'm sure I don't know what I've done to be married to a man of such principles. No: and the whole house *doesn't* taste of soap-suds either; and if it did, any other man but yourself would be above naming it. I suppose I don't like washing-day any more than yourself. What do you say? *Yes, I do?* Ha! you're wrong there, Mr. Caudle. No, I don't like it because it makes everybody else uncomfortable. No; and I ought not to have been born a mermaid, that

I might always have been in water. A mermaid, indeed! What next will you call me? But no man, Mr. Caudle, says such things to his wife as you do. However, as I've said before, it can't last long, that's one comfort. What do you say? *You're glad of it?* You're a brute, Mr. Caudle! No, you *didn't* mean washing: I know what you meant. A pretty speech to a woman who's been the wife to you I have! You'll repent it when it's too late: yes, I wouldn't have your feelings when I'm gone, Caudle; no, not for the Bank of England.

"And when we only wash once a fortnight! Ha! I only wish you had some wives: they'd wash once a week! Besides, if once a fortnight's too much for you, why don't you give me money that we may have things to go a month? Is it *my* fault, if we're short? What do you say? *My 'once a fortnight' lasts three days?* No, it doesn't; never; well, very seldom, and that's the same thing. Can I help it, if the blacks will fly, and the things must be rinsed again? Don't say that: I'm *not* made happy by the blacks, and they *don't* prolong my enjoyment; and, more than that, you're an unfeeling man to say so. You're enough to make a woman wish herself in her grave—you are, Caudle.

"And a pretty example you set to your sons! Because we'd a little wash to-day, and there wasn't a hot dinner—and who thinks of getting anything hot for washerwomen? because you hadn't everything as you always have it, you must swear at the cold mutton—and you don't know what that mutton cost a pound, I dare say—you must swear at a sweet wholesome joint like a lord. What? *You didn't swear?* Yes; it's very well for you to say so; but I know when you're swearing; and you swear when you little think it; and I say you must go on swearing as you do and seize your hat like a savage, and rush out of the house, and go and take your dinner at a tavern!"

"You must swear at a sweet wholesome joint *like lord.* I know when you're swearing, and you swear *when you little think of it.*" Can humour be more hearty, jovial, absurd than this? It is as good as "Mrs. Slipslop" or "Tabitha Bramble."[2]

As Caudle was going up to bed with his shoes off and trembling for the curtain lecture which was awaiting him in the horrid nuptial chamber above Mr. Leech stood in the passage and took his likeness to admiration. The aspect of Mrs. Caudle in the upper room, awake in bed, and in curl-papers—tallow candle throwing a ghastly light round the apartment, and faintly illuminating her stays, petticoats, and—crinoline apparatus; give the beholder a shudder, and impress *Punch's* "Caution to Persons about to Marry—DON'T."[3]

The Fairy Ring is the next Christmas book on our list. It contains a set of new stories, delightfully translated from Grimm's

---

[2] In Fielding's *Joseph Andrews* and Smollett's *Humphry Clinker.*

[3] This famous joke occurs on the first page of volume eight for 1845.

various collections by J. E. Taylor, and charmingly illustrated by Mr. R. Doyle. We read every now and then in these legends of certain princes and princesses who are carried off by the little people for awhile, and kept in fairy land. This must have been surely Mr. Doyle's case, and he must have had the advantage of pencils and paper during his banishment. If any man knows the people and country, he does. A very young man, we believe scarcely twenty, he has produced in the course of a few years, in the pages of *Punch* and elsewhere, a series of designs so remarkable for grace, variety, fancy, and wild picturesqueness— drawings of such beauty and in such profusion, as we believe are quite unexampled hitherto. Callot is a barren inventer by the side of this young artist; and his works have this advantage, which belongs to so few grotesque designers, that there is always the most charming beauty and grace mingled with the fun and uproar and picturesque monstrosities which grow up under his pencil. He has such an intimate acquaintance with dwarfs, ogres, and dragons, that it can only be from nature he has de- signed them: his fairy princesses are the most slender and delicate; his princes the most brilliant and noble; his bears, lions, and foxes have exactly that mysterious intelligence with which they are endowed in the fairy legends. His flowers and little children bloom just as they do in the delightful old stories where you hardly know which is which. His only fault is that a natural gallantry towards the sex, and gentleness of disposition as we take it, prevent him from making the old hags, hunch-backed sorceresses and hideous step-mothers, in which all stories of the "Mother Bunch" kind delight, horrid and ugly enough. Caudle himself has not a greater hatred of his mother-in-law, than we find exhibited towards that character all through the fairy legends.

These, translated newly by Mr. Taylor, are in no ways dif- ferent in nature from their predecessors, but will be liked, as we think, by every person of a simple taste who relishes the old form of the fairy tale, and the child-like simplicity and wonder of narration which constitute its main charm, and which has been ruined by that knowing modern slang and *goguenard* air with which later authors have polluted that sacred fairy ground. To hear a fellow singing "Jim Crow" in the chimney-nook of Cinderella, and brutally addressing the sweetest little creation of poetry as *Cinderelar*, has always been a gross sacrilege in our notion. Were demons and fays not banished out of most places, they would fling the *feller* out of *winder* for attempting such a liberty. Mr. Doyle and Mr. J. E. Taylor have addressed themselves to their work with much more reverence. Little Hop-o'-my-thumbs go on their travels, and overreach giants by their cunning: wicked stepmothers prefer one-eyed children who spit snakes and toads to those who expectorate guineas: king's children are spirited away and restored: hapless damsels are shut up in steel towers, subject to the odious addresses of the landlord, who is an ogre: and ever, when it seems their need is at the sorest, a prince in armour bright comes riding through the forest; and vice is punished, and humble beauty and virtue rescued, as they always are in these kindly stories, which have made their way through all countries, and are told to happy children in every language in the world.

Here is one, not an actual fairy tale, but, as we think, a fine piece of queer owl-like German humour:—

"THE OWL.

"More than a hundred years ago, when people were not so wise and clever as they are now-a-days, a strange thing fell out in a little town. By chance a large owl from a neighbouring wood had stolen at night into the barn of one of the townsmen; and when it was daylight, she did not venture to stir from her hiding-place, for fear of the other birds, which, whenever she shows herself, set up a terrible outcry and clamour.

"When the servant lad went in the morning to the barn, to fetch some straw, he started back in affright as soon as he saw the owl, who sat there in a corner goggling with his large round eyes. Off he scampered as fast as his legs would carry him, and told his master that a monstrous beast, such as he had never before seen in his life, was sitting in the barn, rolling his eyes round and round in his head, and ready to swallow any one without more ado. 'You are a poor chicken-hearted fellow,' said his master; 'ready and bold enough, I warrant, to run after a thrush in the fields; but if you chance to see an old hen lying dead in a barn, you must fetch a stick before you dare come near her. However, I'll go and see myself what this monster is.' So saying, he went into the barn as bold as could be, and looked around. But no sooner did he see the strange animal with his own eyes, than he fell into as great a fright as the lad: he sprang out of the barn in a trice, ran to his neighbours, and begged and prayed them to come and help him against a dangerous wild beast. 'Moreover,' he added, 'there is no telling what mischief may happen to the whole town, if he should break loose from the barn.'

"Then there arose a great tumult and outcry in the streets: the townsfolk came running, all armed with pikes and pitchforks, scythes and axes, ready to go and do battle with the enemy. Last appeared also the aldermen and council, with his worship the mayor at their head, and all the tipstaffs and constables of the town at their heels. When they were drawn up in order in the market-place, they crept cautiously to the barn, and surrounded it on all sides. Upon this, one of the boldest stepped forward, and, pike in hand, ventured into the barn; but in a minute after he came running out again, screaming with fright, pale as death, and unable to utter a word. Then two others ventured in, but they fared no better.

"At last a man came boldly forward—stout and strong—who had been in the wars and was famed for his bravery, and said, 'You'll never drive away the monster by staring at him: this is a time for action— we must take the matter seriously in hand: but I see you are all a parcel of old women, and not one dares to take the bull by the horns: 'tis well you have one man at least among you.' So he brought out his armour, sword and spear, and buckled them on: and all the folks praised his courage, although many of them trembled for his life.

"The barn-doors were thrown open, and there sat the owl, which had meanwhile perched itself on one of the cross rafters. Our hero called for a ladder, placed it against the rafter, and set about climbing up. Then all the people shouted out, and bade him take heart and behave himself manfully, and commended him to St. George, who killed the dragon. He climbed up the ladder gallantly; but the owl, who saw him coming, was confused by the clamour of the people, and did not know how to escape; so she rolled her eyes about, ruffled her feathers, flapped her wings, clattered her bill, and cried Whit-a-whoo? whit-a-whoo! in a rough tone. 'Run him through!' shouted the people to their champion. 'All very fine for you to cry run him through!' answered he, 'but if you were in my place, you'd soon alter your note!' He climbed one step higher, but then began to tremble from head to foot, and half-fainting he made his way back as quick as he could.

"No one now remained who dared to meet the danger. 'The monster,' said they to one another, 'has poisoned and deadly wounded the bravest man amongst us; shall we too risk our lives?' So they all laid their heads together to consider what should be done to save the town from destruction. For a long time everything seemed vain, till at length the mayor hit upon a way to get out of their trouble. 'My advice,' said he, 'is, that we should all put our money together, and buy the barn, with all that is in it—corn, straw, and hay—and burn it down to the ground; thus nobody need risk his life. This is not a time to spare our pence— better to lose our money than our lives.' All applauded his worship's wisdom: so they set fire to the barn at all four corners, and the poor owl perished miserably. If any one doubts the fact, let him go and inquire for himself."

[31 DECEMBER 1845]

CHRISTMAS BOOKS.—No. III.

The Comic Blackstone. By GILBERT ABBOTT A'BECKETT
[Published at the *Punch* Office.

The Snow Storm, a Tale of Christmas. By Mrs. GORE   [Fisher.

A dangerous propensity to be didactic may be remarked amongst many modern humourists and writers of fiction, both here and in France, and we have more than once before protested against the practice. Facetious or sentimental works, in which a reader hoping for mere amusement finds himself suddenly called upon to investigate questions of great social or political interest, such as rick burning, the Game-laws, the Jesuits, the Factory Bill, the claims of the Roman Catholic and Established churches, &c., have been thrust upon us in great numbers, and ought to be generally and strongly exposed and condemned. For it no more follows, because a man is a clever novelist that he should be a great political philosopher, or an historian, or a controversialist, than that he should be able to dance the tight rope or play the flute. All virtuous indignation against grinding aristocrats, artful priests, &c., all sentimental political economy, ought, we think, to be marked and branded. It is not only wrong of authors thus to go meddle with subjects of which their small studies have given them but a faint notion, and to treat complicated and delicate questions with apologues instead of argument—it is not only dishonest, but it is a bore. If Professor Faraday were to produce a comic novel to his audience at the Royal Institution, or Paul de Kock publish lectures on chemistry, it is certain that the admirers of either would be disappointed, and would have a right to cry out against the imposition.

It is not one of the smallest merits of Mr. A'Beckett, as a humourous writer, that he does not in the least pretend to regenerate the world, and shows no disposition for the sublime. There is no doubt that in the public estimation the sublime has the *pas* of the ridiculous, and that Milton, for rank and brains, must certainly be classed before Rabelais. Writers of fun must live in the world and go out of it with this woeful conviction, that there is a kind of art incomparably higher than theirs, and which is not to be reached by any straining or endeavour. But

101

theirs is no bad position after all. It is something to be *Mercutio* if you can't be *Romeo*—to be a gentleman, if not a hero—to have a shrewd, kindly, wit without the least claim to be a sublime genius or a profound philosopher—to have kind affections and warm feelings, but to be very cautious and diffident in parading them;—in fine, though a man can't produce Paradise Lost or Newton's Principia, it is by no means disagreeable to be able to write the "Comic Blackstone."

A lord chief justice skating on a tight rope, two barristers dancing and stamping over equity in the shape of the mace and seals at their feet, and august Themis in the back ground, bursting with laughter, and shaking on her centre of gravity, are the figures which George Cruikshank has placed in the frontispiece of this new commentary on the laws of England. Mr. *Punch* has issued few works from his printing-house which are so perfectly worthy of his patronage and of the public favour. A'Beckett upon Blackstone is a treatise, from beginning to end, of the most happy and ingenious absurdity. To read the book through would be, we should say with respect, almost an impossibility; but every single chapter is inimitable for queerness and folly. Thoughts are knocked about; history turned over head and heels; law and doctrine upset into the most sudden, unlooked-for ludicrous attitudes, the author of all the mischief superintending it with the most incomparable gravity. And a great comfort it is that he occupies himself steadily and modestly with his joking, and with nothing else. He does not make one single attempt to be sublime, or to hint to his reader, "Hark you, though I *am* making fun for you, I beg you to understand that I am one of the finest poets, and deepest and tenderest moralists in the world." There is nothing moral in this book, from which no wiseacre has a right to conclude that the writer is not a moral man, but simply that he does not choose, under present circumstances, to write about ethics any more than about hydrostatics or geology. If laughter, without the least malice—laughter springing out of the sheer absurd—laughter the most unrestrainable be worth cultivating for Christmas-holidays, this should be the Christmas book of the season.

To give any analysis of it is quite a vain task. "The Comic Blackstone" treats of all sorts of points of English history, since and before the time when "William the Conqueror having defeated Harold at Hastings, left that delightful watering place and came to London." He dedicates his book to the Commissioners of the Court of Requests, who, having so often made law a burlesque and justice a farce, are the very persons to appreciate the new commentator of Blackstone; and he follows that grave lecturer with unbounded gravity through all his expositions of the law. What can be more lucid than this explanation of it?— "The judges, in fact, make the law by saying what it means, which, as it scarcely ever means what it says, opens the door to much variety." He points out—

A BEAUTIFUL PROVISION OF ENGLISH LAW.

"It is one of the beautiful provisions of the English law, that not knowing it forms no excuse for not obeying it. It is an ingenious fiction of British policy that every person in the kingdom purchases every act of Parliament, and carefully reads it through; therefore, there can be no possible excuse for being ignorant of the laws that are made every session."

THE THREE FORMS OF GOVERNMENT.

"There are three forms of government—a democracy, where the mass takes such liberties in the lump that there is no liberty left for allotment among private individuals—an aristocracy, which we need not particularly describe—or a monarchy, where one individual is absolute within a certain space, like the square-keeper of a square, who is fortunately the only specimen of pure despotism that this free country possesses."

THE THRONE HEREDITARY.

"First of the Title. It is of the highest importance to avoid those unseemly scrambles for the crown, which, while forming capital subjects for dramatic representation—*vide* Richard the Third—would be a great interruption to the business of every day life if they were at the present time liable to happen. The grand fundamental maxim, on the right of succession to the throne, must be taken to be this, that the crown is hereditary in all cases except those in which it isn't."

And we conclude with a piece of satire as good as anything in Swift.

THE LAW OF PUNISHMENTS.

"In England it has always been difficult to apportion the quantity of punishment due to different crimes; but some general rules have been usually acted on. Thus, stealing a loaf on account of hunger is a grave and serious offence; for it is a melancholy business, and the punishment is no joke; but wrenching a knocker from a door and running away with it, is neither grave nor serious, because there is some fun about it, and the penalty, to be in character, is proportionably ludicrous. The criminal law of this country formerly made hanging a matter of such fatal facility, that 'Hang me,' and 'I'll see you hanged first,' are to this day familiar phrases amid all classes of English society. Excess, however, always brings an end to an evil; and the sanguinary system of capital punishments having been allowed a frightful abundance of rope, has at last nearly worked out its own destruction."

Mrs. Gore's Christmas story of "The Snow Storm" bids fair for a considerable popularity. Whenever this clever author writes fictions, she is sure to introduce us to the very best of company. We move in a select circle of lords and ladies, about whose conversation and behaviour there is such an unmistakable easy air of high fashion, that the common reader can't but be edified; and who would not pay five shillings to be presented to such "distinguished society?" Here, for the above trifle, any genteel family in Baker-street may pass an evening with Lord Castlehurst, "president of the Board of Control;" Lord Charles Milbanke, an ex-lord of the Treasury, and her ladyship, his amiable wife; "that famous fellow Bob Shoreham," Lord Castlehurst's private secretary; young Sir William Meredyth, and the Honourable Sidney Howard (Lord Nottingham's son) "two thoughtless, off-hand young fellows of the day," whose polite ease and undeniable high-breeding form a perfect contrast with the uneasy sycophancy of the wretched *parvenu* Sir Richard Ribstone; and the gross vulgarity of that horrid Lady Gumbledon and her daughters—mere people of yesterday, who can't be supposed to behave like the real old nobility. If Meredyth and Howard (Lord Nottingham's son) ever came to visit Sir Richard Ribstone at all, it was of course because they "took Sir Richard for granted as an old country baronet," and had no notion that he was an odious knight, a fellow who had only just bought the estate about which he was giving himself such grand airs. The gravity with which all these fine people are brought on the stage, and the *naïf* respect with which the writer who has invented them regards these creatures of a truly genteel fancy, form no small portion of the amusement which the volume affords. Castlehurst, Mrs. Gore says, was rather "slow" in conversation, and so in truth she represents him. Milbanke's brilliancy we don't think so well hit off; nor indeed does that famous fellow Bob Shoreham figure to very great advantage: he may do very well among lords possibly, or his wit may be too refined for common people to understand. It is a painful thing to be obliged to confess that such a famous fellow should be tedious, but so it is. Well, even the author of "Historic Fancies" and the "Sidney of his Generation" are slow sometimes, though young men of the highest fashion.

Besides the *noblesse* and *parvenus*, a tale would scarcely be complete now a-day's without some of "nature's nobility," to whom we are presented in the shape of an excellent Aunt Dinah, who cultivates every virtue, though she has but been a housekeeper "to a rich family in Bedford-square" (think of virtue in such a neighbourhood!), who is noble and high-minded, though she says I *were*, and they *is*, and makes other grammatical blunders of the most delightful humour; and a lovely Grace Welland, whose "quiet, lady-like manner" makes her the equal of "Lady Charles" herself.

Grace has a lover, the heir of Hackleton, the son of Ribstone, of Ribstone, who has turned old Welland off the estate on which, under its first owners, the Reveleys and the Wellands had been tenants before the memory of man: and who has very different feelings from those of his upstart of a father. Perhaps a more galling sarcasm never was uttered than that which is delivered by a mysterious old gentleman, who says, The Ribstones, who are the Ribstones? I never knew an old family in Yorkshire of that name, except the Ribstone *pippins*—or words to that effect: a comparison which almost drives the young hero frantic.

This mysterious old gentleman has just come *from India*, and turns out to be—but never mind what he turns out to be. When a mysterious person comes back from India, or from "the golden Americas," just in the nick of time—after fifty years' absence—after he has been forgotten and thought dead by everybody—after oppressed virtue is at its last gasp, and is on the point of being sold up—after vice has had a career of prosperity, and has reached a disgusting climax of luck—you may be sure that somebody is going to be rewarded, and somebody else to meet with his just punishment. It was Kotzebue who invented the uncle from America; the *Peregrine* of *John Bull*, who comes in and gives the £10,000 to *Job Thornberry*;[1] the "brown sailor fellow" of "The Cricket," &c., the ministering angel who always pulls out the bundle of bank notes. Mrs. Gore calls him Paul Reveley,— one of the old old Reveleys, and no mistake. And it is marvellous

---

[1] *John Bull* (1803), a comedy by George Colman the younger, has as its chief character the honest but irascible tradesman Job Thornberry.

to read how, in a village from which he has disappeared for fifty years (and with rather a bad character), such a commotion and jubilation are raised on his return as would scarcely befit his arrival if he were going to present them with ten thousand pounds all round. "Give us back our old nobility," as the Sidney of his Generation sings;[2] that is the real thing the English rustics want— they are always thinking of the old families—they are so fondly attached to them, and with so much reason—they are so happy!

They are happy on the stage, where they grin in *tableaux* before the footlights, and scatter calico garlands before their lord, who pledges them in a bumper of sparkling pasteboard, and, happy in the Christmas-books that are constructed upon the theatrical model: let this pass as one of the jokes of Christmas—to live at the very least until Twelfth-day.

The best piece of writing, perhaps, in the book, is the description of a supper, which is exceedingly luscious and agreeable: the table-cloth and knives and forks; the old ale, broiled fowl and mushrooms, and fried potatoes, are described with great care and relish; and there is an account of some hot elder wine, and a dish of pancakes (not your common pancakes, but served after the old Yorkshire fashion, over the bowl of an inverted basin, having a *slight* layer of winesour jelly between, &c.), which is told with uncommon humour and fidelity to nature; but as the above are the principal points, and the description is a little long, we shall content ourselves by pointing the delighted reader's attention to pages 134 to 141. From the passage beginning "As aunt Dinah had ensconced her bib and apron," to that ending "a genuine wassail bowl, said Shoreham, sniffing the rich aroma of cinnamon and cloves."

Those who have a desire to bestow or purchase more expensive works, should examine the illustrated edition of "Goldsmith's Poems," by the Etching Club; and the book of "Pictures and Poems," published by Mr. Burns, than which English typography has produced nothing more beautiful. Some other Christmas books on our table had best be passed over; such as the "Wedding Bells," of which the illustrations, however, are remarkable; and a "Sentimental Tour in search of the amusing, picturesque, and agreeable," in which the author has certainly not succeeded in the object of his search.

---

[2] See above, p. 82.

[16 MARCH 1846]

Carus's Travels in England.   [Chapman and Hall.

Such a great and profound work as this of Doctor Carus ought not to be lightly taken in hand by any reader or critic. In the first place, it is not only a very bulky work, the large pages of which are quite painfully crowded by type, but also, to a casual glance, it appears to be absolutely stale, and entirely stupid and vacuous. Its descriptions appear, on first reading, not only foolish and unnecessary, but also entirely unlike. There seems something prodigious in the prosiness of the book. The staleness and dulness of the author's reflections amount almost to a marvel. The gravity and self-content with which the Doctor lays down the law—the pomp with which he serves out his small-beer—the happy, blundering skill which leads him to miss the great points and occupy himself laboriously with the small—all these considerations may deter many readers, at first, from a book which appears quite unexampled for drivelling stupidity. Mac Flecknoe is in the flesh again, in the person of a German doctor: the famous Doctor Dillon himself did not write a tour so foolish.[1] Any groom or footman, any person, however stupid or ignorant, could not have made a journey and observed to so little purpose as this laboriously imbecile and educated man of science. You fancy this on a first reading of the incomparable Carus (there is the danger the great book runs); it is only after study and labour that you penetrate the outer dulness, and see what a magnificent treasure is before you.

Carus is one of the greatest humorists that ever lived, that is the real truth. Some authors of this sort try and provoke laughter by wit and ingenuity. The doctor takes quite the opposite, and far more difficult line. No one can say there is a word of wit in this book, that he ever deviates into cleverness,[2] that he is ever for one moment anything but incomparably *dumm*; and yet the properly-prepared reader must explode with laughter at every

---

[1] *The Lord Mayor's Visit to Oxford* (1826) gained its author, Robert Crawford Dillon, D.D., an unenviable notoriety, because of the absurd pretentiousness with which he therein describes an official visit to that city made by the Lord Mayor of London, to whom he was chaplain.

[2] An echo of Dryden's "Mac Flecknoe" (l. 15):

"But Shadwell never deviates into sense."

page, and follow with delighted interest the thoughts, actions, and emotions of this charming, grave wag.

A desire of seeing "Albion," Carus says, had long possessed him. The journey of his Majesty King Frederick Augustus, in the year 1844, gave the doctor the long wished for opportunity. Day by day, and night by night, as he went he chronicled the passing events. He didn't wait; he seized time by the forelock, sometimes once, sometimes thrice a day; he served up his thoughts hot and hot as they came glowing from his brain. Whirling about from sight to sight, gorged with good dinners every day, you would fancy he might *sometimes* be sleepy or overworked, or miss a day—not he. There is no greater proof of the industry of men of genius than this Carus journal. From "*Hildesheim, May 22, Midnight,*" to "*August the 9th, the return to Villa Cara*" (mark the pleasantry, Villa Cara, the beloved feminine of Carus), he does not miss a single day—not one. Sometimes he writes five immense pages, sometimes six, sometimes one; but one or six, they are always dull and delightful.

The royal party to which he was attached (and blessed is the King who has such a companion) left Leipsic on the 22d of May, and, travelling briskly by railroad and other contrivances, passed by Cologne, Brussels, and Ostend, to Albion. The doctor had some qualms, suggested by the rapidity of the travelling and the greatness of the occasion—what man has not?—but he kept up his spirits pretty well, all things considered, resolving, with Goethe, to look the moment in the face, and bear up.[3] At Brussels he showed his coolness, and even made a pun. Seeing a medical work by a promising young gentleman of the name of *Lost*, he pleasantly said, "I hope his efforts will not be *lost* to science." It was this admirable joke, which occurs at the outset of the book, that made us appreciate and study it. Nothing is more characteristic of greatness than coolness in the hour of perplexity.

At Brussels Carus was taken ill. "For the first time," says he, "since the commencement of our journey I felt myself indisposed.

---

[3] In *Faust* (ll. 1699-1702) Goethe's hero remarks, after agreeing to the bargain offered by Mephistopheles:

"Werd ich zum Augenblicke sagen
Verweile doch! Du bist so schön!
Dann magst du mich in Fesseln schlagen,
Dann will ich gern zugrunde gehn!"

The night had been passed almost wholly without sleep, and I only recovered—*on reading Timoleon in Plutarch*. How powerfully does the conscious life of the soul work on the unconscious! During the tedium of the night I longed for my Plutarch, but unfortunately there was nothing at hand except Kohl's Travels in England, and it is impossible to state *how much worse I became* on reading the accounts which the book contains of Manchester and the treadmill of its prison. Early in the morning Plutarch breathed around me *the fragrance of balsam*, and soon after I was actually well again." O, Carus, Carus, in every way dear— what a mercy it was that that dose of balsam of Plutarch restored your precious health!

In spite of want of sleep and long travelling Carus was writing this delightful passage the very next morning at half-past five, and at seven, away! The Princess Alice bore Frederick Augustus and his Carus to Folkestone. The "ship-life" was new and interesting to Carus: he resisted the tendency to sea-sickness, while most of the royal Saxon suite were "sacrificing to Neptune," as the sly rogue says; but the pleasure caused by contemplating "the magnificent high-rolling and foaming waves" kept Carus all right, and presently "the houses in Dover became visible, *painted of a singular brown or olive colour*, with their grey-slate roofs." There's a description of Dover for you! How the place is at once presented to the eye!—a singular brown or olive-coloured place. You feel as if you had been there all your life. "The small houses, the lofty and numerous chimneys, the strange *names over the doors and shops*," now struck him instantaneously—how he seizes on a thing at once!—what an eye it is!

The party being landed, what was the first thing that happened? "A *déjeuner dinatoire* (the great Carus says), *which the English call lunch*, was served at the inn. The richness and abundance of plate surprised us Germans, unaccustomed to such displays in our inns; and many national peculiarities in the viands were *immediately observable*; the rich ox-tail soup, the massive piece of admirable beef, fish of all descriptions, and together with sherry and port, common at all English tables, genuine porter, which, in consequence of its aromatic bitter, was peculiarly well calculated to restore the discomforts of sea-sickness." After a fatiguing "sacrifice to Neptune," it is pleasant to imagine to one's self these honest Saxons swigging the aromatic bitter. The party were off immediately to Buckhurst, the seat of Lord

De La Warr, where, on that very day, Carus wrote eleven immensely heavy pages of journal.

Heavy pages to write, and, indeed, to read; but how delightful to think on afterwards, and to muse over that which has been acquired with so much difficulty! A journey, were it to Rome or Egypt, is often pronounced by travellers to be a bore—the annoyances and discomforts daily and incessant; but in aftertimes the memory of these disappears, and the pleasures of the journey alone remain. So it is with the discovery of Carus. You are bored, but you are repaid for it in the end. You have matter for endless thought and fond and delighted reminiscence. How great his remarks are upon all subjects connected with England! how he at once penetrates to the pith of a subject! There is a physical, metaphysical, political, and archæological description of England, which is a perfect wonder of composition. Carus discovers Albion as it were, and all that in it is—the bays, seas, mountains, language, fossils, vegetables, birds, and beasts. "Regarding sheep (says he) I can only allow myself *to indulge in a very few words.* There are about six different varieties of sheep, from the small white sheep of Sussex to the black-headed sheep of Wiltshire, and the *particularly high-flavoured sheep of Wales.*" Who can choose epithets in this way but dear, dear, Carus?

"Servants with rich liveries and powdered hair," stowed away Carus very comfortably at Buckhurst, and he appears to have enjoyed himself considerably there. The dinners were "rich and cheerful," the "order of living highly agreeable," the beautiful lawns, the magnificent oaks, the splendid flower beds close to the house, it was quite charming! Carus was taken to Knowle, and to Mr. Wells, of Redleaf, who has made an immense fortune in India by ship building, and now lives in this beautiful place alone, in dignified retirement, surrounded by a tasteful collection of choice trees, plants, and pictures.

Carus admired the Landseer in this gentleman's famous picture gallery, and the early pictures of Wilkie; but the garden above all delighted him. As he wandered in it amidst a luxuriance of vegetation, such as he never beheld before, the strangest idea came into his mind:—

"Now into the garden! A luxuriance of vegetation such as I here saw, I had not yet beheld. The magnificent oaks, undisturbed for ages, the large beech trees, the luxurious ivy, the Gothic green-houses for orange and lemon-trees, concealed by shrubs and climbers; the masses of rhododendrons, the clumps of beautiful white flowering broom, and red Alpine roses; then, again, a couple of young wide-spreading cedars of Lebanon; azaleas in full bloom, such as I had never anywhere seen, a leafy alley of psorallea; hothouses, with grapes already nearly ripe, and with shaddocks (*citrus decumanus*) trained on the walls, interspersed with the splendid *clematis grandiflora*, *calceolaria* in hundreds of varieties, in the richest bloom. The sight of all these magnificent plants made me long to spend days in the contemplation of their beauties, and *inspired me with an innocent desire to become the adopted heir of the childless Mr. Wells*, of that small and aged man, whose years, and short gray mantle formed a striking contrast to all this splendid foliage and richness of bloom with which he was surrounded. The circumstance suggested to me the fable of Tithon and Aurora! Here, too, beloved nature, ever new, displayed her charms in all the splendour of youth and beauty; whilst, on the other hand, her lover became hoary and withered! Do we not everywhere read the history of unenduring happiness?''

He wanted to become Mr. Wells' adopted heir! the affectionate rogue! Why didn't he propose the thing to Mr. Wells? Perhaps that gentleman reads the *Morning Chronicle*, and may see the proposal in these very columns. Perhaps it is not too late, and we may have Carus over from Villa Cara. What a blessing if he should come, and that this paper should be the cause of an arrangement so advantageous to all parties. Carus is a great connoisseur in pictures, and speaks in fitting terms of various collections which he saw in London—the Duke of Sutherland's, Lord Westminster's, Mr. Hope's, Sir Robert Peel's, and those of "a rich private individual." "*The gentleman's name was Rogers*," Carus adds, with that blessed *naïveté* of his.

Carus is a great admirer of beauty, and expresses himself concerning the English ladies with a warmth which perhaps will not be much relished by a certain Frau at Villa Cara. Of the Marchioness of Douro, daughter-in-law of the Duke of Wellington, he says, happily "her head is of great beauty, and *when seen in profile* worthy of the goddess Juno." Her grace the Duchess of Sutherland is also "of Juno-like beauty and majesty;" and one of these noble ladies evidently affected Carus's mind a good deal, for he subsequently blesses his good star for putting him at dinner opposite "*that* English beauty whom I have before mentioned as being the most perfect in my mind from the beautiful tracing of a countenance like a painter's Juno." Which is to have the apple? Which is to make Mrs. Carus unhappy?— or is it that lady at Portsmouth, of whom the wretch confesses that she had "a head and bust so beautiful and grandiose, that they might have served as a model for Paul Veronese's famous picture of the marriage at Cana in Galilee, and which *it was impossible to cease contemplating and admiring*."

As for extracts, it is impossible by mere stray specimens to give a notion of this author. It is the mass of dullness which is so great and surprising in him: the continuous gravity and never failing flow of common place. The jokes are frequent and prodigious, as for example that one regarding a doctor, of whom Carus says, "he hopes his *receipts* are better than the *receipts* he gives his patients," &c. The observations are profound, as for instance, "The English divide their edifices perpendicularly into houses, while the Germans divide them horizontally into floors." Take his description of Ascot races:—"This time a jockey in orange was in advance, but a green one kept close behind him, and was evidently holding in his horse. When not far from the winning-post, the latter gave his horse head, and urged him to his greatest speed, so as to reach the goal first." Can anything be more lively, more happy, or give a more complete idea of Ascot races? Here is what our Carus calls "*an anthropognostic notice*:—

"SIR ROBERT PEEL.

"A man of about fifty years of age,—of good figure, powerfully made, and rather full; the form of his head remarkable, on the whole, rather for breadth than height. The relation of the three portions of the brain, so far as I could judge from a cursory view, somewhat prevented, too, by a considerable quantity of grayish hair, tolerably harmonious; the middle part of the head low, as is usual with heads of a broad form. The countenance expresses much firmness, joined with a decidedly prosaic appearance, but great sound common sense. In conversation with crowned heads, the expression, with all its firm reserve, passes readily to a smooth tone, and his bodily attitude easily assumes the same expression. His language is, however, select, comprehensive, and well expressed. Whenever I had the opportunity of seeing him, he was dressed in black, with white neckhandkerchief, and without any orders. I here subjoin, in conclusion, some remarks which were made to me concerning his qualifications for his important duties as prime minister: 'Sir Robert Peel is quite fit for his situation. By birth, belonging to the people, by his early connection with Oxford, entirely devoted to the conservative cause, he seems to have been made for his situation, and for his age. There can be but *one* opinion respecting his talents; he possesses, at the same time, a sufficiency of physical power, and has property enough to secure himself a complete independence (the English say, 'an empty sack will not stand upright'). In his daily intercourse, he is considered cold and stiff, and has no intimate personal friends.'"

"THE DUKE OF WELLINGTON.

"Completely the representation of an old soldier! Stiff, half-deaf, but cheerful; it is easy to be seen that he must have been what is called a well-built, handsome man. The form of his head, as well as that of his face, is principally long, the shape of the skull not very remarkable, the front and back portions rather high. His hair is quite white, and he has rather too much for his age, particularly in a country where baldness is more common than elsewhere. The sockets of his eyes are wide, and it is obvious from his appearance that he is rather to be regarded as a *man of eyes* than a *man of ears*, on which remark the history of his life offers the best commentary. I saw him generally in uniform, and decorated with many orders. He still rides, and was at the head of his regiment at the review, and although the windows of his residence were broken some years back, he still appears a favourite with the people, for wherever he makes his appearance, the cry 'Hurrah for the old Duke,' is general.

"Among the many traits of courage and presence of mind which are related of him, none seemed to me more characteristic, and at the same time greater and more profound, than the following:—At the battle of Waterloo, when the decisive moment was come, at which, according to the calculations of the generals, the enemy must necessarily give way, Wellington put in motion the whole English column. Waving his hat he rode in advance, urging officers and men to advance rapidly. His adjutants remarked that he was exposing himself to great danger from the enemy's fire; but he answered: 'Let them shoot away; the battle must be won, at any rate.' "

The battle must be won at any rate. So, with an admirable consistency, our friend blunders; he can't tell a common story, or understand a common point. He is not fit to be trusted to describe a kitchen poker. But nothing daunts him; on he goes, day by day, writing, writing—never doubting: always missing, always blundering, always stupid and happy.

....

[23 MARCH 1846]

Life and Correspondence of David Hume.

[William Tait, Edinburgh.

Some people may find this biography even more dangerous than the works of Hume. A sceptic, an utter worldling, a man entirely without imagination, a free thinking supporter of absolutism and high church principles, a fluent rhetorician sitting in a judge's place, attacking an adversary, and advocating a case with a dazzling show of candour, and a consummate skill of disguised sarcasm and covert panegyric; a master-hand at insinuating a doubt and hinting a sneer; a poisoner of the wells of truth and history—you find the possessor of such perilous talents, to be in his private character one of the most generous, simple, honest, and amiable of men. His life is quite a model of prudence, amenity, and decorum; no man could be more high-minded when poor, more generous and moderate when prosperous; his disposition and social qualities are so eminent kindly playful and agreeable, that the reader of Hume's life finds himself almost as much attached to Hume at the end of the biography as Robertson and Blair were ninety years ago. Some years since a writer in the *Quarterly* consigned to obloquy (and perhaps worse) "those distinguished ministers of the Gospel for encouraging the scoffs of their familiar friend, the author of 'The Essay on Miracles,' and echoing the blasphemies of their associate the author of the 'Essay upon Suicide.'" The writer of the present excellent biography of Mr. Hume, shows that the reviewer is quite in error in denouncing those eminent divines and philosophers of the last age for "echoing blasphemy" (the phrase is surely as ingeniously Jesuitical as any one by Hume himself), or approving suicide; and that it was only with the virtues and goodness of Mr. Hume they sympathised.

Mr. Burton adopts the same charitable view. Having very strong religious faith apparently, and different and more advanced philosophical opinions, he does not excommunicate the sceptic of the last century; nor, indeed, will any but the most orthodox of haters and men, exclude this most amiable of worldly philosophers from the pale of fellowship. Why should he? Any one who reads Hume's own account of his life, an example of smooth self-contentment, unmatched even by any French philosopher—every body who knows Adam Smith's account of Hume's death, may be sorry for him, but has no right to hate him surely. His life is consistent, at least, and he is the same from sixteen to sixty, insensible to a future seemingly, and untroubled by conscience or remorse, or doubt even about his doubts.[1] He quits the world so easy, good-natured, and flippant; and approaches the future as it were with a smile and a bow. A blind man may walk joking over a precipice, but it is because he

---

[1] Thackeray reproduced this combination of skepticism and good-nature in Mr. Binnie of *The Newcomes,* a character avowedly "a disciple of David Hume (whom he admired more than any other mortal)" (*Works,* XIV, 109).

can't see it. You might hate the one with just as good reason for his bodily infirmity, as the other for his deplorable undoubted mental incapacity.

Mr. Burton's biography has compiled and arranged his materials with great care and skill, and furnished a book which is exceedingly entertaining and contains much to stimulate literary curiosity. Most of the great names of the last century appear here in intimate relation with the subject of the biography. A hundred old acquaintance from the dead world arise and play their parts. We have the Scotch philosophers, so simple and good-humoured—the French *petits-maîtres* and marchionesses, so portentously philosophic—the dandy Walpole pines and frets at the success of his uncouth rival—the orthodox Johnson damns him as a sceptic and a Scotchman. Numberless well-known characters make their appearance—Dr. Smollett and Madame de Pompadour—Wilkes, Lord Bute, and the Young Pretender—Lord Chesterfield enters for a moment, and "the ingenious Irish gentleman, Mr. Burke"—Hurd and Warburton, nay, such other famous controversialists as Broughton and Slack find a place in Hume's biography, and relieve the graver portions of Mr. Burton's work with details that are exceedingly lively, pleasant, and curious. And when the reader has come to the end of the volumes, and has followed Mr. Hume through his life of admirable manliness and simplicity, undeviating probity and good humour, he will be at no loss to understand how it was that divines and philosophers, young people, and men of the world, all agreed in regard for a person so thoroughly trustworthy and amiable.

Not the least affecting of the testimonies to Hume's good qualities is this letter to him, on his death-bed, from his friend Colonel Edmonstonne. Edmonstonne was a member of a Mohock Club, called the Ruffians—a very tender-hearted reprobate to all appearance. Hume says, "Poor Edmonstonne and I parted to-day, with a plentiful effusion of tears; all those *Beelzebubians* have not hearts of iron."

"Linlithgow, Wednesday.

"My dear, dear David—My heart is very full. I could not see you this morning. I thought it was better for us both. You can't die, you must live in the memory of all your friends and acquaintances, and your works will render you immortal. I could never conceive that it was possible for any one to dislike you or hate you. He must be more than savage who could be an enemy to a man of the best head and heart, and of the most amiable manners.

> O toi, qui de mon ame es la chère moitié;
>   Toi, qui joins la délicatesse
>   Des sentimens d'une maitresse
> A la solidité d'ûne sure amitié,
> David, il faut, bien-tôt que la parque cruelle
>   Vienne rompre des si doux noeuds,
>   Et malgré nos cris et nos voeux
> Bien-tôt nous assurions une absence eternelle.
> Adieu! adieu!"—MS. R.S.E.

The heathenism of the French had only augmented since the time when poor Chaulieu had parted from his friend (and the friend of the Regent Orleans) the chaste Lafare, and yielded himself up with a shrug to the "Parque immortelle;" and the account of Hume's reception at Paris, forty years later, is something very curious to read. "No lady's toilette at Paris," Lord Charlemont says, "was complete without Hume's attendance," and a very amusing extract is given by Mr. Burton from the letters of Madame d'Epinay, describing the behaviour of the "grand et gros historiographe," at a party where he was made to assume the robe of "a Sultan between two slaves," the two slaves being the prettiest women in Paris. The Scotch Sultan had nothing better to do or say but to rub his stomach and knees and cry out, "*Well, ladies, here you are, ladies—well, ladies, here you are.*" After a quarter of an hour of which amusement one of the Sultanas got up in a huff, and quitted him, saying, "*Je m'en suis toujours doutée cet homme n'est bon qu'à manger du veau.*" He looked in uniform like a grocer of the trained bands. His speech in English was rendered ridiculous by the broadest Scotch accent, and his French, if possible, was still more remarkable; but in spite of this the French made him their idol, and it is amusing to read of the complacency with which Hume received their homage. He writes to Adam Smith from Fontainebleau:—

HUME TO ADAM SMITH.

"Fontainbleau, 26th Oct., 1763.

"My dear Smith—I have been three days at Paris, and two at Fontainbleau, and have everywhere met with the most extraordinary honours which the most exorbitant vanity could wish or desire. The compliments of dukes and marischals of France, and foreign ambassadors, go for nothing with me at present; I retain a relish for no kind of flattery but that which comes from the ladies. All the courtiers, who stood around when I was introduced to Madame de Pompadour, assured me that she was never heard to say so much to any man; and her brother, to whom she introduced me,— But I forget already that I am to scorn all the civilities of men. However, even Madame Pompadour's civilities were, if possible, exceeded by those of the Duchesse de Choisseul, the wife of the favourite and prime minister, and one of the ladies of the most distinguished merit in France. Not contented with the many obliging things she said to me on my first introduction, she sent to call me from the other end of the room, in order to repeat them, and to enter into a short conversation with me; and not contented with that, she sent the Danish Ambassador after me, to assure me, that what she said was not from politeness, but that she seriously desired to be in friendship and correspondence with me. There is not a courtier in France who would not have been transported with joy, to have had the half of these obliging things said to him by either of these great ladies; but what may appear more extraordinary, both of them, as far as I could conjecture, have read with some care all my writings that have been translated into French—that is, almost all my writings. The king said nothing particular to me when I was introduced to him; and (can you imagine it) I was become so silly, as to be a little mortified by it, till they told me that he never says any thing to any body the first time he sees them. The Dauphin, as I am told from all hands, declares himself on every occasion very strongly in my favour; and many people assure me that I have reason to be proud of his judgment, even were he an individual. I have scarce seen any of the geniuses of Paris, who, I think, have in general great merit, as men of letters. But every body is forward to tell me the high panegyrics I receive from them; and you may believe that [. . .] approbation which has procured me all these civilities from the courtiers."

And to Robertson, he narrates his wonderful reception by the Dauphin and his family:—

"Do you ask me about my course of life? I can only say that I eat nothing but ambrosia, drink nothing but nectar, breathe nothing but incense, and tread on nothing but flowers! Every man I meet, and, still more, every lady, would think they were wanting in the most indispensable duty, if they did not make a long and elaborate harangue in my praise. What happened last week, when I had the honour of being presented to the Dauphin's children at Versailles, is one of the most curious scenes I have yet passed through. The Duc de Berri, the eldest, a boy of ten years old, stepped forth, and told me how many friends and admirers I had in this country, and that he reckoned himself in the number, from the pleasure he had received from the reading of many passages in my works. When he had finished, his brother, the Count de Provence, who is two years younger, began his discourse, and informed me that I had been long and impatiently expected in France; and that he himself expected soon to have great satisfaction from the reading of my fine history. But what is more curious, when I was carried thence to the Count d'Artois, who is but four years of age, I heard him mumble something which, though he had forgot in the way, I conjectured, from some scattered words, to have been also a panegyric dictated to him. Nothing could more surprise my friends, the Parisian philosophers, than this incident. . . . . It is conjectured that this honour was paid me by express order from the Dauphin, who, indeed, is not on any occasion sparing in my praise."

Thirty years later they received Franklin similarly,[1] this luck-less race which was pursuing a fashion that was to end in the downfall of all of them.

With a true British independence, the great people of his own country and our's (which he detested most heartily, designating the English as "the barbarians who inhabit the banks of the Thames"), seeing him so well received by the French aristocracy, began to condescend to notice him, and even to ask favours of him. The surly philosopher shook off these genteel parasites; and, indeed, in the midst of his splendour, confesses occasionally that he sighs for his arm chair at Edinburgh, and the ease and homeliness of the Poker Club.

But a newspaper cannot afford space to analyse these books, or to extract more than one or two of the thousand interesting passages and anecdotes which they contain. They are an excel-lent and most amusing contribution to literary history, most carefully compiled by a competent scholar.

[1] See *Works,* VIII, 166-171, for Thackeray's burlesque version of Franklin's reception at the French court.

....

[6 APRIL 1846]

Travels in the Punjab. By MOHAN LAL,[1] Esq.

[London: W. H. Allen and Co.

The travels of Mohan Lal, Esq., *aus dem Stamme der Fürsten von Kashmir,* are not remarkable for accuracy of details or novelty of information. The descendant of Kashmerian princes performed the first part of his journey in the suite of Burnes, who has left us, in one of the noblest books of travels in our language,[2] an

[1] Thackeray perhaps remembered this name when he christened the swindling Indian merchant of *The Newcomes* "Rummun Loll."

[2] Sir Alexander Burnes's *Travels into Bokhara; Being the Account of a Journey from India to Cabool, Tartary, and Persia,* three volumes, 1834.

account of the countries which were visited in his company by the youthful Lal. Mr. Lal was not, in 1831, Mohan Lal, Esq. (except perhaps as Mr. S. Panza in the suite of a certain noble-man of La Mancha, was S. Panza, Esq.). A lad brought up in the English college at Delhi, he was employed by Burnes as Persian secretary or clerk; he is mentioned irreverently by the latter as "the Hindoo lad we brought with us," and there is no more heard of the future Knight of the Lion and Sun. Mean-while the ingenious young Lal was making notes of his own: composing a journal, in the drollest and most amusing English; noting down those incidents of travel which struck his opening mind; receiving the legends told him by Afghans and Sikhs with a charming simplicity of belief, and recording the compliments paid to his own personal beauty and abilities with the most delightful credulous complacency. His memoirs do not complete Burnes's, or give us any new information about Bokhara and Persia; but they illustrate "Gil Blas" very well, and confirm the truth of "Hajji Baba"[3] completely. The bachelor of Santillana was just such another simple *gobemouche* of a youth as young Mr. Lal, of Delhi College. Hajji Baba, Esquire, was just such another easy moralist, with the same engaging modesty and unalterable good humour. After reading the history of one or other adventurer, respect is not perhaps exactly the feeling one is led to entertain for the subject of the memoir. His virtues are certainly not of the austere kind; but there are many other qualities which make a man agreeable, and we can fancy Abbas Merza, the Prince Royal of Persia, patronising Mohan Lal, Esquire, as an English Prince Royal delighted in Falstaff. He is always amusing. In all the circumstances of his life, as here narrated by him, Squire Lal presents himself under an aspect indescribably ludicrous and pleasant. He appears in his portrait with his orders of the Dourannee empire, and the lion and sun, his Kashmerian turban and pelisse, and a very handsome Eastern physiognomy; but his handsome face is lighted up with such a killing Kashmerian ogle that it is impossible for the beholder of the miniature to refrain from laughing at it. His gravity is funny beyond expression: his dignity is as irresistible as Keeley's, in that great tragedian's most solemn moments; and there is a

---

[3] James Justinian Morier's romance of Persian life, *The Adventures of Hajji Baba of Ispahan* (1824).

charming, unreality, grimace, and buoyancy about his very grief, which makes his tears more comical than the jokes of most people. If the "stamm" of Kashmerian princes produced many Lals, they must have been a race of wags unexampled in royal genealogies.

Having taken leave of his friend Mr. B. Fitzgerald, who "took Lal in his arms," &c., sighed and shed a flood of tears at parting from him (we presume it is the wont of English gentlemen in the Indian service to weep in the embraces of their Hindoo retainers), young Mr. Lal set out from Delhi on the 29th December, 1831, on the commencement of his career in life. At Painpat, on the 23d December, one of his relations gave him an excellent dinner followed by a dance. How the amiable young hypocrite joked and laughed with his companions, though in reality melancholy; and next day at Kurnaul, whilst conversing with one of the hostlers about a lodging, "a beautiful young girl came gracefully to him and said, 'Come with me in the next room, where I will prepare a clean bed for you;'" upon which Master Lal confesses that he "*slept very comfortably.*" On the 6th of January, having joined Mr. Burnes at Loodhianah, Lal was at Judgarh, close to the Sutlej. The weather was cold. Cow-dung, he remarked, was burned for fuel by the people after it was sun-dried. "I am surprised," he justly says, "at the foolish prejudices of the Hindoos, who worship cows and eat cow-dung to purify themselves, and at other times burn it."

The traveller now entered the Punjaub: "The inhabitants," Lal says, "are filthy; they never bathe or wash their faces, on account of which they are much afflicted with fever and cold." Some exceptions, however, there were: at Biki, he saw a woman, a perfect model of beauty. Her person was clean, she charmed the spectators by her modesty. Her raiment being blue, added lustre to her beauty.

Remarks of this profound kind and amiable egotisms occur at every page, and it is only occasionally that the reader gets a glimpse of the country in this book of travels, the writer being incessantly occupied with the person of Mr. Mohan Lal.

Charming as his person no doubt is, and as M. Lal, Esq., perpetually declares the eastern people found it to be, yet those who have not had the blessing of knowing him cannot expect to be so fascinated by this beautiful Indian gentleman. It may even happen that the compliments paid to Mr. Lal, and noted down in his journal, will not simply be found tedious and foolish, but perfectly disgusting by English readers. He should be entreated to omit them in future editions of his work, and to forget how Mr. Fitzgerald wept over him; how Kwajah Mahommed wrote him love verses; how the Maulvir, at Peshawur, shedding another flood of tears, called him his "incomparable taper, or beloved"— if they did, which after all may be questioned—for who knows how far figures of speech may be allowed to go in Oriental language; and whether these touching incidents may not be simply imaginative poems by M. Lal, Esq.?

From Peshawur Lal went to Bokhara, thence to Mashad and Herat, making conquests wherever he appeared. From Herat he turned to Candahar, back to Peshawur again, and thence to Calcutta by way of Delhi, where his old fellow citizens, instead of loving him as every body else had done, abused and envied him on account of "the fame he had won," and where he appears to have made consequently a very brief sojourn. This journey occupied him two years. In 1835 Mohan Lal set out on a second mission to Kabul, where he remained till 1842. Some of the greatest triumphs and disasters that ever befel our power in India occurred while he was acting as political agent. But of these Mohan Lal, Esq., gives no account. He says that he freed the Afghan prisoners; he says that he escaped himself, after the noble Burnes' massacre (to which he scarcely condescends to allude)—escaped in a miraculous manner; but his relation is so vague as to be past comprehension, and to puzzle even belief; and he threatens another work, which, if it be like the volume before us, will be perfectly unexampled for vacuity of intelligence, for a happy faculty on an author's part of believing and imparting absurdities, and for an indomitable self-complacency which supports him under all difficulties, and keeps him buoyantly floundering amidst blunders.

He came to England and Ireland, where he was received with that discriminating cordiality which our country always accords to distinguished foreigners. He is profuse in his professions of gratitude, and records his impressions of the country in the following brilliant manner:—

"DEC. 20.—After passing through several manufactories in Manchester, where all sorts of flowered and plain muslins, as well as chintzes, are made for the Indian market, I came to Birmingham. I there saw manufactories of guns, cannon, and needles, all done by the steam-machine. The towns of Manchester and Birmingham are not very clean, but are marts of considerable trade.

"JAN. 1, 1845. London.—Sir Robert and Lady Inglis possess really kind and benevolent hearts. They invited me frequently, and I was introduced to some very high men at their table. The relations of the late Sir William Macnaghten treated me with great kindness, and I often dined with his good sister, Mrs. Chapman, and also with Mrs. F. Macnaghten, the sister of my most lamented friend Captain John Conolly, to whom I was much attached. It is hardly in my power to describe the cordial treatment I received from Lord and Lady Palmerston, Sir John Hobhouse, the Marquess of Lansdowne, and Lord Auckland. They invited me to their evening parties, and to dinners, and showed themselves desirous to promote my interests.

"MARCH 4.—Mr. G. E. Anson, secretary to his Royal Highness Prince Albert, sent me a note desiring me to wait upon his Royal Highness, at Buckingham Palace. The elegant and agreeable manners, mingled with kind and generous feelings, of the Prince, are beyond any praise. His knowledge of passing events in Asia, and the outbreak at Kabul, surprised me. The popularity and affection which he has gained from all parties in England are wonderful, and show very rare and extraordinary qualities. He received me very kindly, and after a long conversation I left the Palace with sentiments of deep respect and grateful satisfaction. I had the honour of meeting the Prince at Lord Northampton's *soirée*, and other places, frequently afterwards, and the more I saw of his Royal Highness the more kind I found him.

"MARCH 5.—Mr. (now Sir Emerson) Tennent wrote a very kind note, stating that the Earl of Ripon, president of the India Board, had a high opinion of my humble services; but that as the result of my claims was pending upon the decision of the Court of Directors and his lordship, it would be advisable that I should be presented to her Majesty through some channel independent of the government. It was therefore that the noble and benevolent Lord Ashley took me in his carriage and presented me to her Most Gracious Majesty Queen Victoria. I was also invited to her Majesty's ball in Buckingham Palace. The court was very full, and the rooms exceedingly warm. All the ministers of state, the foreign ambassadors, and the nobility and gentry of England, in their different costumes, bowing and passing before her Majesty, exhibited a magnificent sight; but the rooms are not well adapted, nor sufficiently spacious. The drawing-rooms of her Majesty, where all the ladies are presented, exhibit a great profusion of beauty, of rich dresses and jewels. The royal balls are beyond anything of the kind in the world. One who is as fortunate as myself to be invited will see an assembly of noble ladies with charming countenances, and elegant robes covered with diamonds, joining in the dance, which, although dazzling, yet becomes brighter and more beautiful when her Majesty and her royal consort, Prince Albert, take part in the dance. In so large a company the Queen appeared to me the most graceful in the dance, smiling and looking now and then graciously towards her royal husband. I kept my humble eyes unweariedly fixed upon her Majesty and the Prince, while they were dancing, and I read with inexpressible delight in their countenances that they have a deep attachment to each other."

Five hundred and thirty pages of such description of European and Asiatic courts are at the service of the readers of the "Travels of Mohan Lal, Esq."

....

[11 APRIL 1846]

The Novitiate; or, a Year among the English Jesuits. By ANDREW STEINMETZ.   [Smith, Elder, and Co.

The author of this book having, at one or two-and-twenty years of age, seen the end of a small and embarrassed patrimony, finding himself in London with considerable talents and learning, and strong devotional ardour, acquired in early life at a Roman Catholic school, bethought him, not unnaturally, of turning Jesuit; and applied to the resident Jesuit agent in London, for leave to enter their society's ecclesiastical seminary at Hodder Hall, in Yorkshire. He was received with a very good grace; exchanged his threadbare clothes, rather profitably, for the black Jesuit uniform, and commenced his clerical novitiate with great warmth and vigour. But between his terms of residence at Ushaw and Hodder, Mr. Steinmetz had seen the world, and shared in its struggles and pleasures, and tasted of freedom. At the end of a year's novitiate, the Jesuit rule was too severe for him, and he came out into the world again, and bade farewell to the society. He writes a most singular and interesting account of the Hodder seminary, and his way of life there. A pretty little neatly gilt picture of a chain and a scourge are on the face of his book. He revolted against that miserable moral and bodily discipline, and is a man once more, and not a Jesuit. Perhaps, considering that the reverend fathers fed him, and gave him a year's loan of a cassock, paid his lodging-house bill in London when he wished to quit the world, and gave him a little money when he wished to return, Mr. Steinmetz should have held his tongue, and not published the Jesuit arcana. Such will unquestionably be the opinion of their reverences, under whose roof he was housed not unkindly or uncomfortably; but the public would have lost a very singular and useful book had he remained mute. We are very glad he has peached, for our part. He seems to be a perfectly honest and credible informer, and his testimony may serve to enlighten many a young devotional aspirant, who is meditating "submission" to Rome and the chain and scourge system.

There is nothing in the least resembling invective in the volume, nor does it contain any of those charges of monstrous craft and cruelty with which one is accustomed to meet among enemies of the order. One figure of those introduced into the dismal ascetic picture, that of the "father of the novices," a gentle and pious old man, is even charming: at least there is something human and kindly left, which all the training of the society with its infernal ingenuity has not been enabled to eradicate. But all besides in the description of the commencement of the Jesuit life is inexpressibly sad and disheartening. Let us briefly give an account of Mr. Steinmetz's career, and of that (necessarily) of every other member of the body which he intended to join.

Having signified his wish to the Jesuit agent in London, it was forwarded to headquarters, and the aspirant was in the meanwhile told to study the constitutions of the society, but to *signify to no one* his intention of joining it. The agent would not even help Steinmetz to get a recommendation to the British Museum, for the purpose of reading the constitutions, so cautious was he not to appear to stir in the matter. The candidate being accepted hastened down into Yorkshire, and was immediately inducted.

After a "retreat" of a few days, he joined the rest of the novices. As he entered Hodder House, the father of the novices seized his hand with rapture and kissed it, and leading him to the little chapel, they prayed together. A brother novice was then appointed to show the new-comer the house and its ways, to which he was called upon absolutely to conform. The novices are robed in black cassocks and caps, and by way of humility they wear the cast-off raiment of the students of the college.

Their day's work begins at five o'clock in the morning, when the porter (a novice also) comes to the curtain that hangs before the little compartment that each occupies in the common dormitory, and scratching it, says, "Deo gratias," to which every novice answers, "Deo gratias," and rises instantly. "Collecting himself," that is, thinking of God or uttering some pious ejaculation, he dresses himself. So dressed, each solemnly descends to the kitchen, where there is a pump and a trough, and performs a silent toilette. As they move about no word is spoken; they keep their eyes steadily down to the ground (this is called the "custody of the eyes") and this rule is never relaxed except in hours of recreation.

The first duty is performed in chapel, where, after prayer, comes an hour's "meditation." A subject connected with religion is given out by the porter, who reads the "points" which the student is to consider. He is to keep his mind to this subject, and no other; to revolve everything connected with it; and so he meditates obediently, kneeling, standing, sitting, then kneeling again for an hour. Mass is then performed, after which each walks back to his cell for half-an-hour's spiritual reading. Then comes a breakfast of porridge and milk, swallowed with downcast eyes; then a lecture in chapel, on the subject of which the students converse in the dormitory, until the porter cries "Deo gratias," when conversation ceases, and all begin to make their beds. All the domestic functions of the establishment are then gone through by the novices, the manner of which Steinmetz describes in the following edifying way:—

"In-door manual works consisted in all the functions of domestic economy. You went to the porter and said 'Deo gratias!' He replied, 'sweep the dormitory, clean knives, clean shoes, sweep the recreation-room, sweep up the hearth, dust the chairs,' &c.

"Sometimes the 'Deo gratias' would be answered by 'go to Brother So-and-so, in the refectory.' Brother So-and-so would then order you to sweep the room, or set the benches, or lay the cloths, or plates, or knives and forks; and when he had nothing more for you to do, he would answer your 'Deo gratias!' by another 'Deo gratias!' and you went again to the porter.

"The porter would then, perhaps, order you to go to another brother. This brother, on hearing the 'Deo gratias!' might order you to go and fetch the 'tub;' or perhaps he would go with you, as it required two persons to lift it. This tub was set ready by the lay-brother at the kitchen door. You carried the tub to the back region of the house, and then you washed, and wiped the utensils there deposited; and then you scrubbed the *sedilia*, swept out the adjacent localities, made all neat and tidy, and returned the tub aforesaid to where you found it. This part of manual works was considered the most trying to pride; and, consequently, it was not ordered to new novices. For my part, I often longed for the order, in my fervour; and when it was vouchsafed me, I was rather grieved to think that perhaps the companion selected for me was chosen in order to diminish my repugnance—which certainly did not exist. At all events, my companion was a son of Lord ——, a Catholic nobleman. I may mention that at the time of which I am speaking there were in the Novitiate, besides the gentleman just alluded to, the son of a baronet, and two near relatives of another Roman Catholic nobleman. Before I left I think we numbered about twenty novices in all.

"Other occupations consisted in dusting the books, cleaning out the chapel, polishing plate, &c. &c.—in a word, every domestic work was performed by the novices, excepting cooking; which was, however, in the hands of the lay-brother, and an assistant who was a lay-novice.

"When the appointed hour was passed, we were ordered into the garden. Here we were sent to dig potatoes or root up weeds—to pick fruit, or sweep away dry leaves, to roll the play-ground, or clean the walks—according to the season."

Time for work in the garden now comes; it is performed in silence, and the eyes of the labourer are not removed from the cabbage or potato bed on which he digs. The garden work over, they return, take off the old clothes worn in the garden, and put on cassocks and slippers; for slippers are more favourable to silence than shoes are. Then they study for an hour, translating a book of divinity; then they go to chapel and examine themselves.

"The reader may perhaps fancy that we have not had much time for sinning; but he is mistaken: we went to chapel for the examination of conscience. We remained kneeling during this quarter of an hour.

"It may be asked what we examined our consciences to find? I will state a few novice-sins; and the result of this proceeding will render the matter perfectly intelligible. Suppose a novice walked rather hurriedly—it was a fault. If he contradicted his brother in conversation—it was a fault. If he failed in the custody of the eyes—it was a fault. It might happen that he spoke more to one than another—it was a fault. He laughed too loudly—that was fault. In fine, he has not 'done his best' in every public duty—this is a fault."

And now dinner takes place, in a decent and plentiful manner. Meanwhile, some of the novices, kneeling in the middle of the room, are confessing their faults to the Superior. One says, "Holy father, I neglected the custody of my eyes, and looked up once or twice, in the garden;" or, "Holy father, I talked too loud in recreation," &c.; and he assigns himself a penance. This one says a prayer or psalm, kneeling in the room with outstretched arms: that goes round and kisses the feet of all present: another eats his dinner, kneeling in the middle of the room.

Once (this was on a grand day) the good old pious white-haired superior knelt down in the middle of the young men, and so took his meal, and went and kissed their feet all round afterwards. This must have been a delightful spectacle of humility indeed. Whilst each student is confessing his fault, those whose turn is not yet come are lying about the room grovelling in the ground, with their arms stretched out.

This cheerful repast concluded, "recreation" is allowed. They lift up their eyes, and talk actually for an hour. At the sound of a bell the talk stops; the eyes go floorwards; they march again to chapel; then to "manual works" in the house or garden; then to reading and writing in the dormitory (no books are read but with the authority of superiors by *any* Jesuit—no letters sent or received but open); then comes chapel, and another examination of conscience; then supper and an hour's recreation; then, finally, bed. You might hear all the beds creaking on their hinges, and all are in bed and asleep in a minute; unless—unless it is mortification night—*flogging night*—as now in Lent, when all these young men fall to with the scourge on their naked shoulders—a noble occupation in this present stage of the world.

When by this godly and manly course of life an English gentleman has utterly trained down his mind, his eyes, his senses, his notions of right and wrong; when he has learned obedience, and has brought his body to be *perindè ac cadaver*—a carcass at the entire subjection of his superiors; when he has learned chastity like holy Aloysius, "who never would stay alone *with his mother* in her chamber, and such was his virginal modesty, that he was afraid to let a servant see so much as his foot uncovered;"—when he has reached, not this absolute perfection, but as near it as his fallible nature will allow, at any rate has learned to bare his shoulders to the lash with a zeal sufficiently cowardly, and to grovel in the dust and relish it with a becoming humility, there is a chance then of making a JESUIT of him. And then who knows but that he may have the glory of receiving the "submission" of Anglican divines fresh from Oxford, and inducting them into the noble practices in which he himself is a proficient?

[21 APRIL 1846]

The New Timon. [Colburn, 1846.

This poem has reached a third edition, and appears gloriously attired in a sea-green cover and gilt edges. The voice of critics has been loud in its praise. "There has not been better writing since Churchill," says one; "It belongs to the school of Crabbe," a second declares; a third, still more enthusiastic, augurs from this poem "a resuscitation of our bardic glories," and says that "it combines the characteristics of Crabbe and Byron." Finally, a fourth hand testifies that "a great poet is *at length* before the world," that "his accents fall like manna on the heart," in fact, that "he is to be a standard study beside Byron." All these panegyrics are placed in the first page of this immortal gilt-edged work, after the fashion of our old poets and dramatists ("our ancient bardic glories"), who used to affix copies of laudatory verses, in Latin or English, to their plays and poems, hoping by this simple method that the subject of their letters of recommendation would be welcomed by the public patron.

After all these vouchers for glory, these repeated editions and gilt edges, out comes Sir Bulwer Lytton, to whom universal fame has ascribed the authorship of the poem, and denies positively the bantling that is sworn to him. Mr. Colburn is authorized to give the disclaimer on the part of the reputed father. It is in vain the incredulous say, "Look at the child. It has Sir Lytton's eyes, every glance of them. It is Sir Edward's nose to a T; it has Sir Bulwer's expression, his complexion, the very trick of his walk and mould of his limbs." But there is the publisher's affidavit to quash the charge, and that gentleman's testimony is doubtless sufficient. There have been such remarkable resemblances before in the world. History books and the Causes Célèbres narrate such. There was the famous case of Martin Guerre, in which the wife did not know which of the two claimants to her hand was her actual husband; the case of Kynaston, in Charles II.'s time, who was so like Sir Charles Sedley, that the knight one day pulled the actor's nose and beat him in Hyde Park, pulling his double's nose and spiting his own face as it were. There was the case of Nero's freedman, as told by Tacitus, who was so like him in countenance, and could sing and play on the cittern so dexterously, that he led away multitudes of people, and caused dreadful riots and disturbances. Hence we should not marvel that a Protean poet, who has been compared to Churchill, and to Byron, and to Crabbe, and to a mixture of the two latter, should be also likened to Sir Bulwer Lytton.

The "New Timon" is in the manner of the Cambridge prize poems, the inventors of which exercises wisely confined the young bards who competed for honours to compositions of a few score of lines in length. For the prettinesses, the clevernesses, the classical allusions and epigrams, the grave pertness, the jingling antithesis, the feeble recurrence of the perpetual twanging rhythm, would grow unbearable if protracted beyond a few pages;—and there are two hundred and twenty of these in the "New Timon." To our mind, the impression caused by reading the poem right on end is one of intolerable tedium. The hero is an Indian Quadroon, of whose early life and parentage the following marvellous account is given:—

> "From childhood fatherless, and lone begun
> His fiery race beneath as fierce a sun,
> Where all extremes of love and horror are,
> Soft Camdeo's lotos bark, grim Moloch's gory car.
> Where basks the noon-day luminously calm,
> O'er eldest grot and immemorial palm;
> And in the grot, the Goddess of the Dead
> And the couch'd strangler, list the wanderer's tread,
> And where the palm-leaves stir with breeze-like sigh,
> Sports the fell serpent with his deathful eye.
> " 'Midst the exuberant life of that fierce zone,
> Uncurbed, self-willed, to man had Morvale grown.
> His sire (the offspring of an Indian maid
> And English chief), whose orient hues betrayed
> The Varna Sankara* of the mixed embrace,
> Carved by his sword a charter from disgrace;
> Assumed the father's name, the Christian's life,
> And his sins cursed him with an English wife;
> A haughty dame, whose discontented charms
> That merchant, Hymen, bargained to his arms.
> In war he fell: his wife—the bondage o'er,
> Loathed the dark pledge the abhorred nuptials bore—
> Yet young, her face more genial wedlock won,
> And one bright daughter made more loathed the son.

"*The Sanscrit term (familiar to those who, like the writer, have resided in the vast empire that we govern and forget), denoting the mixture or confusion of classes; applied to a large portion of the Indian population excluded from the four pure castes."

> Widowed anew, for London's native air,
> And two tall footmen, sigh'd the jointured fair:
> Wealth her's, why longer from its use exiled?—
> She fled the land and the abandoned child;
> Yet oft the first-born, midst the swarthier race,
> Gazed round, and miss'd the fair unloving face.
> In vain the coldness, nay, the hate had been,
> Hate, by the eyes that love, is rarely seen."

In this description, we take it, the only lines that have the least truth or naturalness are the pair, "widowed anew, for London's native air, and two tall footmen sighed the jointured fair;" which are terse and happy as a satiric couplet of Pope. But how unsatisfactory all the rest of the description is—how turgid, and how weak! How utterly untrue the last sentiment; how absurd the notions of the East, and "the *Varna Sankara*, the Sanscrit term familiar to all those who have resided, like the author, in India;" as if Sanscrit was the spoken language there, and Thugs and tigers in every bush! Some man leaves this young savage a fortune, which finds him "couched in the shade that rear'd the tiger's lair." He quits the jungle, and comes to Europe, where his mother, dying, repents of her coolness towards him, and leaves his sister, "the lorn Calantha, to a brother's care." This couple come to London, and occupy a mansion somewhere near St. James's Park. But there is some melancholy hanging over "the Peri-child"—as the author (familiar with the Sanscrit) calls the young lady—a secret, a corroding care. She is respectful and tender towards her brother, but not familiar, and that gentleman still pines for something to love.

Walking through Pall-mall at day-break one May morning, Morvale finds a young girl seated on some door-steps, as stone-like as the stone on which she sate. "The son of the desert"—so the writer (familiar with, &c.) *will* call the East Indian gentleman—examines the young outcast.

> "With orient suns his cheek was swarth and grim,
> And low the form, though lightly shaped the limb;
> Yet life glowed vigorous in that deep-set eye,
> With a calm force that dared you to defy;
> And the small foot was planted on the stone
> Firm as a gnome's upon his mountain throne;
> Simple his garb, yet what the wealthy wear,
> And conscious power gave lordship to his air.

"Lone in the Babel thus the maid and man;
Long he gazed silent, and at last began:—
'Poor homeless outcast—dost thou see me stand
Close by thy side—yet beg not? Stretch thy hand.'
The voice was stern, abrupt, yet full and deep—
The outcast heard, and started as from sleep,
And meekly rose, and stretched the hand, and sought
To murmur thanks—the murmur failed the thought.
He took the slight thin hand within his own:
'This hand had nought of honest labour known;
And yet methinks thou'rt honest!—speak my child.'
And his face broke to beauty as it smiled,
But her unconscious eyes, cast down the while,
Met not the heart that opened in that smile;
Again the murmur rose, and died in air.
'Nay, what thy mother and her home, and where?'
Lo, with those words the rigid ice, that lay,
Layer upon layer within, dissolves away;
And tears come rushing from o'erchargèd eyes:—
'There is my mother—there her home—the skies!'
Oh, in that burst, what deeps of lone distress!
O desolation of the motherless!
Yet through the anguish how survived the trust,
Home in the skies, though in the grave the dust!
The man was moved, and silence fell again;
Upsprung the sun—light reassumed the reign;
Love ruled on high! Below, the twain that share
Men's builded empires—Mammon and Despair!
  "At length, with pitying eye and soothing tone,
The stranger spoke: 'Thy bitterer grief mine own;
Mine the full coffers, but the beggared heart,
Amidst the million, lonely as thou art;
But gold—earth's demon, when unshared—receives
God's breath, and grows a God, when it relieves.
Thou trust'st our common Father, orphan one,
And he shall guide thee, if thou trust the son.
Nay, follow, child.' And on, with passive feet,
Ghost-like she followed through the death-like street.
They paused at last a stately pile before;
The drowsy porter oped the noiseless door;
The girl stood wistful still without;—the pause
The guide divined, and thus rebuked the cause:—
'Enter, no tempter let thy penury fear,
We have a sister, and her home is here,' "

Here comparisons will suggest themselves, and who that is
familiar with Sir Edward Bulwer Lytton's novels will not recognise a hero of the Lyttonian order? The calmness of his force,

the prodigious pomposity of his language, and *the smallness of his feet,*[1] at once stamp the tragic Pelham. That touch, at which the poet just hints at Morvale's boots, is worthy of the great painter of heroic dandies; the comparison, "firm as gnome's upon his mountain throne," exquisitely incoherent, and most poetically vague. The sickening Peri-child, Calantha, takes charge of the orphan Lucy. She becomes the delight of the whole house. "The very menials" stop to listen to her singing. She is the dove in the ark, and her behaviour is described in the following pretty and unaffected lines:—

> "It was not mirth, for mirth she was too still,
> It was not wit, wit leaves the heart more chill;
> But that continuous sweetness which with ease
> Pleases all round it from the wish to please."

Lucy's history is mysterious and melancholy. Her mother was a clergyman's daughter, who had trusted a young reprobate of a nobleman, and contracted a marriage with him, which afterwards turned out to be sham. The victim's father died of grief. She fled into seclusion, perished in the direst poverty, and died, leaving Lucy a miniature of her papa, whom, though on her death-bed, the fond mother never rebuked. Morvale hears her tale, loves her, and, as a matter of course, Lucy returns the love of her benefactor.

Morvale has a friend, an ex-diplomatist, a palled sybarite of a man, who has talents and some good points, nevertheless, and for whom the son of the desert has some liking. Arden tells the latter his story. He has led, latterly, a sad dissipated life in the principal courts of Europe; numerous are the women who have yielded to his fascinations, and pined afterwards at his indifference. But of all those who have made an impression upon him, a case in early youth affects him most. Dependent then upon his uncle, he had fallen in love with a clergyman's daughter, married her in secret, and left her. But he found afterwards, from the friend who arranged the marriage for him, that the latter had engaged a sham parson. He had succeeded to his uncle's titles, and sought his wife once more; but she was gone, no traces were left of the injured and innocent Mary, and Arden,

---

[1] Bulwer-Lytton was proud of the smallness of his feet and gave this attribute to many of his heroes from Pelham on. See Thackeray's caricature in *Letters,* III, 21, where he claims that his depiction of Bulwer-Lytton's tiny boots is "very fine."

though he endeavoured to drown his remorse in dissipation (and in spite of his successes among the fair sex of the highest quality), never could forget his guileless and beautiful clergyman's daughter.

The reader of prose and verse novels knows the rest. Arden is Lucy's father, as is proved by the miniature she possesses; but, alas! the rogue has also given *another* miniature to the Peri-child Calantha, who dies broken-hearted at his lordship's neglect of her. All talk of marriage is over now, between Lucy and the son of the desert—there is death between them (—Death! as the poet writes, one of the most liberal poets for capital letters and notes of exclamation this age has produced); they part, Lucy goes home with her papa, and Morvale is a comfortless wanderer. In the fifth act they meet again, however. Arden is dead; Lucy (victim a second time of the bastardy laws), is without a shilling, and—can it be doubted—they rush into one another's arms: Mr. and Mrs. Morvale's children are grandsons of the desert.

This is called a romance of London. Clever sketches of O'Connell, the Duke of Wellington, Lord Stanley, Lord John Russell, and Sir Robert Peel, are introduced in the early part: but for these "the New Timon" might be a romance of Jericho, or any other city. "The New Timon" is not like Timon at all; the poetry, to our mind, is not like nature, though it is sometimes something like poetry. It has the loudness, but not the passion— the rage without the strength. It is ingenious, often pretty and fanciful; scarcely ever, as we think, natural and genuine. The style is tawdry to a wonder, and the use of the English language supereminently coxcombical. When the writer wishes that the word "even" should be read as a word of two syllables, he is good enough to write it *evèn*. Even the unfortunate personal pronoun "he" is overloaded in this manner, and we read at page 37, "*Hè* had won Venus, but escaped the net." Adjectives, by the help of a capital are elevated to substantive rank—the Good, the Beautiful, the True, the Past, the Future, &c. By this easy typographic artifice nouns substantive are exalted to extra importance—"And with the Heart its temple Reason shook;" "But Grief, the Egoist, yearneth to confess;" "But the calm dwelling by the Streams of Life;" "Ease on the wing, and Labour at the wheel," &c. Why should labour with a big L be sitting at a wheel with a little w? Why not advance to capital rank, as the Germans do, all the substantives in the dictionary? Finally, substantives are farther denaturalized, and made to figure as verbs—"Glass'd on its bosom shot the sparkling stream;" "The wise perplex'd, yet glimpsing still sublime;" "All that his heart has *templed* overthrown." Who has a right to take liberties in this way with our venerable mother, the English grammar?

Sir Edward Bulwer Lytton has done so repeatedly, that is the fact; and in his prose and poetry glassing, and glimpsing, templing, and the like, a lavish expenditure of capitals; a proper use of the Truthful, the Unreal, the Beautiful, the Ugly, and what not, will be found. These defects the author of the "Modern Timon" has adroitly adopted, and he has taken the Bulwerian characters, and so sedulously imitated the tone of thought and jingle of verse, and is so *citharæ ac cantus peritus*, like Nero's freedman before-mentioned, as to persuade the commonality that he can be no other but Nero. He ought to be treated as Sir Charles Sedly treated Kynaston—but let us provoke no breach of the peace.

The protest here is against the critics rather than against Timon. He is *not* a great poet come amongst us: he is not a resuscitator of our bardic glories, &c. Great poets we have amongst us perhaps; and the best thing the writer of Timon has done in this the third and gilt-edged edition, is to expunge an impertinence towards one of them, which appeared in the former issues[2] of this most bepuffed of poems.

---

[2] *The New Timon* was first published in four one-and-six-penny parts in December 1845 and January 1846. Part Two contained a diatribe against the poetry of "School-Miss Alfred" Tennyson, which was suppressed in the book issue.

....

[27 APRIL 1846]

THE EXHIBITIONS OF THE SOCIETIES OF WATER COLOUR PAINTERS.

The usual throng of fashionable visitors attended on Saturday at the water-colour exhibitions, on which day both the societies opened their doors. The day before, we believe, the two galleries were open for the solitary inspection of royalty.

The exhibitions have not more than the average merit. At the

THE EXHIBITIONS OF THE SOCIETIES OF WATER COLOUR PAINTERS

old society's room a great *Forest Scene* by Mr. CATTERMOLE is the picture of chief mark. It is perhaps the most powerful and vigorous work that has been ever produced by water-colour painters. It appears to us to be a work of great genius and peculiar poetical power. There is something *enormous* in the scene, huge, rude, and solitary. A lonely knight winds his way through a wood of great, unheard-of trees, from the boughs of which "darkness looks downwards with a hundred eyes." Nobody, not the most extensive traveller, can say he has ever seen trees like these. Their trunks are more gnarled and twisted than olives, their leaves are larger than the leaf of a cabbage, they look so old that mammoths must have rested under them, and their branches must have tossed in the storms of ten thousand equinoxes; in a word, they are entirely impossible trees. But so are the giants of Ariosto, and so is *Caliban*—impossible; we give them, however, a poetic credence. A great artist has a right to these gigantic extra creations; and we stipulate for Mr. Cattermole's privilege as a poet, and against a number of critics, such as there will infallibly be, and who will object to this tremendous supernatural timber. No person can see such trees as these, certainly, in any wood in England; but suppose the painter's traveller to be a knight riding through a fairy wood, and you are instantly reconciled to the picture. Nor is the thought alone strange and beautiful: the picture is a marvel of manual skill. Like Paganini's "single string," the painter's brush performs wonders of strength, harmony, and rapidity. His work looks as if it were dashed in whilst the artist laboured under a sort of poetic fury. The effect of the whole is sombre and melancholy.

A half dozen of minor sketches by Mr. Cattermole, if they don't possess the same poetical power as the large picture, give evidence of equal skill. Carelessly as these figures and tints seem dashed in, every one must know how difficult of acquisition this careless mastery is, and how much the artist must think before he begins to work on the paper.

Mr. Cattermole's works seem to be now painted entirely in body colour. It is a pity that artists, if bent on painting with opaque colours, should not use them with varnish and oil in place of water. A few weeks of a damp room would be fatal to all these noble drawings, the colours of which are only held on the paper by a feeble binding of gum. After Mr. Cattermole one should mention his imitator, Mr. RAYNER, who has at this exhibition some vigorous and clever drawings.

Mr. HARDING's large drawing, No. 118, the *Range of the High Alps*, is one of the very finest by this master. It is most superbly and dexterously painted, and the innumerable details of the vast landscape are full of brightness, air, and sunshine. It is a capital piece. Mr. COPLEY FIELDING had his usual number of works—Scotch sketches chiefly; Mr. PROUT his accustomed town-halls and gable-ended houses. Both artists seem to us weaker and less efficient than in former years. Mr. DEWINT's showery landscapes and Thames scenes have found rivals in the works of Mr. GEORGE FRIPP, some of whose drawings are very good.

Mr. FREDERICK TAYLOR's pictures are, as always, delightful. Their skill is not more remarkable than their charming grace, character, and humour. Mr. Taylor is a colourist with a style entirely his own; an English Watteau. The characters which he indicates rather than draws out are touched with admirable grace and truth. Witness the baby's head in the *Old Soldier*; the dogs in the highland sporting scene; the beautiful brilliant figure of the Baron of Bradwardine, in the delicious little drawing from Waverley. *The Poultry Yard* is a perfect idyll; and one is at a loss whether to admire most the truth of the figures of animals, or the wonderful ease with which they appear to be painted, or the fresh sparkling harmony of the whole piece. Mr. Taylor's portraits, and we are glad of it, are not so successful. A gentleman who can paint so well does not deserve to succeed in the mercantile branch of the art.

Mr. NASH's *Lincoln's Inn Hall* must be mentioned as a triumph of this species of composition. The Queen and Prince Albert, very like, are advancing down the hall. There seem to be at least a thousand barristers assembled in that hall; all, no doubt, portraits, with their wigs and gowns. The pineapples, gold plate, spermaceti candles, and cold collation are depicted with amazing accuracy; and the new damask tablecloths are washed and mangled to a nicety. Considering the subject, the picture could not be better; it is as accurate as a catalogue, and as poetical as a Court-guide.

Mr. A. FRIPP has not, in our opinion, made the advance which was expected from his *début*. *The Irish Harvesters returning after their Voyage to England*, is a dreary sort of caricature. The faces look to be copies from Maclise, without the wonderful power of drawing belonging to that great artist. The faults of the drawing of the figures is exaggerated by the faulty perspective of the landscape; the lights on the heads are dirty patches of heavy opaque white. A number of the water-colour artists are now dipping into this dangerous white-pot, and the peculiar charm of their branch of the art is ruined by the use of it. It is as if a guitar-player persisted in performing an oratorio: they are always taxing their powers beyond their strength, and endeavouring to carry their art farther than it will go.

There is a young gentleman eating bread and cheese in a barn, a dog watching him, who is the only one of Mr. HUNT's famous boys who struck us in this exhibition. He has a number of interiors painted with astonishing accuracy. There is a room at Knowle, a drawing-room with a flock paper full of pictures, a stable full of chips, shavings, faggots, and hampers, all of which are depicted with a skill which is so curious as to be absolutely ridiculous. There is the usual bird's nest and blue eggs. And in another piece grapes, half a pomegranate and a little deal fruit basket; the purple grapes and the deal basket are such astonishing portraits that they might hang up in a fruiterer's window in Covent-garden.

Mr. GEORGE HARRISON, a new name, we believe, in this catalogue, must be mentioned with praise for his beautiful and poetical landscapes; Mr. WRIGHT's delicate heads; Mr. BENTLEY's coast scenes; Mr. EVANS's rich landscapes; Mr. STEPHANOFF's mysterious compositions, and Mr. RICHTER's full-blown beauties, with that ogle which is familiar to all frequenters of this gallery, will strike, as in former years, those persons who visit it.

At the New Society the artists are greatly more ambitious, and several are yearly endeavouring to expand to the dignity of historical painters. Mr. CORBOULD has two very large drawings— a scripture piece, the *Raising of Darius' Daughter*; and a history piece, *Henry VI.'s Entry into Paris*. Both pictures are remarkable for cleverness; the latter especially, in which some hundred figures are introduced, is full of ingenuity, picturesqueness, and animation; and as one looks into these enormous drawings and sees that the whole surface of the paper is worked over with the stippling of the most laboriously fine pencil, one may admire the perverse industry of the hand that works so much to make so little effect. M. WEIGALL has his historical picture from Richard II. Mr. WARREN is still in the East, at Jerusalem, or in the desert on his usual dromedary excursion. A critic in the *Observer* has remonstrated so pathetically with Mr. RIVIERE about his *Scene from the Waters of Babylon* (where the Jewish women seem not to be weeping but howling), that he will no doubt in another year take care to draw his figures better.

In Mr. WEHNERT'S large pictures all his figures seem to be in a state of frantic muscular excitement. In the picture of *Wickliff abusing the Mendicant Friars at Oxford*, the monks look almost frenzied to rage by the violent remarks of the furious old maniac writhing on the tester; and in the picture of *Henry IV., Emperor of Germany, escaping from an Assassin*, (who by some accident broke his own neck instead of the King's), the limbs of the nude assassin and the monarch (who has no other garment but an exceedingly light red tunic) are quivering with an agony frightful to witness. Who can desire to possess pictures on such subjects is the question, but there can be none as to the power, vigour, and careful execution of the painter who has chosen to illustrate these most uninteresting and unpleasant points of history.

Mr. HUGHES's chief picture, of *Rubens painting in his Pavilion*, is not so important, or indeed so good as some of his former large works. He has two other admirable drawings, as deep and sunny as De Hoogh, of which the figures are the only feeble part. Mr. KEARNEY's *Cromwell* may be mentioned as excellent in depth and harmony of colour and tone, and skill in painting. The best of Mr. JENKINS's pictures is *Watteau showing his Sketches*— a beautiful work—the large piece of the French tragedy. *Soldier telling of his Wars*, in red trowsers, is a comparative failure; and what shall be said of the figure called the *Homini Salvator*? It is as great a mistake as the Latin. We do not like Mr. ABSOLON's *Fair Rosamond* as well as his delightful scene from the *Barber of Seville*, and the beautiful *Haymaker's Dance*.

The chief charm of the exhibition, however, lies in a number of little pictures copied directly from nature, and in these the river-pieces and landscapes of Mr. DUNCAN eminently excel, and the admirable drawings of Miss FANNY STEERS. This lady, with another, Miss JANE EGERTON, may divide the honours of the exhibition. All the latter's three pictures of female figures are beautiful for sentiment, very good in drawing, and excellent for vigour, richness, and harmony of colour.

The young society has no artists of the strength of CATTERMOLE and TAYLOR; but put these champions away, and it is more than the rival of the old institution.

....

[4 MAY 1846]

Sketches of English Character. By Mrs. GORE.   [Bentley.

How Mrs. Gore can write so much, so often, and so well, must have been a question often ere this asked with wonder by every frequenter of the circulating library. She is the most productive of English writers. Even the prolific James is sterile compared to this parent of a thousand volumes; and it is only in France that you find a pen so active as hers. "Cecil," "Agathonia," "A Prize Comedy," "An Essay on Roses," "A Christmas Book," "A Dissertation on Witchcraft" (under the pseudonym of Albany Poyntz).[1] Who knows what this indefatigable author does or does not do? She is capable of the Lives of the Chancellors or a volume of sermons. Many well-informed persons insist that she wrote "The Vestiges of Creation,"[2] and there is a strong and influential party which attributes to her the "New Timon."

And what surprises one is not merely the quantity but the quality of her performances. How does she come by her knowledge is the wonder. She knows things which were supposed hitherto to be as much out of the reach of female experience as shaving, duelling, or the bass viol. There are quotations in Latin and Greek in "Agathonia" that the most learned of our

---

[1] Mrs. Gore is the acknowledged author of *Cecil: or the Adventures of a Coxcomb* (1841); *Agathonia: a Romance* (1844); *Quid Pro Quo: or the Day of Dupes* (1844); *The Rose Fancier's Manual* (1838); and a Christmas book of 1845 called *The Snow Storm. A World of Wonders with Anecdotes and Opinions concerning Popular Superstitions,* ed. A. Poyntz (London, 1845) was never claimed by her; and Thackeray's attribution may be simply a joke.

[2] The famous *Vestiges of the Natural History of Creation* had been published anonymously in 1844. It was not until much later that Robert Chambers acknowledged its authorship.

novelists could scarcely match. It is next to impossible that she should have ever been a member of a club; but she is as well acquainted with all the mysteries of those institutions as the oldest Pall-mall lounger. She talks about Ude and Soyer with a familiarity and justness of appreciation perfectly frightful; she is so familiar with the bow-window of White's, that you might fancy she had, by special permission, been allowed to take a place amongst the exceedingly venerable dandies there. Nor is it only with the great she is familiar; with the mysteries of Crockford's and the carte of the Travellers'. She does not forget the small. Her eye, with fatal keenness, penetrates the secrets of the servants' hall. John the footman is revealed to her both in and out of livery. In his characters as Man and John she reads him through and through. There is a chapter in the present Sketches about that valuable and confidential class of men butlers, which describes their history in such a way as to astound a reader who cannot think how this knowledge has been acquired, and whether it is the patient consequence of labour or the brilliant result of a great intuitive genius. From the butler the omniscient author skips away to the banker: she is as familiar with his mystery as with that of the gentleman who waits at his sideboard, and she discourses about loans, and discounts, and Consols, with a prodigious vivacity and ease.

Little lords, lady-killers, linkmen, lady patronesses, hotel keepers, diners-out, clubmen, and a host more of male and female characters appear in these sketches. A smart and brilliant introduction ushers the collection into the world, in which preface the only omission is that the sketches are reprints from old magazines. That they have appeared before in print is a fact not somehow mentioned by the author in the brilliant introduction to the volumes. But her admirers recognize their old friends, as we sometimes do the vicar's old sermon, without blaming his reverence for not informing his dearly beloved brethren from the pulpit that his discourse has been preached many times before. Mrs. Gore's worldly lectures quite bear a second hearing. They are not a little curious as pictures of the present world, and of the author's mind. They are clear, sprightly (too sprightly), coarse, and utterly worldly. A direct morality is not called for, perhaps, in works of fiction, but that a moral sentiment should pervade them, at least, is no disadvantage. People's minds will not be refined or exalted by the perusal of this book. The subjects, to be sure, are not very refined or exalted. But if you want a tolerably faithful picture of Pall-mall in 1840, of the dandies who frequented Crockford's, the dowagers and virgins who resorted to Willis's, their *motus et certamina*,[3] intrigues, amusements, and ways of life, their lady's maids, doctors, and flunkies both in and out of livery, such may be beheld in the present microcosm of Mrs. Gore.

Here is a specimen of her style and views of society:—

"People eat, drink, sleep, talk, move, think in millions. No one dares to be himself. From Dan to Beersheba, not an original left! All the books published seem to have been copied from the same type, with one of Wedgewood's manifold-writers. All the speeches made might be stereotyped in January by an able reporter, to last out till June. In society, men are packed one within the other, like forks or spoons in a plate chest, each of the same exact pattern and amount of pennyweights. Doctor, divine, or devil's-dragoman, (*Ang.* lawyer), all dressed alike,— all affecting the same tastes, pursuits, and habits of life.

"Would Shakspeare have invented Falstaff, or Parolles, in such an order of society? Would Scott have hit upon the Baron of Bradwardine, or Lawyer Pleydell? Would even Fielding or Smollett have extracted the ripe humour of their inventions out of such a sea of batter? The few authors of fiction who pretend to individualize are obliged to have recourse to the most unsophisticated class for elements of character; society of a higher grade being so used down into tameness, as to form one long, long Baker-street, or Guildford-street, of mean, graceless, and tedious uniformity—from number one to number one hundred, a hundred times ditto repeated.

"It is not so in other capitals. Elsewhere, every profession has its stamp, and every grade its distinctions. In Paris, or Berlin, or Vienna, you can no more surmise when you dine out what will be placed on the table, or what conversation will take place around it, than you can pre-assure the morrow's weather. In London, whether the dinner occur at the house of a man of eight hundred a-year, or of eight thousand, you are cognizant, to a dish and a topic, what will be supplied for the delectation of your ears and palate. You eat the turbot and saddle of mutton by anticipation, as you go along; and may chew the cud of the great letters of the ministerial and opposition papers, which anon you

---

[3] From Virgil, *Georgics,* IV, 85-6:
> "Hi motus animorum atque haec certamina tanta
> Pulveris exigui iactu compressa quiescent."

(Yet all this tumult of soul and all this savagery of conflict may be quelled and laid to rest by the scattering of a little dust.) This was a favorite passage with Thackeray, to which he returned many times. See, for example, the conclusion of chapter six, book three, of *Esmond.*

will have to swallow, diluted with milk-and-water by the dull, or vivified by a few drops of alcohol by the brilliant.

"In the evening entertainments, as at the dinners, *'toujours perdrix;'*—Jullien, Gunter, and Lord Flipflap—Lord Flipflap, Gunter and Jullien!—You see the same people waltzing, fiddling, and serving the refreshments, and hear the same phrases exchanged among them, at every fête given at the west end of the town between May and August. May and August?—Rather say from A.D.1835 to A.D. 1850!"

And so, through the two volumes, she dashes and rattles on, careless, out-speaking, coarse, sarcastic, with thoughts the least elevating, and views quite curiously narrow. Supposing that Pall-mall were the world, and human life finished with the season, and Heaven were truffled turkies and the Opera, and duty and ambition were bounded in dressing well and getting tickets to Lady Londonderry's dancing teas, Mrs. Gore's "Sketches of Character" might be a good guide book. And we are wrong in saying it has no moral: the moral is that which very likely the author intended—that entire weariness, contempt, and dislike which the reader must undergo after this introduction to what is called the world. If it be as here represented, the world is the most hollow, heartless, vulgar, brazen world, and those are luckiest who are out of it.

....

[5 MAY 1846]

THE EXHIBITION OF THE ROYAL ACADEMY.

Before giving a judgment upon the works exhibited to the public at the rooms of the Royal Academy yesterday (after the picture buyers have had their private view on Friday, and the great world has been regaled by the annual dinner on Saturday), it is necessary, even for critics, to see the pictures, and this was almost an impossible gratification in the midst of the crowd on Monday. The combat at the paying place, at twelve o'clock, was a ferocious encounter, conducted with that fierce pugilistic competition which distinguishes Englishmen on such occasions. Crowds blocked up the circles round the principal pictures, and it was quite a vain attempt to examine them at leisure. Even the little octagon room, ordinarily so tranquil, was lively with squeezing amateurs; and almost up to the last moment, when the sun was about to quit the gallery altogether, the spectators remained in dogged admiration. Dinner alone caused the enthusiastic spectators to flag in their love for the fine arts; and it was only possible to look at a few of the pictures before the dusk obliged every one to decamp.

If it be true, as we think, that the art has made undeniable progress in England, the present may be considered as the very best exhibition which has ever been held by the Royal Academy. The young painters are coming forward with great force and power, and the elder ones, of the better order (there are some veterans so entirely superannuated that it is a shame they should keep the ground from younger and abler men), are still holding their own, and admirable for the most part in their way. The landscape artists are as strong as ever; in figure or *genre* pictures there is a very great and striking improvement and increase; the portraits only are scarcer—an absence which nobody need regret.

The places of honour are occupied by portraits of *her Majesty and Prince Albert*, from the pencil of Mr. FRANK GRANT. They are cavalry pictures: the Queen on her charger, with embroidered crimson saddle and holster, seems to be directing the evolutions of squadrons of dragoons, who are blazing in the distance. The Prince has not yet mounted his charger, but appears in the uniform of a field-marshal, with the turquoise sabre that has already been painted in the admirable miniature of Mr. THORBURN. The head of her Majesty is fine, and a likeness; the prancing horse, belaboured with gilded trappings, has, however, a kangaroo-like action. The horse in the picture of his Royal Highness is better: but the head of the Prince has not the nobleness and handsomeness of the original. The City of London Club has had the *Duke of Wellington* painted on horseback, by Mr. PICKERSGILL, to counterbalance, no doubt, the famous equestrian statue which already decorates the front of the Exchange. The canvas horse is not so good as the bronze quadruped; but, on the other hand, the figure of the Duke is a much finer one. He wears the historical short cape, which so many painters have depicted; and the cocked hat that has waved in so many exhibitions. Indeed, it is difficult to say much about these state pictures. They are large, handsome, and well done;

but somewhat cumbrous ceremonies, like a Lord Mayor's state coach, which, however, lighter equipages are not allowed to pass, and which always has the largest capitals in the newspaper account of them.

Under the hoofs of the Duke's charger there is a little picture by Mr. MULREADY (the subject taken from a recondite work called the "Vicar of Wakefield") that will, as we have very little doubt, live even when the City of London Club has ceased to exist. If the works of GERARD DOUW and MIERIS fetch enormous prices now, some future Sir Robert Peel will one day pay down a family's handsome maintenance for the possession of this admirable picture. For colour and finish it may rank by any cabinet picture of any master. It does not create pleasure merely, but astonishment. The amazing novelty and brilliancy of the colours of this little piece are not to be described by any words or similes. A blaze of fireworks is not more intensely brilliant: it must illuminate the whole room at night, when everybody is gone, and flare out like a chemist's bottle—one is obliged to resort to extravagancies and caricatures in merely attempting to give an idea of its astounding power and brilliancy. Such a picture as this ought to be sent abroad, for the credit of the country, and to show what English artists can do.

If Mr. MULREADY's *Vicar* may stand by the side of any, the best, Dutch painter, Mr. DANBY's *Dawn of Morning* may take rank with CLAUDE LORRAIN: let any critic make the comparison by walking into the National Gallery. This of Mr. DANBY's, too, is a picture whose quality defies description; but every lover of nature will appreciate its calm truth and beauty, as the artist will admire the wonderful skill with which the painter has depicted the flat homely landscape and water receding into the dawn; and the luminous rosy twilight, in which the moon and stars are still flickering faintly, while the east wakes and flushes with the approach of the sun. The picture is the work of a great and true poet.

And what words are enough to convey the delight and admiration which every one must feel before Mr. LESLIE's noble pictures? His large picture from "Roderick Random," where the young gawky squire is receiving the congratulations of the lawyers, on coming into the entire inheritance, is better than HOGARTH, for it is carried up to a higher and more delicate point of humour. The characters are wonderful for their truth and absence of exaggeration. Each acts his part in the most admirable unconscious way—there is no attempt at a *pose* or a *tableau*, as in almost all pictures of figures where the actors are grouping themselves with an eye to the public, and, as it were, attitudinizing for our applause. In this noble picture everybody is busied, and perfectly naturally, with the scene, at which the spectator is admitted to look. Every single performer is a character and a comedy in himself, the minutiæ of which are somehow revealed to the looker-on by each countenance; and you acknowledge the effect of the whole by a reply of laughter. It is that charming *naïveté* and unconsciousness which makes *Sancho* so delightfully ludicrous: you have a ridiculous sympathy, and jocular regard for the honest humourist; and Mr. LESLIE (who is the finest commentator upon CERVANTES, and on some parts of SHAKSPEARE that ever lived) has seized and understood this point of their art perfectly; he ties you to all these grotesque ways by a certain lurking human kindness; and there is always felt (though not intended) in the midst of the fun a feeling of friendliness and beauty. His is surely the perfection of pictorial comedy. What would you have more than pathos, beauty, wit, wonderful aptness and ingenuity, and the most perfect and generous good-breeding?

In the little picture called *Mother and Child*—a mother playing with a child by a cradle—the comedy rises up to the very highest point, and becomes almost *sacred*. It is a picture all purity, grace, playful tenderness, and exquisite innocent affection.

[To be continued.]

....

[7 MAY 1846]

*THE EXHIBITION OF THE ROYAL
ACADEMY.*

[SECOND NOTICE.]

Mr. MACLISE only exhibits one picture, but it is perhaps the best and greatest of the artist's works. In the *Ordeal by Touch*, the body of a murdered man lies on a tomb before a Gothic altar, lighted up with tapers and gilding and the gorgeous hues of ancient stained windows. The widow and family of the deceased are gathered round the corpse; a solemn jury, a band of warriors in armour, a crowd of pilgrims, retainers, and peasants, officiating bishops and their attendants, watch the murderer as he places his hand upon the body, of which the wound begins to bleed afresh, and from which he starts back in a convulsion of guilt. The widow, surrounded by her children, who look on unconsciously, cries out for vengeance upon the homicide. This fierce, gloomy pageant is set before the spectator's eye in the most wonderful manner. Many faults may be suggested in the picture. The surface, whether it represent armour, velvet, flesh, or stone, is pummiced down as it were to an universal smoothness. The picture wants air; the characters want individuality; nay, the same face, with a variation of costume, is repeated a half-score of times in the picture. But the very faults seem to exaggerate one's notion of the prodigious power of the painter. As in reading the "Inferno," you see not only the place but Dante looking on, so in Mr. Maclise's canvas you have the subject and the artist too; his manner of imagining and viewing it; he himself throws himself into the legendary past, and wanders about in it and explores it; he makes one of the crowd of peasants; tries the knight's armour; peers at the bleeding body with astonished eyes; and is himself quite frightened and awe-stricken with the story which he invents and tells. The uncertainty of the costume of the figures somehow adds to the mystery, and gives the fable an air of truth. They are a sort of possible dresses, not real, but such as ought to be worn in a time that is only probable, and painted with the most faithful accuracy and belief, as Kühleborn's beard in "Undine," or the Gawrie's wings in "Peter Wilkins."[1] So the picture is at once perfectly real and vague too—a painted dream. All the picture rolls and revolves round the little drop of blood in the centre—how astonishingly it is painted that little shining guilty drop!

Mr. EDWIN LANDSEER has never excelled his pictures of the present year. They possess that brilliant and famous execution which always distinguishes this consummate painter; and a poetical thoughtfulness and seriousness which of late has been

---

[1] Fantastic romances by De la Motte Fouqué (1811) and Robert Paltock (1751).

growing upon him. The clouds and water of the *Stag at Bay*, are nobly painted, as is the gallant animal, who has slain one of his pursuers, while another, howling furiously, prepares to renew his foiled attack. The pictures called *Time of Peace* and *Time of War* exhibit the artist's magnificent skill, and the moral is delicately hinted. In the picture of "Peace," you see a little group of quiet sheep and goats couched on a height over a sunny seashore. A busy, peaceful town lies smoking in the distance, and all round a calm and beautiful blue sea. A lamb is nibbling grass with its head in a rusty howitzer. The useless gun and the little animal are wonders of execution. The picture has an idyllic repose and sunshine. The episode of "War" has quite an opposite character. A cuirassier lies dead, tumbled over his horse, another charger lies by him, in the midst of a *corpse* of a cottage, which has been blown into perdition along with horse and horseman. All about is lurid flame and smoke, silent death and ruin. But in the midst of the carnage a poor little rose-tree and a small trembling geranium peer out, escaped from the general devastation. The lamb and the rose-tree are charming little prettinesses, delightful points of pathetic wit.

Mr. ETTY's large picture of the *Judgment of Paris* flames over the room as gorgeous as the richest canvas of RUBENS. Passages of this picture are unexampled for richness of colour; the dazzling shield and helmet of Minerva, Juno's blazing peacocks and chariot of gold, the wood in the back ground before which Paris is seated, are all painted in this great artist's most splendid manner. Nothing can be finer than his indications of landscape; the distant sea in the picture of Circe quite dazzles the eye with its brightness, that in which the superb bather is dipping is as brilliant and transparent in azure and green as the sunniest water of the Mediterranean. In regard to the drawing of the figures there may be no little question—enormous rotundities, shadows strangely smeared over the face of Circe and the limbs of Juno. The blonde Venus is quite impossibly pink, and the extremities of some of Circe's nymphs are almost as mysterious as Mr. TURNER's own.

What to say about Mr. TURNER's pictures? As the traveller in the desert beholds at a distance pools of the most delightful water and shady palm trees for his camels to rest under, and urging on his footsore dromedary, finds at the desiderated spot that it is all bosh—no water, no date trees, no shade—only sand, rubbish, vanity, and vexation of spirit; so, as you look from afar off at Mr. TURNER's pictures, you behold all sorts of wonderful and agreeable sights—Venice and the Adriatic flash out in the sunshine; ships loom through the haze at sea, or whales frisk and gambol there, &c., but on coming up to the picture, behold it was all an illusion—a few washes of gamboge, putty, and vermillion are flicked over a canvass at hazard seemingly; it is only at a distance that they condescend to take a shape, but near at hand they are as intangible as Eurydice.

Never having been there, we cannot say whether two pictures, one representing the centre of the sun and the other the middle of the sea (with *The Interview between Undine and Masaniello!*), are accurate representations. Undine rising in a whirlpool amidst a chorus of lobsters-pots, mermaids, whitebait, &c., is a marvellous creation, and there is a look of humorous wonder about Masaniello quite worthy of that most intrepid of Neapolitan fishermen. There are no extracts from that sibylline poem, "The Fallacies of Hope," this year.[2]

With every respect for Mr. EASTLAKE's genius, it must be confessed that his work this year is not happy. This piece is called the *Visit to the Nun.* The nun (sister Saint Maudlin) comes forward with a sanctified simper to embrace a friend of a similar style of countenance, with a couple of waxy children. This work ought to be hung up in a namby-pamby Young England oratory, and sung by a dandy Puseyite. Mr. DYCE, in point of art, may be said to have gone over to Rome altogether. His *Virgin and Child* are as rigid a pair as you will see in any of the masters before RAPHAEL. There is no mediæval illumination by Mr. HERBERT this year.

Mr. COPE's little picture of the *Young Mother*, and the piece from Spenser are both capital. His hand is still somewhat heavy, and has not yet attained the easy mastery of his pencil. But the scheme of his picture is always good; the idea clear before him; the sentiment and colour finely imagined and understood, and the figures drawn in the best manner.

All Mr. CHARLES LANDSEER's pictures are good, and painted with his accustomed silvery brilliancy of colour. The little

[2] For examples of Thackeray's parodies of such extracts, see "Academy Exhibition," *Punch,* VI (11 May 1844), 209.

Candidate for a Portrait is charming; and the picture of *Mary Avenel and Mysie Happer* a very finely painted interior. There are fine details in *The Wounded Smuggler*, and excellent painting and tone.

Mr. REDGRAVE has a couple of pictures, which every lover of the milk-and-water of human kindness will appreciate. One, *The Return from Church*, has a great deal of exceedingly pretty painting, in the landscape part especially; but none of the simpering heads seem to fit the shoulders of the prim personages who are represented—an old couple, a young ditto, a young widow with her children, &c. The weakest of Kirke White's poems is not more piously insipid than this piece. In the other picture, *Preparing to throw off her Weeds*, the heroine, in black satin, is examining a new (and most hideous) gown that the milliner has brought her. A white silk bonnet in a handbox has likewise just come home: the bandbox is capital. At the door enters "the capting," taking off his cocked hat. What! when she is just "preparing to throw off her weeds?" O you naughty captain!

(*To be continued.*)

....

[11 MAY 1846]

ROYAL ACADEMY.

[THIRD NOTICE.]

Mr. WEBSTER's pretty little picture of *Please remember the Grotto* always attracts a crowd of delighted spectators, who can't resist this kind-natured artist's appeal to the philoprogenitive organ. *Good Night* is not a less attractive piece of child-life, in which the nursery incidents of Saturday night are indicated with much humorous *naïveté*—thus, papa is embracing one retiring child, another says his prayers between his grandmother's knees, the *tub*, with flannel and brown soap, are prepared for a third. Every frequenter of a nursery will admire the accuracy of that basin and flannel. The old people in this picture, as in most others by the same artist, are admirably characteristic; the children and adults smile a little too laboriously to our notion; they seem to be aware, as it were, of the looker-on's presence, and wink at him archly from the canvas. There is none of this knowingness in the works of that great dramatic painter and humorist, Mr. LESLIE—look at the girl's figure in his picture of *Mr. Dickens as Bobadill*: what a simple, delightful, mirth-provoking-face it is!

All artists admire, and every spectator must acknowledge, the admirable skill and brilliancy of Mr. POOLE's picture, *The Surrender of Syon Nunnery to Henry the Eighth's Commissioners*. A rich and dazzling effect, a great number of figures, a quantity of the prettiest Gothic properties and decorations, carvings, illuminations, tapestries, and stained glass, are painted with the utmost brilliancy and dexterity, and grouped together in the cleverest manner. A great many of the heads are very good, but it is hard to understand the drama which is supposed to be enacted from the expressions of the various characters. Most of the nuns (and they are as like each other as eggs), most of the pretty prim young nuns, are smiling among each other, as if the breaking up of the convent were a jocular affair, which the commissioners, too, seem to think.

Mr. HARVEY's *First Reading of the Bible in the Crypt of Old Saint Paul's* is a very fine and richly toned picture of the Scotch school. Its sombre tones, and some of the figures, remind one of Wilkie's latter style. Mr. JOHNSTONE's *Introduction of Flora Macdonald to Prince Charles Edward*, is another good specimen of Scottish art. Mr. LAUDER's *Gow Chrom and the Glee Maiden*, from "The Fair Maid of Perth," is rich and deep in colour—but the Gow Chrom is a theatre-hero, and the Glee Maiden, in pink stockings, looks as if her discomfiture arose from her vain efforts to keep her clothes on her back.

Mr. WARD's picture of *Clarendon in Disgrace* has excellent qualities. Some of the figures are beautiful; especially an *Amazon*, with long golden ringlets, standing in a group of periwigged dandies, who are gazing at the disgraced statesman. The artist perfectly understands the outrageous costume of Charles II.'s time, and the figures look at home in their dresses. Mr. FRITH's *Scene from the Bourgeois Gentilhomme*, and Mr. EGG's *Buckingham Rebuffed* are *genre* pictures of the same period. Both are exceedingly pretty; neither, perhaps, has the dramatic character and *genuine* look of Mr. WARD's picture, but the details of Mr. FRITH's picture are painted in the most facile and brilliant manner. *Dorante* is capital, as are the beautiful female figures in Mr. EGG's canvas.

Mr. ELMORE's *Scene from "Much Ado about Nothing," Claudio renouncing Hero at the Altar*, has very great merit—the fainting *Hero* is beautiful: the tone, drawing, and arrangement of the picture excellent. Mr. F. STONE's *Sweet Hour* (a summer evening group of ladies and lords on a terrace), charms from its want of subject perhaps, and gives perfectly the sentiment of repose and beauty. A little more vigour of drawing would have done the picture no injury, and would especially benefit the figure of the lady reclining in the foreground, whose limbs and drapery have an almost ghostly airiness. Every body will admire Mr. GOODALL's beautiful *Going to Vespers*. The lamplight and starlight effects are excellently painted, and the moonlit architectural mass in the foreground touched with great skill and truth. Mr. CROWE, a new exhibitor we believe, has a picture, 534, *Prynne searching Laud's pockets*, which promises very well. The puritan and the bishop are capital figures, the head of the latter especially fine. The artist is as yet deficient in pictorial dexterity, but the picture has energy, good drawing, and character. So famous a painter and so fine a picture as that of M. ROBERT FLEURY, of Paris, 498, *Rembrandt's Study*, ought to have met with a better welcome from the English Academy. There is perfect delicacy and much grace and beauty in Mr. FROST's *Diana and Acteon*. His pictures remind one of HILTON and HOWARD, and are better than either of those respectable painters.

An enormous broad-chested female, in a copper-coloured cloud, takes up a deal of space in the principal room, and is the work of Mr. PATTEN. A family portrait by the same artist (in one of the heads of which we seem to recognize the athletic Pandora before mentioned), is as excellent and well painted a picture as the former is a disagreeable one. The portraits are not of very great mark. Two by Mr. NEWENHAM (44 and 92), are very good; they are honestly and excellently painted: as is Mr. LAWRENCE's *Archdeacon and Mrs. Berners*, which is hung, however, almost out of sight. Mr. WATSON GORDON's portrait of *Lord Robertson* is, perhaps, the best of the collection: his picture of *Mr. F. Grant* is likewise good. The great charm, perhaps, in the works of the latter most popular painter is the air of high breeding which he gives to his portraits. All his gentlemen have the most unmistakeable aristocratic look; and his ladies are, without exception, slim, pensive, graceful, and genteel. Mr. BUCKNER has a pretty full-length (52) of a beautiful lady and child, but one regrets the absence of drawing and substance in the picture, a want which must be felt in almost every one of Mr. GRANT's works likewise. The portrait 270, by the latter artist, is, however, an exception—an excellently drawn and coloured figure—a capital picture. Most of Mr. KNIGHT's portraits may be mentioned with praise for their power, depth, and brilliancy in tone. Mr. HART's *Jessica* may be placed among the portrait class: it is beautiful, as is another female portrait (363), in quite a different style, by the same painter.

The landscape painters keep their places, and the admirers are still as numerous as ever of this delightful branch of English art. The veteran COLLINS has not painted a finer picture than his *Early Morning*: it is full of natural poetry, freshness, and beauty. His other pictures are not less charming. No pictures convey the landscape sentiment better; no painter seems to have a more hearty appreciation of nature. Mr. LEE's scenes of rural England give the spectator almost the same feeling of pleasure. Mr. CRESWICK, with a hand more skilful than either, has, perhaps, an equal appreciation of English landscape poetry. These pictures represent much more than the mere objects—a river or a willowbank, a country road or a sandy bay—they leave the spectator's mind in the happiest mood somehow, and suggest all sorts of peaceful thoughts and pleasant contemplations. Such pictures always appear to us as the best of room decorations. No figure pieces can be such companions as these unobtrusive and charming images of cheerful repose. Mr. HARDING, Mr. BRIGHT, Mr. WILLIAMS, Mr. JUTSUM, and Mr. HILDITCH must not be omitted as excellent painters of landscape, and there is a little landscape by Mr. REDGRAVE which must make everybody regret that he should not practise more in this style of composition. Mr. STANFIELD's pencil is as brilliant as ever, and his son is an excellent pupil of this admirable master. Every person will admire the superb pictures of Mr. ROBERTS, and the Eastern traveller will recognise the beautiful and splendid scenes which the painter re-produced with masterly skill and truth.

As usual, the works of the miniature painters attract as many admirers as any other branch of the art. Sir WILLIAM ROSS'S little portraits are almost perfect specimens of minute skill, and truth, and beauty. Mr. THORBURN is scarcely inferior, in some respects even better than the older artist. His portrait, for instance, of Lady FRANCIS EGERTON, gives one the impression of a large picture. It is as sober, elegant, and harmonious as a full length of Sir JOSHUA. Mr. CARRICK is as excellent as ever— witness his admirable miniature of *Lablache*. Mr. RICHMOND'S subjects have not been quite so favourable, and as for Mr. CHALON, he has a portrait of a *West Country Baronet* in a dove-coloured shooting jacket lined with satin, with a bouquet in his button-hole, which is the perfection of comedy. It is wonderful what a simper this gentleman can impart to the gravest face, and what a killing Jemmy-Jessamy air he can give to any figure.

In the Sculpture-room there is no statue of great mark. Mr. WYATT'S female figure is scarcely worthy of his great reputation. Mr. DAVIS'S *Madonna* is a beautiful head. Count D'ORSAY has a clever statue of the *Marquess of Anglesey*. The busts are good, as they always are, especially those of Mr. WEEKES, Mr. WESTMACOTT, Mr. CAREW, and Mr. JONES. The busts of *Mr. Pierce Mahony* and *Sir William Betham*, by the latter, are capital as likenesses, and as works of art.

....

[19 JUNE 1846]

Haydon's Lectures on Painting and Design.
                    [London: Longman, Brown, and Co.

Mr. Haydon's lectures are most amusing and interesting. They relate to Mr. Haydon and Phidias, Mr. Haydon and Fuzeli, Mr. Haydon and Wilkie, and to various subjects connected with the fine arts, the central point of interest being always Benjamin Robert Haydon, historical painter. He is full of bravery and *bonhomie*—as *naïf*, vigorous, and egotistic as Benvenuto Cellini himself; and these lectures, and the sketches of painters' life which they contain, form very entertaining and curious chapters of artistical biography. There can be no doubt that the man who painted the "Judgment of Solomon" was a great painter.

Concerning the fiddling Nero, the gulfing Curtius, &c., there may be questions; but Mr. Haydon's literary performances contain many a page, as we fancy, that is likely to outlive works which *one* man in England considers perfect. Benvenuto hardly finished a cup or a statue but he sang out, in a similar manner, his *exegi monumentum*.[1] His book is worth even more than his Florentine Perseus; and we hope to see B. R. H. on paper more frequently even than on canvas. His style of writing is large and striking: he has a grim humorous way of narrating, which is very pleasant, for it amuses you not merely with the story, but with the writer; and putting out of the question the perfections of B. R. H., he always praises heartily and generously.

Here is his account of the three legitimate designers of the British school:—

"Fuzeli, Flaxman, and Stothard, were the three legitimate designers of the British school, and yet not one of them was perfect master of the figure.

"Flaxman's designs from the Iliad, Odyssey, and Greek tragedians, are his finest works, but when first they appeared, the Continent asserted (as no Briton has any imagination), they were invented by an Italian!

"It is extremely hard to say whether some are sublime or ridiculous, but there are groups of Houris, Nymphs, and Nereiades, very sweet and vase-like.

"As a designer, his works place him as much before Canova, as Canova's power of cutting marble placed Flaxman below him; since Praxiteles, no man changed marble into flesh like Canova; no man perhaps ever worked up a single figure as a bit of fleshy execution, equal to this distinguished man.

"Though Flaxman in his lectures talks pompously of muscles and construction, he knew in reality not deeply of either, as his anatomical designs prove.

"His lectures on the whole, though containing many useful hints, are shallow, and display clear evidence of no very high intellectual power.

"It is not surprising that Johnson should estimate a sculptor's power of deduction very lightly, when Nollekens was his friend; and surely these lectures of Flaxman, with conclusions so feebly made, tend rather to confirm than refute Johnson's prejudice.

"The value of Fuzeli's and Opie's Lectures, in comparing them to Flaxman's and Barry's, is extraordinary, and the superiority of Reynolds's to all more extraordinary still.

"Stothard, as a composer, was sometimes beautiful, but he could not

---

[1] Horace, *Odes,* III, xxx, 1:

"Exegi monumentum aere perennius."

(My work is done, the memorial more enduring than brass.)

paint any more than Fuzeli, and knew less of the figure than Flaxman: he could not tell a story by expression, yet there was an angelic sweetness in every thing he did.

"He seemed to have dreamed of an angel's face in early life, and passed the remainder of his days in trying to combine, in every figure he touched, something of its loveliness."

How pretty and delicate is the sentiment of the last sentence! Hazlitt uses a similar image about Correggio's innocent sweetness, and the delicious beauty of colour—the tints do not look as if they were laid by the brush on the canvas, but as if they settled there from an angel's breath.

One-and-forty years ago B. R. H. was in Devonshire, whither his friend Jackson wrote to him of the arrival at the Academy of a queer, tall, keen-looking Scotchman, with "something in him, called Wilkie." B. R. H. set off for London, hoping that this keen-looking Scotchman was not going to be an historical painter:—

"Well, the next day I hurried away to the academy: Jackson was delighted to see me, and so were others, and they all told me there was certainly something peculiar in this new student. Jackson said he drew too square; another said his style was vulgar. 'What does Fuzeli say?' said I. Fuzeli said, 'Dere is something in him.' I was rather uneasy all night, for Jackson said he had done something from Macbeth, which all agreed must be a picture in high art.

"The next day I went as usual, when, in about an hour after we were all drawing, in came David Wilkie: he was tall, pale, quiet, with a wonderful eye, short nose, and vulgar humorous mouth, and a look of great piercing energy of investigation.

"In the course of the morning, he began behind me to get into some argument in a whisper, of which he was always very fond, and after a little, I am proud to say, he got up and quietly looked over me; he then sat down, and I got up, and looked over him: however, I am delighted to say, he moved first.

"The next day we got into a fierce dispute, in which neither gave in, and we went away and dined together.

"He used to dine at an ordinary in Poland-street, where a great many Frenchmen assembled: here he got that old man with glasses, reading the paper to himself, in the Village Politicians.

"By the time the vacation commenced, the habit of dining together, drawing together, and arguing, had generated a sort of necessity to be together, which insensibly grew upon us.

"When the academy closed, Wilkie came up to me, and said in the broadest Scotch—'Whar d'ye stay?' and invited me to breakfast. I went to No. 8, Norton-street, knocked at his ground-room door, and a voice said—'Come in.' In I walked, and to my utter astonishment, instead of a breakfast, there sat Sir David, 'In puris naturalibus,' drawing himself in the glass! 'Good heavens!' said I, 'where am I to breakfast?' Without the slightest apology for this position, he replied, with the greatest simplicity, 'Its copital practice, let me tell you: jist tak a walk.' I took my leave and walked till he was ready.

"At the first meeting he showed me his picture of the Fair: the colour was bad, but the groups exquisite. But I was so full of Raffaelle, I had a sort of contempt for a young man so devoting himself: the fact was, I did not know enough of art to see its great value. I had a very different opinion when I did.

"Though Wilkie drew at the academy with great power, there was a smart touchy style, peculiar to himself, and not fit to be put into the hands of a student for high art. It did well with him, was a part of himself, but could not be ventured on by any other without risk of manner.

"Wilkie brought to London a letter to Mr. Greville, a relation of a noble lord (Lord Mansfield), and, through Mr. Greville, Lord Mansfield called and gave him the commission for the Village Politicians, his first important work here."

Grotesque as this picture of Wilkie enjoying capital practice is, it is not such a caricature as that which the painter furnishes of himself in his letter to Sir Robert Peel from Jerusalem, and which Sir Robert thought did the artist "so much honour." He writes to Sir Robert, he says, "as to one endowed with every faculty to relish and appreciate what, with all his eyes, he, Wilkie, felt himself so feebly qualified to do justice to." He thinks with tenderness how Lady Peel and Miss Peel (hoping that they, with Sir Robert, enjoy their usual good health) would be pleased with the reminiscences which Jerusalem presents, and especially with "those realities of the past which the *pious Empress Helena* has done so much to recall and to justify;" and after many really sensible remarks on the benefits which painters might derive from Eastern travel, if they purposed to represent Scripture history, he concludes "*entreating Sir Robert's most condescending excuse*," and stating his address, should Sir Robert "*deign to write.*" Surely there is no other country in Europe where a great and famous painter would so demean himself before any person of any importance, or make such an exhibition of pitiful humility.

Mr. Haydon urges strenuously several means for elevating his darling profession:—that the English aristocracy should be made decently acquainted with the first principles of the arts; that there should be professors of the fine arts appointed at the universities; that annual government grants should be awarded for modern pictures, and the public works of taste placed under the guidance of effective and competent committees. In all of his generous, rambling discourses there is much that is sound and useful, and a great deal that is amusing; the biographical and anecdotic matter, especially, queer, interesting, and pleasant.

....

[4 JULY 1846]

The Gastronomic Regenerator.   [London: 1846.

Everybody who knows him, everybody who has sat before his dishes, everybody interested in the promotion of the Reform cause, or who likes to have a good dinner at home, has long since said in his heart "Why does not Soyer write a book about cookery?" When reform was flagging, when Peel had it all his own way, before a country party was thought of, or a revolt seemed possible, when the idea of the Whigs coming in was hopeless, and the party therefore needed consolation, what did Soyer do? At that moment of general depression Alexis Soyer invented *cutlets à la réforme. He* didn't despair, *he* knew the *avenir* that was before the party. He rallied them round the invigorating table, from which they rose cheered and courageous; flushed with victuals, their attack upon the enemy was irresistible (as under such circumstances the charge of Britons always is), and Downing-street may be said to be the dessert of the dinners in Pall-mall. He is one of the greatest politicians and pacificators in the world. If they had him in Conciliation-hall, even there they would leave off quarrelling. Look at his influence upon the diplomacy of our country! In this very day's paper appears an account of a dinner at that very Reform Club which Soyer loves, and which has stood as sponsor to the great cutlets which he invented—of a dinner at which Lord Palmerston and Ibrahim Pacha had their hands in the same dish of pilaff, and the maker of that dish was Alexis Soyer. To such a noble and magnanimous spirit as Soyer's evidently is, such a meeting will cause pride and thankfulness indeed. It is a happy omen. They have eaten salt together, and the peace of the world is assured.

How it was that Gibbon came to write the Decline and Fall; under what particular circumstances Newton conceived the theory of gravitation; how Scott invented his works, &c., are historic anecdotes with which all persons interested in literature are familiar. It is always pleasant to know how and where a great thought came into the brain of a great man, and so it is agreeable to know how this cookery book, which all the world longed for, was suggested to Soyer. It came about as follows:—

"At the request of several persons of distinction who have visited the Reform Club, particularly the ladies, to whom I have always made it a rule never to refuse anything in my power, for indeed it must have been the fair sex who have had the majority in this domestic argument to gain this gastronomical election,—Why do you not write and publish a Cookery-book? was a question continually put to me. For a considerable time this scientific word caused a thrill of horror to pervade my frame, and brought back to my mind, that one day being in a most superb library in the midst of a splendid baronial hall, by chance I met with one of Milton's allegorical works, the profound ideas of Locke, and several *chefs d'œuvre* of one of the noblest champions of literature, Shakspeare; when all at once my attention was attracted by the nineteenth edition of a voluminous work: such an immense success of publication caused me to say, "Oh; you celebrated man, posterity counts every hour of fame upon your regretted ashes!" Opening this work with intense curiosity, to my great disappointment, what did I see—a receipt for Ox-tail Soup! The terrifying effect produced upon me by this succulent volume made me determine that my few ideas, whether culinary or domestic, should never encumber a sanctuary which should be entirely devoted to works worthy of a place in the Temple of the Muses.

"But you must acknowledge, respected readers, how changeable and uncertain are our feeble ideas through life; to keep the promise above mentioned, I have been drawn into a thousand gastronomic reflections, which have involved me in the necessity of deviating entirely from my former opinion, and have induced me to bring before the public the present volume, under the title of 'The Gastronomic Regenerator,' throughout which I have closely followed the plain rules of simplicity, so that every receipt can not only clearly be understood, but easily executed.

"I now sincerely hope, ladies, that I have not only kept my promise, but to your satisfaction paid tribute to your wishes.

"You have not forgotten, dear reader, the effect that monstrous volume, the said nineteenth edition, produced upon me, therefore I now sincerely beg of you to put my book in a place suited to its little merit, and not with Milton's sublime Paradise, for there it certainly would be doubly lost."

Surely this preface is one of the most remarkable documents that ever ushered any book into the world. Soyer has made it a rule never to refuse anything in his power to the ladies (the rogue!)—and, amongst other favours, they asked him for a cookery-book. The request caused him "a thrill of horror;" but being in a library in the midst of a hall, where he met with *one* of Milton's allegorical works, Locke's profound ideas, and several *chefs d'œuvres* of that noble champion of literature, Shakspeare, what should his eye turn to but a cookery-book closeted in such company! "The terrifying effect of that succulent volume" made him determine that he never would write a book of the culinary sort.

What was the consequence? The very determination not to write, forced him into "a thousand gastronomic reflections." Write he must, and it was sheer modesty that generated the regenerator. Mark the pleasantry upon the word "lost," the last word in the preface, and fancy Soyer lost in Paradise. Tempter! if you had been in any such place, to what could you not have persuaded the first gourmand! In fine, Soyer determined to write this book, because he justly "considered that the pleasures of the table are an every-day enjoyment, *which reflects good and evil on all classes*." And when we remember that he has written the work in ten months, during which he has also supplied twenty-five thousand dinners to the gentlemen of the Reform Club, and thirty-eight dinners of importance, comprising 70,000 dishes; that he has had to provide daily for sixty servants, and to do the honours of the club to 15,000 visitors, one may fancy what genius and perseverance can accomplish. He says he is "entirely satisfied with the composition, distribution, and arrangement of the volume." *Exegit monumentum* in fact. He has been and done it. He gives you his signature, his portrait *en buste*, and another full length, in which he is represented in his parlour at home (where, in spite of his avocations, he has leisure to receive his friends and consume a most prodigious quantity of victuals*) surrounded by a select society of private friends,

---

* "In my kitchen at home," he says, "I can roast a neck or haunch of venison, *depending on which is presented to me* (670). Knuckle of veal is a very favourite dish of mine (648). I make very good soups at home in a black saucepan or stewpan (652). I often roast a small leg of pork as, &c. (648). At home I usually content myself with the chump of veal; I content myself at home with a nice piece of streaked bacon, about two pounds in weight (647). At home I often have ribs of beef (see beef). I frequently serve legs of mutton with harricot beans (645),"

dispensing to them some of the luxuries which he describes in his 700 pages.

After a few prefatory observations about carving, for which he has invented a new and apparently successful, though unintelligible method; about larding, which he recommends to the English "middle classes"—the seasons of fish and game, &c., the utensils for the kitchen—Soyer plunges into sauces at once, as the great test of culinary civilization. The key-sauces are the White Sauce, No. 7, and the Brown Sauce, No. 1. They are the *principia* of the science—they are the sauces which Soyer daily and principally uses. If the reader suspects that we are going to transcribe the formula for the preparation of these sauces, he is disappointed. No; let those who want the sauce buy the book, and enjoy both.

From sauces we go to "Potages or Soups" (and what are these, in fact, but diluted and agreeable sauce?), commencing with the clear light broth, or FIRST STOCK of soup, and proceeding to a hundred delicious varieties—the Louis Philippe, the Jerusalem, the Marcus-Hill, the Princess Royal, &c. Nothing can be more delicate or worthy of a young princess than this latter little soup; whereas the "potage à la comtesse," beginning with "cut half a pound of lean ham with an onion," is of a much stronger character. All these soups are flavoured with appropriate observations, as, for instance—"In fact it is much better for all thick soups to be too thin than too thick." Louis Philippe soup, he says, should contain "Brussels sprouts, *boiled very green*." There is surely some wicked satire here.

From soup we come to fish, as in the order of nature; thence to the hors d'œuvre and removes, to the flancs, the entrées, the roasts, the vegetables, the sweets or entremets, and the second course removes. As the critic reads from page to page his task becomes absolutely painful, so delicious is the style, so "succulent" are the descriptions, and so provoking the hunger which they inspire. Every now and then you get anecdotes, historical and topographical allusions, &c. Here is one:—

"Périgord is the only place renowned throughout the world as the favourite soil for this recherché vegetable, and our celebrated diplomatist, Talleyrand de Périgord, was indeed a worthy owner, for he was not

&c., &c. "I frequently make an excellent dinner from a meat-pudding. For plovers' eggs, my favorite, I have," says this Heliogabalus of a cook, "paid three shillings and sixpence each."

only a great diplomatist, but likewise a great gourmet. Having an interview with any distinguished personage upon any question of political importance, after patiently hearing, his usual reply was, I will consider of it after dinner; perhaps your excellency will favour me with a call to-morrow morning; and ringing the bell often call for his bill of fare, and order some of his most favourite dishes. But in eulogizing Talleyrand and the produce of his estate, I must not forget to mention that the truffles of Piedmont, though partly white, are very excellent, likewise in Burgundy, and many very good ones are now found in the southern counties of England, especially in Hampshire, but none are equal to those from Périgord. The white are dressed the same as the black.

How finely it is written! "Will *your excellency* call to-morrow morning?" Talleyrand's friend says nothing, but you see his rank at once, and when his excellency is gone, the Prince of Benevento rings the bell and—orders some of his favourite dishes. There is an account in the volume of crawfish aux truffes à la sampayo, which makes one almost frantic with hunger.

And what will the reader say to this dish, which is the invention, not of Soyer the cook, but of Soyer the poet:—

"the celestial and terrestrial cream of
great britain.

"Procure, if possible, the antique vase of the Roman capitol; the cup of Hebe; the strength of Hercules; and the power of Jupiter;
"Then proceed as follows:—
"Have ready the chaste vase (on the glittering rim of which three doves are resting in peace), and in it deposit a smile from the Duchess of Sutherland, from which terrestrial déesse it will be most graceful; then add a lesson from the Duchess of Northumberland; the happy remembrance of Lady Byron; an invitation from the Marchioness of Exeter; a walk in the fairy palace of the Duchess of Buckingham; an honour of the Marchioness of Douro; a sketch from Lady Westmoreland; Lady Chesterfield's conversation; the deportment of the Marchioness of Aylesbury; the Affability of Lady Marcus Hill; some romances of Mrs. Norton; a mite of gold from Miss Coutts; a royal dress from the Duchess of Buccleuch; a reception from the Duchess of Leinster; a fragment of the works of Lady Blessington; a ministerial secret from Lady Peel; a gift from the Duchess of Bedford; an interview with Madame de Bunsen; a diplomatic reminiscence from the Marchioness of Clanricarde; an autocratic thought from the Baroness Brunow; a reflection from Lady John Russell; an amiable word from Lady Wilton; the protection of the Countess de St. Aulaire; a seraphic strain from Lady Essex; a poetical gift of the Baroness de la Calabrella; a welcome from Lady Alice Peel; the sylph-like form of the Marchioness of Abercorn; a soirée of the Duchess of Beaufort; a reverence of the Viscountess Jocelyn; and the good-will of Lady Palmerston.

"Season with the piquante observations of the Marchioness of London-derry; the stately mien of the Countess of Jersey; the tresor of the Baroness Rothschild; the noble devotion of Lady Sale; the knowledge of the fine arts of the Marchioness of Lansdowne; the charity of the Lady De Grey; a criticism from the Viscountess of Melville:—with a musical accompaniment from the whole, and portraits of all these ladies, taken from the Book of Celebrated Beauties.

"Amalgamate scientifically, and should you find this *appareil* (which is without a parallel), does not mix well, do not regard the expense for the completion of a dish worthy of the gods!

"Endeavour to procure, no matter at what price, a virtuous maxim from the book of education of her Royal Highness the Duchess of Kent; a kiss from the infant Princess Alice; an innocent trick of the Princess Royal; a benevolent visit from the Duchess of Gloucester; a maternal sentiment of her Royal Highness the Duchess of Cambridge; a com-pliment from the Princess Augusta de Mecklenbourg; the future hopes of the young Princess Mary;—

"And the munificence of her Majesty Queen Adelaide.

"Cover the vase with the reign of her Most Gracious Majesty, and let it simmer for half a century, or more, if possible, over a fire of immortal roses."

If this dish was provided for his Highness Ibrahim Pacha last night, no eastern prince since the days of the Barmecide was ever so entertained. *Ardebit Alexim.*[1] His Highness will be bribing away this Gascon genius at any price to Cairo. He will become ——— Pacha, and the cause of Reform will begin to droop.

Besides poetry, there are pictures in this incomparable volume. The dindonneau à la Nelson (of which the croustade is the bow of a ship, in compliment to the hero of Aboukir) is a picture worthy of Turner. The engraving of Soyer's own parlour, where a pretty maid is in waiting (and an exceedingly pretty girl, by the way, is seated by the great artist) is an enticing interior, in which any man would like to let his portrait appear. The pic-ture of "Salade de Grouse à la Soyer," is a capital portrait, and will be recognized by all who know and love the original. Soyer's own portrait we have mentioned before. But perhaps the finest and most interesting work of art in the volume, is the plate at 294, which represents, of the natural size, a mutton cutlet, a pork cutlet, and a lamb cutlet. This cut—this plate of cutlets we should say—is incomparable.

---

[1] Virgil, *Aeneid,* II, 1:

"Formosum pastor Corydon ardebat Alexim."

(Shepherd Corydon was all aflame for fair Alexis.)

[20 AUGUST 1846]

Moore's History of Ireland; from the earliest Kings of that Realm down to its last Chief. 4 vols.   [Longmans.

The "last Irish chief," with whose deeds Mr. Moore concludes the fourth volume of his history, is Colonel Owen Roe O'Neill, a gentleman in the Spanish service, who came to Ireland at the close of Charles I.'s reign, when the island was trebly distracted by the Puritans, the Catholics, and the Protestant lord-lieutenant holding for the King, and who, joining the confederate Catholic army, won with it the brilliant battle of Benburb, over Leslie and the Scotch Parliamenteers. Owen Roe had no right to be ranked amongst Irish chiefs, the last and greatest of whom was Hugh O'Neill, Elizabeth's Earl of Tyrone, the famous Ulster prince, who, after nearly conquering his native island from the English, left it a broken-hearted exile in 1607, and died at Rome. Regarding Tyrone we have some new information in Mr. Moore's last volume, and a history that is the most pathetic, brilliant, and surprising. It has been told elsewhere—not without talent, but with the most furious partisanship, and in the style of Mr. Carlyle, imitated with the brogue, as it were—by a strenuous declaimer against the Saxon, Mr. Mitchel.[1] Mr. Moore writes it with the grace and beauty which belong to every page that comes from his famous pen. The last is by far the most interesting of the four volumes of Mr. Moore's history.

The antiquarian dissertations of the first part deterred many an English reader, who cared little about the Phœnicians, or Ollam Fodhla, or the state of Ireland before the days of St. Patrick. Nor were the love of the Brehon laws and the praises of tanistry and gavelkind, fostering and gossipred, so fashionable ten years ago in Ireland, when the first part of Mr. Moore's history was published, as they since have become among certain ardent young patriots there. With all the convictions of a· young Saint Just, or a spotless Robespierre, and all their angelic meekness, these young writers lately launched their indignation against Mr. Moore for the tone of his history, and without remorse or pity seized the old patriot, the liberal who was tried and proved

---

[1] John Mitchel's *Life and Times of Aodh O'Neill, Prince of Ulster* had been published in Dublin not long since.

when liberalism was dangerous, the most famous man of letters of their country, the brilliant and tender genius whose poetry has done more to reconcile England to Ireland than any law, parliaments, or orators, and clapped him under the national guillotine. *Maxima debetur pueris.*[2]—It was a characteristic trait of generous young blood.

If this party has banned Mr. Moore's work, we cordially hope the English reader of history will study it. It is a frightful document as against ourselves—one of the most melancholy stories in the whole world of insolence, rapine, brutal, endless persecution on the part of the English master; of manly resistance, or savage revenge and cunning, or plaintive submission, all equally hopeless and unavailing to the miserable victim. There is no crime ever invented by the eastern or western barbarians, no torture of Roman persecutors or Spanish inquisitors, no tyranny of Nero or Alva but can be matched in the history of the English in Ireland. The noble English lords come riding amongst the simple Irishry, like Cortes among the wondering people of Montezuma. The English law and custom is set down and colonizes the Pale; it calls the kernes beyond "the Irish enemy," and makes inroads in the savage outlying country, burns its crops and simple wattled huts and castles, and murders and rifles, without any idea of remorse or pity, according to the regular and admitted practice of feudal war. In the time of Essex we don't recognise Ireland to be more cvilised than the French consider Algeria. The Scotch cross the narrow seas, and set up colonies and make razzias. James sends over Scotch and Englishmen, who make settlements and fortify them, and clear their holdings of Irishry as they would of timber. The King's Highness parcels out the country without scruple, as the Pope's Holiness had done before; and sends over a religion, with orders to the Irish to accept it, and burns, and hangs, and massacres all obstinate recusants who decline it. Not that we are any worse than our neighbours of Europe in this respect. All Europe acts under the same principle; every government hangs and murders for the government religion; and with the Book of Kings for a

---

[2] Juvenal, *Satires,* XIV, 47-8:

"Maxima debetur puero reverentia, siquid turpe paras."
(If you have any evil deed in mind, you owe the greatest reverence to the young.) Compare *Works,* XIV, 9.

reference, the Scotch Covenanters hang up Montrose with as little scruple as Louis XIV., backed by church authority, dragonnades the Protestants. Is it to be supposed that Cromwell had any scruples of conscience as he struck down the English Catholics at Drogheda? or that Tilly was disturbed in mind when he put the Magdeburgers to the sword? Persecution was a condition of faith in the past period, axe and fire the weapons of argument all the world over, in those wicked middle ages of which romancers like to make chivalrous pageants, and we madmen in Young England and Young Ireland prate about. Surely no Englishman can read the Irish story without shame and sorrow for that frightful tyranny and injustice, that bootless cruelty, that brutal and insolent selfishness which mark, almost up to the last twenty years, the whole period of our domination. In spite of its savage task-masters, the oppressed Irish people multiplies and grows strong; and we may learn humility at least by defeat, and common prudence and expediency, as well as by the consciousness of shameful wrong.

And if, after remorselessly applying brute force towards Ireland for seven centuries, this country gives it up as useless, and acknowledges it to be wicked, and proclaims at last that equality and justice are the only possible conditions of government—this granted, peace may surely follow, and arms be laid down on both sides. When another Cromwell meditates a female massacre at Wexford, it will be time for Irish champions to defend the ladies of that town. Mr. O'Connell admits as much. Perhaps Young Ireland will be brought to own a similar truth; or the history of the country has been read to very little purpose by those ardent young students. It may suit them to describe mere scuffles as great combats, and the death of *octodecim equites splendidi** as the utter ruin of the English cavalry[3]—(Mr. Mitchel

---

* "Then from the Irish ranks arose such a wild shout of triumph as those hills had never echoed before: the still thunder-cloud burst into a tempest: those equestrian statues became as winged demons: and with their battle-cry of 'Lamh-dearg-aboo,' and their long lances poised in Eastern fashion over their heads, down swept the chivalry of Tyr-owen upon the astonished ranks of the Saxon. The banner of St. George wavered and went down before that furious charge. The English turned their bridle-reins and fled headlong over the stream, leaving the field covered with their dead, and, worse than all, leaving with the Irish that proud red-cross banner, the first of its disgraces in those Ulster wars."—Life of Hugh O'Neill, p. 114-15. And Mr. Mitchel gives, in a

writes about an affair in which Hugh O'Neill was successful in this absurd ranting way). But the upshot always comes, and, in spite of courage and wrongs, the weaker party goes down, and the conqueror tramples upon him. Nor does foreign assistance (which the above-named author seems to demand, yearning for "Spanish troops and blades of the Toledo tempering") ever benefit the luckless Irishman in arms. Hugh O'Neill had an army, and a principality almost, until forced to come to the assistance of his useless Spanish ally at Kinsale. But for Rinuccini, Owen Roe, after the battle of Benburb, might have mastered the Scotch and Irish parliamenteers in Ireland: the Frenchmen that acted with Sarsfield only marred the best efforts of that gallant and brilliant leader—the *Nation* may console itself for not having closed with the offers of Ledru Rollin.

Is this country weaker, or is the other better prepared, or are its wrongs greater, its enemies more tyrannous now than in former days?—now, when for the first time you have got the ruling party in England to declare that equality for Ireland can henceforth be the only means of governing it—now, when for the first time the English people are sincerely and warmly interested in its behalf? A hundred Benburbs or Blackwaters, the slaughter of Lord Cardigan's *equites superbi regii* in the Phœnix, and of fifty regiments to boot, would never have wrung those acknowledgments from the British people which justice, peace, and the peaceful genius and labours of great men—be they orators or poets—have brought us to own.

Mr. Moore's History must make many an English and Irish convert. What have arms ever done for Ireland, and how much has peace not done? Here is a story of seven centuries of ceaseless violence, renewed defeat, and complicated hatred, bigotry, and oppression. If injuries wrought during such a period cannot be healed suddenly, at least they are acknowledged and over; nor surely can honest men say, when they look at the present temper of this country towards Ireland, that she is not sincere in her recantation.

---

note, his authority for the above wonderful description. *Circum Sedgreium* OCTODECIM MILITES SPLENDIDI *regii succumbunt, et signum capitur.* O'Sullivan.

    ³ Thackeray later devoted one of the best of his comic ballads, "The Battle of Limerick," to a mock-heroic account of such an Irish skirmish, in which Mitchel and other Young Irelanders were involved. See *Works,* VII, 150-3.

[27 AUGUST 1846]

Ravensnest; or the Red Skins. By the Author of "The Pilot," &c.
3 vols. 1846.   [Bentley.

The social position of Brother Jonathan does not appear to
be just as comfortable as his best friends could wish. His fusion,
not only with the denizens of the Old World, but with his fellow-
citizens in the New, is but in progress, and much boiling and
bubbling, and rubbing and roughing, must take place before it
is complete. Abroad, we all know how uncomfortable an American is. His writings abound with complaints of slights and of
ill-usage received at the hands of an antiquated, ignorant, and
purse-proud aristocracy. Returned home, spoiled with the con-
taminating influence of European prejudices—prejudices in
favour of the rights of property, the claims of respectability,
and the natural influences resulting from both—he has to suffer
still deeper indignities from a tyrant democracy.

Mr. Fenimore Cooper has afforded us an able exposition of
both these unhappy positions in the works which he has put
before the public. A few years ago, after visiting this country,
he published a memoir of his travels,[1] in which he showed how
gracefully he could receive attentions and enjoy the hospitality
of English noblemen and gentlemen—attentions offered as a
tribute due to talents which had been already generally acknowledged by the public at large. Here was the deference paid by
the aristocracy of title and wealth to the aristocracy of genius.
It was, at least, in this spirit that the fêting and feasting of Cooper
took place, for although we may just have some misgivings as
to this gentleman's claim either to aristocracy or genius in a
catholic peerage of either—still, as he was undoubtedly the one
bright name in the literature of the land whence he came, he
may be accepted as its representative of the aristocracy of genius.
How gracefully the aristocracy of genius accepted the attentions
of the genius of aristocracy, and how graciously he requited
them, is known to all who read Mr. Fenimore Cooper's three
volumes, entitled "England," published some nine years ago.
How he received every little act of hospitality as a simple right—
how he construed every mark of politeness into an effort of
servile homage—how he denounced every little symptom of

---

[1] *Gleanings in Europe: England,* three volumes (London, 1837).

neglect or indifference as a positive *lèse majesté*—how he grinned, and gratulated himself and his readers when an earl knocked at his door, or a lady of title offered him Dutch herrings after dinner—and how he growled because an old nobleman was suffered to hobble up-stairs before him, and because, on another occasion, through his own stupidity, he happened to walk down last to dinner; in short, how ill his uncivilized nature assimilated with the general tenor of civilized life, and how little he understood the real spirit of equality and independence which regulates the association of gentlemen in the worn-out old world, are matters all fully set forth in the pages of the three notable little volumes referred to.[2]

Mr. Cooper quitted England a thorough-going equality-man, and a hater and despiser of everything connected with the land in which he had experienced so much misapplied hospitality. All this at least in his own conceit; for, alas for poor weak human nature! how little are we aware of the encroachment of evil influences upon us. Can we touch pitch and not be defiled? And was it possible that a man of the fine proud spirit of Mr. Cooper could see so much of the effect of pride and ostentation without imbibing some little taste for it? Besides, there were family circumstances to favour such a weakness. Mr. Cooper may hold in supreme contempt the prescriptive honours of such English houses as Howard and Percy, but he must hold in proud distinction "the old house" of Littlepage, which he tells us was founded in 1785. We may observe, before proceeding further, that we assume the author himself to be identified with the person of his hero, Littlepage, who speaks throughout in the first person; and so assuming, we must say that a finer specimen of a Brummagem aristocrat never came under our notice. How grand is his burst of patriarchal enthusiasm as he contemplates the land of his forefathers, land which has been in the family of the Littlepages for nearly three-score years! The small capitals, be it observed, are the author's own:—

"From childhood I had regarded that place as my future home, as it had been the home of my parents and grandparents, and in one sense, of those who had gone before them for two generations more. The whole of the land in sight—the rich bottoms, then waving with grass—

---

[2] Thackeray amusingly burlesques these foibles of Cooper in "The Stars and Stripes. By the Author of 'The Last of the Mulligans,' 'Pilot,' &c." See *Works*, VIII, 166-174.

the side-hills, the woods, the distant mountains—the orchards, dwellings, barns, and all the other accessories of rural life that appertained to the soil, were mine, and had thus become without a single act of injustice to any human being, so far as I knew and believed. Even the red man had been fairly bought off by Herman Mordaunt, the patentee, and so Susquesus, the Redskin of Ravensnest, as our old Onondago was often called, had ever admitted the fact to be. It was natural that I should love an estate thus inherited and thus situated. No CIVILISED MAN—NO MAN, INDEED, SAVAGE OR NOT—HAD EVER BEEN THE OWNER OF THOSE BROAD ACRES, BUT THOSE WHO WERE OF MY OWN BLOOD. This is what few besides Americans *can* say; and when it can be said truly, in parts of the country where the arts of life have spread, and amid the blessings of civilisation, it becomes the foundation of a sentiment so profound, that I do not wonder those adventurers-errant who are flying about the face of the country, thrusting their hands into every man's mess, have not been able to find it among their other superficial discoveries. Nothing can be less like the ordinary cravings of avarice than the feeling that is thus engendered; and I am certain that the general tendency of such an influence is to elevate the feelings of him who experiences it."

His uncle Ro, too, who never owned a foot of the property, entertains the same fine sentiment. "He took pleasure," says the author, "in remembering that *our race* had been the only owners of the soil on which he stood, and had that very justifiable pride which belongs to *enduring respectability and social station.*" And then Old Ro goes on to explain the secret of this sentiment in this way:—"Beyond all contradiction, boy, there is a strange perversion of the old and natural sentiments on this head among us. But you must bear in mind the fact that of the two millions and a half the state contains, not half a million, probably, possess any of *the true York blood*, and can consequently feel any of the sentiments connected with birth-place and *the older traditions* of the very society in which they live." A little further on we have a record of the honours of the Littlepage family in its three generations, a record full of the same sentiment of exclusiveness, a sentiment which, having been denounced time out of mind by the movement party in the old world, is just beginning to be taken up by the aristocratic party in the new:—

"*Now, there had been three generations of generals among the Littlepages, counting from father to son.* First, there had been Brigadier-General Evans Littlepage, who held that rank in the militia, and died in service during the revolution. The next was Brigadier-General Cornelius Littlepage, who got his rank by brevet, at the close of the same war, in which he had actually figured as a colonel of the New York line. Third, and last, was my own grandfather, Major-General Mordaunt Littlepage; he had been a captain in his father's regiment at the close of the same struggle, got the brevet of major at its termination, and rose to be a major-general in the militia, the station he held for many years before he died. As soon as the privates had the power to elect their own officers, the position of a major-general in *the militia ceased to be respectable, and few gentlemen could be induced to serve.* As might have been foreseen, the militia itself fell into general contempt, and where it now is, and where it will ever remain until a different class of officers shall be chosen. The people can do a great deal, no doubt, but they cannot make a 'silk purse out of a sow's ear.' As soon as officers from the old classes shall be appointed, the militia will come up; for in no interest in life is it so material to have *men of certain habits, and notions, and education,* in authority as in those connected with the military service."

And that there may be no mistake as to what the author considers to constitute "respectability," and those "habits and notions" which should entitle a man to authority over his fellow-citizens, we take the following from amongst many similar passages recurring in the course of the work:—

"I say that, in a country like this, in which land is so abundant as to render the evils of a general monopoly impossible, *a landed gentry is precisely what is most needed for the higher order of civilization,* including manners, tastes, and the minor principles, and is the very class which, if reasonably maintained and properly regarded, would do the most good at the least risk of any social caste known."

What strange vicissitudes occur in the history of our race! A premium upon landowners in democratic America, just at the very time the country-gentleman party have been turned to the right about in aristocratic England! We will not allow ourselves to be tempted to dwell upon this theme suggestive of so many speculations for the future. Doubtless there are the elements of social change at work in the vast continent of America, which will pass through many phases before her domestic economy can be said to be consolidated.

These changes will not be accomplished without much of trouble and struggling—the struggle of two abstract principles, both very strongly rooted in the American mind, namely, the principles of equality on the one hand, and of right of property on the other, both principles being controlled, as virtually they now are, by a third principle—the right of the majority to control, coerce, and bind the minority by a simple resolution. And effectively one of the great bones of contention existing between the majority and minority forms the staple of the present volumes.

In a word, it is a land-tenure question, a question of the right of a landlord to receive the rent for his lands, or of the tenant to occupy it rent-free, or upon commuted terms of purchase. It appears that in the States a great portion of the land was let by the original owners upon perpetual leases, a rent being reserved, payable partly in kind, partly by service, both being redeemable at their money value. Against these payments a very strong opposition has been made, and is now making, by the anti-rent party, who have gone to great excesses, disguising themselves as red Indians, and spreading fire and terror over whole neighbourhoods. "Men appeared in a sort of mock-Indian dress, calico shirts thrown over their other clothes, and with a species of calico masks on their faces, who resisted the bailiff's processes, and completely prevented the collection of rents. These men were armed, mostly with rifles; and it was finally found necessary to call out a strong body of the militia, in order to protect the civil officers in the execution of their duties."

Without entering into any argument upon the subject we will merely give a passage from the author's preface in reference to it:—

"It is pretended that the durable leases are feudal in their nature. We do not conceive this to be true; but, admitting it to be so, it would only prove that feudality, to this extent, is a part of the institutions of the state. What is more, it would become a part over which the state itself has conceded all power of control, beyond that which it may remotely possess as one out of twenty-eight communities. As respects this feudal feature, it is not easy to say where it must be looked for. It is not to be found in the simple fact of paying rent, for that is so general as to render the whole country feudal, could it be true; it cannot be in the circumstance that the rent is to be paid 'in kind,' as it is called, and in labour, for that is an advantage to the tenant, by affording him the option, since the penalty of a failure leaves the alternative of paying in money. It must be, therefore, that these leases are feudal because they run for ever! Now the length of the lease is clearly a concession to the tenant, and was so regarded when received; and there is not probably a single tenant, under lives, who would not gladly exchange his term of possession for that of one of these detestable durable leases!"

It appears, however, that the State of New York has passed an act for the redemption of these services, as of a mortgage, which is a subject of loud complaint with the author.

Another subject of complaint is that they should have imposed a tax upon the rents on long leases—in short, a sort of property-tax—which the author denounces as "a measure discreditable to civilisation and an outrage on liberty."

Soured with the contemplation of these wrongs, Mr. Littlepage and his uncle (or rather Mr. Fenimore Cooper) turn about in search of all sorts of abuses, and denounce pretty freely nearly every political institution and executive function of the land of which they are so proud. Basil Hall, Trollope, Dickens, and other European libellers never spoke more strongly or more unceremoniously on these points. A few specimens are worth extracting, as evidences of the progress of opinion in the great republic:—

" 'I wonder the really impartial and upright portion of the community do not rise in their might, and put this thing down—rip it up, root and branch, and cast it away, at once.'

" 'That is the weak point of our system, which has a hundred strong points, while it has this besetting vice. Our laws are not only made, but they are administered, on the supposition that there are both honesty and intelligence enough in the body of the community to see them *well* made, and *well* administered. But the sad reality shows that good men are commonly passive, until abuses become intolerable; it being the designing rogue and manager who is usually the most active. Vigilant philanthropists *do* exist, I will allow; but it is in such small numbers as to effect little on the whole, and nothing at all when opposed by the zeal of a mercenary opposition. No, no—little is ever to be expected, in a political sense, from the activity of virtue; while a great deal may be looked for from the activity of vice.' "

The jury system:—

"I had heard this before, there being a very general complaint throughout the country of the practical abuses connected with the jury system. I have heard intelligent lawyers complain, that whenever a cause of any interest is to be tried, the first question asked is not 'what are the merits?' 'which has the law and the facts on his side?' but 'who is likely to be on the jury?'—thus obviously placing the composition of the jury before either law or evidence. Systems may have a very fair appearance on paper and as theories, that are execrable in practice. As for juries, I believe the better opinion of the intelligent of all countries is, that while they are a capital contrivance to resist the abuse of power in narrow governments, in governments of a broad constituency they have the effect, which might easily be seen, of placing the control of the law in the hands of those who would be most apt to abuse it; since it is adding to, instead of withstanding and resisting the controlling authority of the state, from which in a popular government most of the abuses must unavoidably proceed."

The Court of Errors:—

"The Court of Errors is doomed, by its own abuses. Catiline never abused the patience of Rome more than that mongrel assembly has abused the patience of every sound lawyer in the state. 'Fiat justitia, ruat cœlum,' is interpreted, now, into 'Let justice be done, and the court fall.' No one wishes to see it continued, and the approaching convention will send it to the Capulets, if it do nothing else to be commended. It was a pitiful imitation of the House of Lords' system, with this striking difference: the English lords are men of education, and men with a vast deal at stake, and their knowledge and interest teach them to leave the settlement of appeals to the legal men of their body, of whom there are always a respectable number, in addition to those in possession of the woolsack and the bench; whereas our Senate is a court composed of small lawyers, country doctors, merchants, farmers, with occasionally a man of really liberal attainments. Under the direction of an acute and honest judge, as most of our true judges actually are, the Court of Errors would hardly form such a jury as would allow a creditable person to be tried by his peers, in a case affecting character, for instance, and here we have it set up as a court of the last resort, to settle points of law!"

Lastly, of cant and demagogism, which, it appears, are sapping the foundations of the social state in America. Our extracts are from two distinct portions of the work:—

"There is not at this moment, within the wide reach of the American borders, one demagogue to be found, who, if he lived in a monarchy, would not be the humblest advocate of men in power, ready to kneel at the feet of those who stood in the sovereign's presence. There is not, at this instant, a man in power among us, a senator or a legislator, who is now the seeming advocate of what he wishes to call the rights of the tenants, and who is for overlooking principles and destroying law and right, in order to pacify the anti-renters by extraordinary concessions, that would not be among the foremost, under a monarchical system, to recommend and support the freest application of the sword and the bayonet to suppress what would then be viewed, aye, and be termed, 'the rapacious longings of the disaffected to enjoy the property of others without paying for it.' All this is certain; for it depends on a law of morals that is infallible."

"The talk is all aimed at the leases; everything that can be thought of, being dragged into the account against us poor landlords, in order to render our cause unpopular, and thus increase the chances of robbing us with impunity. *The good people of this State little imagine that the very evils that the enemies of the institutions have long predicted, and which their friends have as warmly repudiated, are now actively at work among us, and that the great experiment is in imminent danger of failing, at the very moment the people are loudly exulting in its success. Let this attempt on property succeed, ever so indirectly,* AND IT WILL BE FOLLOWED UP BY OTHERS, WHICH WILL AS INEVITABLY DRIVE US INTO DESPOTISM, AS A REFUGE AGAINST ANARCHY, AS EFFECT SUCCEEDS TO CAUSE. The danger exists, now, in its very worst form—that of political demagogueism—and must be met, face to face, and put down manfully, and on true principles, or, in my poor judgment, we are gone. Cant is a prevailing vice of the nation, more especially political and religious cant, and cant can never be appeased by concessions."

We think there may be a good deal of truth in these observations, and, coming so mildly from whence they do, will doubtless be received in a kindly spirit. With regard to the book generally, we must observe that, although printed in the usual fashionable novel form, it is the least lively affair of the kind we have ever met with. Indeed, we do not see how it could be otherwise, the incidents being few and common-place, and the dialogue all turning upon political and social questions.

....

[1 SEPTEMBER 1846]

Life at the Water Cure.

An elaborate picture of a pump ornaments the preface of this volume, which a good deal resembles the emblem which the good-natured author has prefixed to it—the contents being exceedingly brisk, fresh, voluble, wholesome in tendency, and, it must be added, insipid in flavour. If the chronicling of small beer[1] has afforded matter for satire, what can be said of a man's persevering, through 380 pages, to register his month's history at a hydropathic establishment; how he sitz'd, and sweated, and douched; how the flies tickled his nose when he was lying helpless in the packed blankets; how he ran on amiable little errands for penny buns to Malvern; what nimble little practical jokes the gentle company at the water-cure performed on each other; what exceedingly harmless conversations they indulged in,—all which is here noted down with a prodigious simplicity,—what praise ought to be awarded to such a patient *naïf* hydrographer?

Besides the picture of the pump, there are many more pleasant ones connected with the noble science of water healing. There is a picture of a sitz-bath, of a shallow bath, of a douche with the fighting gladiator *arrosé* by its waters, of a wrung-out towel in a basin (an admirable piece), of the author's own bath at home, his sponge, and the horse upon which he hangs his sheets to dry, and sundry more representations of other great and remarkable objects in nature which have attracted our artist's eye. The book, as it exhibits the author, with his prattling simplicity,

---

[1] *Othello,* II, i, 147.

his wonderful simple jocularity, his mind, which, if contented with itself, is assuredly benevolent and kindly to all men, is not a little curious as an autobiographical sketch, and you get to know Mr. E. J. Lane, A.R.A., as you know Lackington,[2] or Cibber, or Benvenuto Cellini. And what is more, the effect is produced; and as in his admirable drawings, which are only completed with innumerable minute strokes and extreme patience and labour, so somehow his laborious minuteness of detail makes out a complete picture of life at the water-cure at Malvern. After having read the book you feel as if you had been there, as if you had undergone the sitzing and packing, the busy idleness, the mild effervescence of spirits, which these meek disciples of Priessnitz seem to enjoy, had broken out into the harmless joking stage (one of the regular *crises* which, among others less agreeable, the water patients undergo)—and were come home again, much purified, and perhaps not sorry to get away.

And now that the season has come to a termination we can imagine no better book for all the London world to study. Dowagers, senators, the dyspeptic, the gourmand fatigued by dinners, the young lady worn out by six months' inveterate balls, might find a refuge and a novelty in the native waters of Malvern, which the German Abanas and Pharphars,[3] Kissingen, Baden, and the like, may fail to supply. The great merit of the system seems that the mind is constantly occupied while the body is being healed. You are always either drying yourself or wetting yourself, or packing or unpacking, or getting hot or getting cold. These incessant labours and emotions preclude all other mental exercises. A tired lawyer will find a rattling douche tumbling down on his shoulders from a mountain a real refresher; a hipped politician, plumped in a sitz bath for a couple of hours, may sit there and reflect calmly upon the vanity of ambition and the faithlessness of parties. We can fancy Mr. Disraeli in one pail, talking quite benevolently to Sir Robert, placed on his centre of gravity in an opposite can; and the ladies will learn with pleasure that this Malvern water is the very best of cosmetics, the real kalydor, and gives that "charming bloom to the complexion,"

---

[2] James Lackington, author of *Memoirs of the First Forty-Five Years of the Life of J. L. . . .* Written by Himself, in a Series of Letters to a Friend (1791).

[3] A Biblical phrase (II Kings, 5, 12) often used by Thackeray. Compare *Letters,* I, 283.

and "imparts that brilliancy to the neck and arms," which the best condiments from Bond-street or Hatton-garden vainly endeavour to restore. Mr. Lane even says that his *hair* began to grow again under the pump, in which case Rowland and Son[4] had best shut up their shop in despair.

Here is what another aqueous disciple, Sir E. B. Lytton, says of the water cure in his magniloquent way:—

ARISTON MEN HUDOR.

" 'The first point which impressed me was the extreme and utter *innocence* of the water cure in skilful hands—in any hands indeed not thoroughly new to the system.

" 'The next thing that struck me was the extraordinary ease with which, under this system, good habits are acquired, and bad habits are relinquished.

" 'That which, thirdly, impressed me was no less contrary to all my preconceived notions. I had fancied that, whether good or bad, the system must be one of great hardship, extremely repugnant and disagreeable. I wondered at myself to find how soon it became so associated with pleasurable and grateful feelings, as to dwell upon the mind as amongst the happiest passages of existence.'

"Now for his experience of the impulse and the enjoyment resulting from the wet sheet, the bath, and the drinking, the every morning's introduction to a Malvern day:—

" 'The rise from a sleep as sound as childhood's; the impatient rush into the open air, while the sun was fresh, and the birds first sang; the sense of an unwonted strength in every limb and nerve, which made so light of the steep ascent to the holy spring; the delicious sparkle of that morning draught; the green terrace on the brow of the mountain, with the rich landscape wide and far below; the breeze that once would have been so keen and biting, now but exhilarating the blood, and lifting the spirits into religious joy: and this keen sentiment of present pleasure, rounded by a hope sanctioned by all I felt in myself, and nearly all that I had witnessed in others, that that very present was but the step— the threshold—into an unknown and delightful region of health and vigour—a disease and a care dropping from the frame and the heart at every stride.' "

The following are Mr. Lane's personal reasons for considering that

THE WET SHEET IS THE TRUE LIFE PRESERVER.

"It was not the experience of the half-packing that caused me to awake early, but a certain dread in anticipation of the *whole* wet sheet;

---

[4] Proprietors of Rowland's "Kalydor," a well-known hair oil, advertised in the monthly numbers of *Vanity Fair* and elsewhere.

and at six the bath attendant appeared with what seemed a coil of linen-cable, and a gigantic can of water, and it was some comfort to *pretend* not to be in the least degree apprehensive. I was ordered out of bed, and all the clothes taken off. Two blankets were then spread upon the mattress, and half over the pillow, and the wet sheet unfolded and placed upon them.

"Having stretched my length upon it, and lying on my back, the man quickly and most adroitly folded it—first on one side and then on the other, and closely round the neck, and the same with the two blankets, by which time I was *warm*, and sufficiently composed to ask how the sheet was prepared of the proper degree of dampness. [I was told that being soaked well, it is held by two persons—one at each end—and pulled and twisted until water has ceased to drop; or that it may be done by one person putting it round the pump-handle, or any similar thing, and holding and twisting it at *both* ends]. Two more doubled blankets were then put upon me, and each in turn tucked most carefully round the neck and under me. Upon this the down bed was placed, and over all another sheet or counterpane was secured at all sides and under the chin, to complete this hermetical sealing. By this time I was sure of being fast asleep in five minutes, and only anxious to see Ned as comfortable, for he was regarding the operation with silent horror. He, however, plucked up and before Bardon (the attendant) had swathed him completely, favoured me with his opinion, conveyed in accents in which a slight tremor might be detected, that 'packing is jolly.'

"What occurred during a full hour after this operation neither man nor boy were in a situation to depose, beyond the fact that the sound, sweet, soothing sleep which both enjoyed was a matter of surprise and delight, and that one of them, who had the less excuse for being so very youthful, was detected by Mr. Bardon, who came to awake him, *smiling*, like a great fool, *at nothing*, if not at the fancies which had played about his slumbers. Of the *heat* in which I found myself I must remark that it is as distinct from perspiration, as from the parched and throbbing glow of fever. The pores are open, and the warmth of the body is very soon communicated to the wet sheet, until, as in this my first experience of the luxury, a breathing, steaming heat is engendered, which fills the whole of the wrappers, and is plentifully shown in the *smoking* state which they exhibit as they are removed; still it is not like a vapour bath. I can never forget the calm, luxurious ease in which I awoke on this morning, and looked forward with pleasure to the daily repetition of what had been quoted to me, by the uninitiated with disgust and shuddering.

"The softness and delicacy of the skin under the operation is very remarkable, and to the touch clearly marks the difference between a state of perspiration or of fever. I cannot conceive the long existence of any *cutaneous* disease under this process.

"Bardon had brought a colossal can of water, and, always ready to bathe, I felt doubly prepared to enjoy the next operation by the smoking satisfactory state in which he found me.

"The shallow bath was repeated as yesterday, and the can emptied on my head as I sat in the water; the same friction used—and the careful and active dry rubbing.

"I then fully experienced the bracing and glowing effect of the bath, heightened by the preceding wet sheet packing.   .   .   .

"The glowing, humid, breathing heat increases, and the fancy, content to wander through all that is exhilarating and joyous, is warmed, and keeps pace with the body. This morning I had awakened with a dry feverish tongue, a parched mouth, and throbbing head; and before I moralized upon the imprudence of 'going it,' as I did yesterday at Worcester, went to the water bottle for relief. In the wet sheet I became gradually calm, and wondered at the speedy effect. I thought of what Dr. Wilson told me, that the action of the wet sheet soothes the nervous system, and improves the texture of the skin; and I was sure of the truth of both assertions. I bade farewell in prospect to my scorbutic spots. I conceived how great must be the luxury of this application, followed by the bath, as a restorative after a long journey, and the comfort in the idea that it can be done anywhere—the materials being in every house.

" 'It is a *poultice* to the whole inflamed surface of the body,'—and, by sympathy, to the *internal* surface.

" 'In fever, as the warmth increases, the pulse becomes soft, and *falls* rapidly.' "

After a month of this practice, Mr. Lane, who had been a martyr to medicine and ill-health, who dreaded blindness, and was plunged in despondency—who had been paying, in fact, to an excess of labour the penalty which others often pay to an excess of pleasure—came home again almost cured of all his ills, braced for new exertions, determined still on pursuing his bath system at home and abroad, making as many converts to it as he could. Very early every morning, be it fair or foul weather— in fact, what is rain but welcome to the water worshipper?— he may be seen mounting Ben Primrose, as *Punch* calls it, and his life, his prospects, his honest hopes for his family have assumed quite a different aspect since he made the acquaintance of water and Doctor Wilson.

In a word, though his book is a great deal too long, yet it answers its end: though it contains many trivialities and digressions, yet somehow they are pleasant, as making you acquainted with a very honest and kindly Christian; and, of those who read, all will be pleased and many converted to his simple and wholesome faith. When Sydney Smith, sitting in the scorner's chair, drinking port wine, asked sneeringly, "Did you ever see a jolly

party round a pump?" Priessnitz[5] and Dr. Wilson were unknown
doubtless, or had not yet taken charge of the handle, and Mr.
Lane had not appeared, the most faithful and good-natured
disciple that ever embraced the spout.

---

[5] Vincenz Priessnitz, author of *The Cold Water Cure, its Principles,*
Theory, and Practice: with Hints for its Self-Application, and a Full
Account of the Wonderful Cures Performed with it . . . at Graefenberg
(London, 1842), a work much discussed at this period.

....

[21 SEPTEMBER 1846]

The Poetical Works of HORACE SMITH.

[London: Colburn. 1846.

All our duty with regard to these delightful little volumes is
to give them a word of welcome. Mr. Smith has long been
known by every reader of English verse. Those admirable "Rejected Addresses" first, which parodied the styles of the poets of
five-and-thirty years ago with such felicity and good humour—
and the fugitive poems subsequently, which have been scattered
over many periodicals, and are here gathered modestly together.
There is not one of these many lyrics that is not pleasant and
pretty: often they rise higher, and in the midst of the easy graces
of this most kindly and unaffected of lyrical poets you come upon
the noblest thoughts, images, and language. But the author is
so modest (or understands his office as a comic poet so well),
that these glimpses of the sublime are but transitory, his business
being social wit and friendly and harmless laughter. Yet, like
that of every generous humorist, his humour is of a plaintive
turn, closes mournfully, like a school-boy's holiday, and leaves a
certain sadness for re-action. Such a sadness, however, is not in
the least bitter, but gentle, kindly, and full of charity. This is
the brotherly Christian privilege of humour. It is impossible to
accompany for any length of time this cheerful philosopher
without being touched and charmed by his hearty and affectionate spirit.

The reader of poetry knows those charming lines at the commencement of Faust, in which Goethe recalls the memory of the

friends to whom he first sang;[1] in a strain of similar melancholy, the sweet and kindly old English poet reviews his long career, and touches on it in a poetical preface full of natural pathos and sweet reflection. We give the verses, because, as we should fancy, the delightful apology is the writer's history too, and a worthy poet's biography:—

"I, though no conjuror, have far outdone
    Such Archimages,
For, as I culled and ponder'd, one by one,
    These scattered pages,
From the dark past, and memory's eclipse,
Up rose in vision clear my life's Apocalypse.

"Mutely each re-creative lay outpour'd
    Its own revealings;
Youth, manhood, age, were momently restored,
    With all their feelings.
Friends long deceased were summoned from the tomb;
Forgotten scenes regain'd their vividness and bloom.

"Again did I recline in copses green,
    Gazing from under
Some oak's thwart boughs upon the sky serene,
    In reverent wonder;
Or starting from the sward with ear acute,
To hear the cuckoo sound its soft two-noted flute.

"Association! thy transcendant power
    What art can rival?
Muse-haunted strolls by river, field, or bower,
    At thy revival,
Return once more, and in their second birth
Bring back each former scent and sound of air and earth.

"In social joys where song and music's zest
    Made beauty fairer,
In festive scenes with all their mirth and jest,
    Once more a sharer,
I see the smiles, and hear the laughter loud
Of many a friend, alas! now mouldering in his shroud.

---

[1] Thackeray has in mind the second stanza of the "Zueignung," a favorite passage with him (see *Works*, III, 280):

"Ihr bringt mit euch die Bilder froher Tage,
Und manche liebe Schatten steigen auf;
Gleich einer alten, halbverklungnen Sage
Kommt erste Lieb' und Freundschaft mit herauf;
Der Schmerz wird neu, es wiederholt die Klage
Des Lebens labyrinthisch irren Lauf
Und nennt die Guten, die, um schöne Stunden
Vom Glück getäuscht, vor mir hinweggeschwunden."

"So, when the hands are dust that now entwine
        These prompting pages,
    Some future reader, as a jest or line
        His thought engages,
    Feeling old memories from their grave arise,
May thus, in pensive mood, perchance soliloquise:

    " 'I knew the bardling; 'twas his nature's bent,
        His creed's chief feature,
    To hold that a benign Creator meant
        To bless the creature,
    And giving man a boon denied to brute,
Loved him to exercise his laughing attribute.

    " 'He felt that cheerfulness, when unalloy'd
        With aught immoral,
    Was piety, on earth, in heaven enjoy'd;
        And wished his laurel
    To be a Mistletoe, whose grace should make
The mirth-devoted year one hallowed Christmas wake.

    " 'In mystic transcendental clouds to soar
        Was not his mission,
    Yet could he mould at times the solid ore
        Of admonition;
    Offenceless, grave, or gay, at least *that* praise
May grace his name, and speed his unpretending lays.' "

Such verses surely give a very favourable idea of man and poet. He is full of love and friendship, mirth and simple reverence—this honest, genial, and humble spirit. All through the poems indeed these delightful qualities of the writer are indicated—the warmest family affections, the most generous social friendliness, the strongest religious feeling breaking out involuntarily at sight of natural objects. Perhaps *sensibility* is the quality, in that much mooted question of the difference between wit and humour, in which the latter's superiority lies.

What charming verses are these! how genuine, how unaffected, how happily the heart aids the artist here in producing his picture of beauty and grief!—

"THE SONG-VISION.

    "Oh, warble not that fearful air!
        For sweet and sprightly though it be,
    It wakes in me a deep despair
        By its unhallow'd gaiety.

    "It was the last my Fanny sung,
        The last enchanting playful strain,
    That breathed from that melodious tongue,
        Which none shall ever hear again.

"From Memory's fount what pleasures past
    At that one vocal summons flow;
Bliss which I vainly thought would last—
    Bliss which but deepens present woe!

"Where art thou, Fanny! can the tomb
    Have chill'd that heart so fond and warm,—
Have turn'd to dust that cheek of bloom—
    Those eyes of light—that angel form?

"Ah no! the grave resigns its prey:
    See, see! my Fanny's sitting there;
While on the harp her fingers play
    A prelude to my favourite air.

"There is the smile which ever bless'd
    The gaze of mine enamour'd eye—
The lips that I so oft have press'd
    In tribute for that melody.

"She moves them now to sing!—hark, hark!
    But ah! no voice delights mine ears:
And now she fades in shadows dark;—
    Or am I blinded by my tears?

"Stay yet awhile, my Fanny, stay,
    Nor from these outstretch'd arms depart;—
'Tis gone! the vision's snatch'd away!
    I feel it by my breaking heart.

"Lady, forgive this burst of pain,
    That seeks a sad and short relief,
In coining from a 'wilder'd brain
    A solace for impassion'd grief.

"But sing no more that fearful air,
    For sweet and sprightly though it be,
It wakes in me a deep despair,
    By its unhallow'd gaiety."

Before closing the volumes let us borrow one extract more:—

THE WRECK OF ROYAL GEORGE.

"For his eyes were seal'd, and his mind was dark,
    And he sat in his age's lateness,
Like a vision throned, as a solemn mark
    Of the frailty of human greatness.

"His silver beard o'er a bosom spread,
    Unvex'd by life's commotion,
Like a yearly-lengthening snow-drift shed
    On the calm of a frozen ocean.

"O'er him oblivion's waters boom'd,
    As the stream of time kept flowing;
And we only heard of our King when doom'd
    To know that his strength was going.

"At intervals thus the waves disgorge,
    By weakness rent asunder,
A part of the wreck of the Royal George,
    For the people's pity and wonder."

The noble image with which these lines conclude, and the touching verses which have been above quoted, will show the reader what qualities go to the making of a comic poet.

....

[25 SEPTEMBER 1846]

Diary and Letters of Madame d'Arblay. Vol. 6.

This sixth and penultimate volume of the memoirs of the indefatigable Madame d'Arblay is the pleasantest of this very pleasant and useful work. It is as amusing as any of the numerous French works of similar nature; and has the advantage, which most of the latter do not possess, of unquestioned authenticity. The letters are genuine letters. You get portraits sketched from the life of many famous personages, who, though they figured but fifty years back, belong to a society as different and remote from ours, as that of Queen Anne or the Restoration—as different as a minuet is from a polka, or the Calais packet, which was four-and-twenty hours on its journey to Calais from Dover, to the iron steamer that can rush thither and back half a dozen times in the day. Some of the letters of the romantic and verbose Evelina to her beloved father, the good old Doctor Burney, did not reach her "dearest sir" for a year after they were written. Some went by way of America, others slipped in by smugglers, or ships from Hamburg. The First Consul had at this time locked up Evelina at Paris, and all intercourse with England had ceased with the breakage of the peace of Amiens.

Evelina saw the First Consul; his appearance of "seriousness or sadness" sank deep into her sentimental mind. She saw all his grenadiers and generals gorgeously attired, and Cambacérès,

Consul No. II., "dressed richly in scarlet and gold, wearing a mien of fixed gravity and importance." The ungrateful hypocrite Talleyrand she had known, but would acknowledge no longer. Madame de Stael she patronised only a very little; the sentimentality of the impetuous Corinne was rather too boisterous for the polite and tight-laced Cecilia. She knew Cromwell-Grandison Lafayette, and shared his generous hospitality. And she wept in secret with Beauveau and Mortemar, and a great deal of the best company (returned from emigration), over the martyrdom of the Bourbon family.

In England, before she went to France, she was also a favourite in the very highest and most august company. Six lovely princesses wept over her immortal novel of "Camilla," read it hastily in their apartments at Windsor, or "comfortably" together at Weymouth. The august eyes of Queen Charlotte moistened with tears over those dingy and now forgotten pages. The King himself had a copy and read in it, and was good-natured to the hysterically loyal Fanny d'Arblay—always ready to gush with tears at the feet of her royal master—always plunging from the embraces of one soft and kind-hearted princess into the closet and arms of another. Peace to their honest big-wigged shades! There is something queer, pleasant, and affecting in the picture which Fanny d'Arblay draws of this primitive and kindly female family of George III.; of the princesses so simple, so tender, so handsome, blooming in powder and pomatum; of the old Queen herself, that just and spotless, that economical but charitable lady. The young princesses are described as having the most romantic attachment for their interesting and romantic brothers, those models of princely chivalry and Grandisonian correctness; and the old King himself appears before us, not only as a monarch whose majestic wisdom strikes Fanny d'Arblay with speechless awe, but as a good, just, and simple father and gentleman, whose qualities inspire her with rapturous and admirable volubility of praise. Considering her gift of speech, indeed, it is a wonder that Madame d'Arblay did so little, and that we had not many hundreds of volumes of novels from her, in place of the mere score which she left behind her.

More interesting sketches than even those of the above-named famous personages are the pictures of Fanny's father and husband, such as her letters and their own exhibit them. The letters of

"My dearest sir," the good old doctor at Chelsea, are as pleasant as any we know—to the highest degree lively, honest, and good-humoured. Even the multitudinousness of poor Fanny's caresses does not overpower his good temper; and after her raptures and wonders, and tears and flurry, it is the greatest relief to come upon the kind hearty prose of the jovial old scholar and gentleman, who is too good-natured even to laugh at his sentimental daughter. In this sixth volume the honest Doctor is busy about an immortal poem on astronomy; some favourite portions of which (relative to the state of the science before the time of Copernicus) he imparted to Dr. Herschel, at Slough. It is a pleasant picture. The old Doctor drives over to Slough in his "car." The ladies only are at home, but insist that Dr. Burney should step down from the car and take his dinner. Fanny's health is drunk after dinner, and Herschel arriving recently, "we walked and talked round his great telescopes till it grew damp and dusk; then we retired into the study to philosophise." Even the snow of their buzz-wigs is grey in the twilight—gloaming deepens into midnight, as the immortal Burney recites a few thousand favourite lines of the great work. Where is it, that ponderous masterpiece?

The d'Arblay portrait is a very fine one. A noble gentleman, and a Liberal, holding high rank in France, he quits the country when the Constitutional King is but a puppet in the hands of the mob. Here he and Fanny Burney give each other lessons in their native language, and correct each others exercises. What follows from this mutual instruction may be imagined: that indomitable virgin Fanny Burney is conquered in a very few lessons—and Lord Orville[1] carries off Cecilia to love and a cottage in the country, where she writes novels and has a little baby. D'Arblay works, gardens, accommodates himself to his altered fortunes: *et s'occuppe uniquement du bonheur qu'il a devant lui.* He is always a philosopher: when Fanny rushes to Windsor to show her darling to "her dearest Princesses," the Chevalier keeps modestly and independently in the back ground, in his old coat, which he carries to Paris to present himself at the bran-new court of the First Consul, when there are hopes of his being restored to his former grade of general officer. But he is a gentle-

---

[1] Lord Orville is the exemplary hero of *Evelina;* Cecilia, the heroine of Fanny Burney's novel of that name.

man too, and, wonderful to say, so grateful to his friends in England, that when offered restoration to his rank (it was upon certain conditions, and in the eminently philanthropic expedition to St. Domingo), he makes a proviso—that he shall never be called upon to serve against this country. Such a condition, of course, was refused, and the noble gentleman instead of his general's epaulets, went into a government office as a clerk, and lived honestly on sixty pounds a year.

These are the main personages and incidents of this present sixth volume. They are set before one with singular liveliness and truth, and will be read, as we take it, with kindly interest. The *plot* of the little drama is not much, but how well the characters are described! Fanny, with her tears and her raptures, and her "tumultuous sensations," and prodigal notes of admiration; pleasant Charles Burney, with his easy shrewdness and *bonhomie*; and the high-minded Chevalier, whom the ruins of fortune *feriunt impavidum*,[2] and who makes a little niche for his wife and child out of them, and cultivates his garden-plot over the *débris*. Beautiful princesses, august kings and heroes, come in and figure as adjuncts in this little simple play. In one act Fox's lovely and charming Mrs. Crewe passes over the stage—in another it is the awful Barbauld, or the tremendous Mrs. Chapone—trim, old-fashioned abbés, blazing republican officers, and prim Windsor bed-chamber lords and women, walk about as *mutæ personæ*. One scene has Windsor Terrace or the Queen's closet—another the First Consul's ante-chamber for a decoration—and there is a grand view of old Herschel's telescope in a third. And then the great dark curtain drops, and the lights are put out—but no, we are promised one act more, and shall keep the moralities for the end of the seventh volume.

---

[2] Horace, *Odes,* III, iii, 7:

> "Si fractus illabatur orbis,
> Impavidium ferient ruinae."

(If the round sky should crack and fall upon him, the wreck will strike him fearless still.)

[5 OCTOBER 1846]

Royal Palaces. F. W. TRENCH.   [August, 1846.

This little brochure, which is appropriately bound in *marble* paper, contains an assortment of pamphlets, speeches, and petitions produced by Sir Frederick Trench upon the subject of Royal Palaces, at different times since the year 1825. For twenty years and upwards the honourable and gallant baronet has made the domestic comfort and external splendour of the Crown the object of his especial solicitude. More than twenty years ago he tried to make George the Fourth uncomfortable in his mind about his lodgings. It was a shame, he said, that the nation should "take advantage of the moderation of his wishes (!) or his kind consideration for his people (! !), to keep him in a state which approached almost to degradation, when compared with the splendid accommodation of the other Sovereigns of Europe." But the only answer to this touching appeal was the building of the miserable and unwholesome hole at Pimlico, and the patching up of Windsor Castle and the Pavilion at Brighton, all at some trifling expense to the nation.

When good King William came to the throne, Sir Frederick Trench again made himself busy about the royal household, and now with a courtier's adroitness appeals to his Majesty's feelings, not only as a monarch, but as a husband. He calls upon him to consider "in all its bearings, a subject so deeply affecting the interests of his people, as well as the future health and comfort of his Majesty and our gracious Queen;" "our most beloved and gracious Queen," as he elsewhere describes her. But still Pimlico Palace stood where it was; and Buckbern Hill remained unadorned with Mr. Wyatt's magnificently designed palace.

Another monarch succeeds to the Crown, and again the Trench and Wyatt scheme is agitated. Sir Frederick, who is as felicitous in style as he is great in his conceptions, again ingeniously adapts his argument to the peculiar domestic circumstances of the case. He appealed to George the Fourth as a splendid but "degraded" prince; to William the Fourth as a husband;—he appeals to Queen Victoria, or her advisers, as a mother, a mother of "lovely children." How pathetic, and how somewhat mystic is he when he tells of the "shifts and expedients," the "miserable expedients which our gracious Queen has been compelled to have recourse *for* the unwholesome and uncomfortable accommodation of her family"—(the plain English intended being that the place is unwholesome and uncomfortable in spite of such shifts and expedients);—how great and generous his sentiments when he expresses a hope "that no false pride, or false economy, will condemn her Majesty and her lovely children to remain in such an objectionable locality."

Before proceeding further, we may observe that if there is any one point upon which men of all parties and in all stations in this country would be found to agree, it would be that her Majesty should have a palace in the metropolis in every way worthy of the dignity of her station, and adapted in every respect to her domestic requirements. But it is one thing to agree that the Queen shall have a palace, and another to consent that the firm of Trench and Wyatt should build it.

Sir Frederick, however, thinks otherwise. He considers himself the genius of palaces, as he is the genius of equestrian bronzes, of candle-lighting, and all other matters in which supreme taste can be displayed. He is, in a word, a sort of Lambert Jones of the west. Sir Frederick is a modest man withal. After unfolding to our astonished minds the vastness and variety of his designs for metropolitan improvement and embellishment, he candidly informs us that much of what he had devised had been thought of before, and he at the same time pays a due tribute to the genius of a man who could anticipate the ideas of a Trench:— "After devoting much time and labour," he says, "to an examination of various parts of the metropolis, and indulging in speculations which I fancied were new, I find that there is scarcely an idea that has presented itself to my mind, or that I have heard mentioned by any one else, which may not be found in a work entitled 'London and Westminster Improved.' This book was written by John Gwynn, an architect, and I believe was published in the year 1766." And then of Gwynn says Trench, as of Trench doubtless would have said Gwynn had he been alive, *"Gwynn seems to have possessed a mind at once capacious and accurate."* And, again, "In a word, the enlarged and intelligent mind of this man seems to have embraced and anticipated everything" (that is "everything" that was subsequently devised by Trench)—

"To him let critics turn their wondering eyes,
Led by his light, and by his wisdom wise!"

(Hear, hear! with "loud cheers," for Trench, from the *arch*-impostor at Constitution-hill!)[1]

Not to go at present into all these vaster matters, the "everything" which Gwynn anticipated, and Trench has subsequently sanctioned, let us confine ourselves to the palace, and that which immediately concerns it.

The gallant baronet lays down two positions. First that the Queen shall have a new palace, and secondly that the said palace shall be built at a place called Buckbern-hill, and a plan for which has been already some time prepared by one Philip Wyatt, architect, and a relative, we believe, of Matthew C. Wyatt, sculptor, and author of the never-to-be-sufficiently-admired Wellington Statue, located "for a limited period" *vis-à-vis* Apsley-house. As early as the year 1825 did Sir Frederick Trench adopt this site and this plan for the Royal palace, and he at the same time unfolded the gigantic project of a street to run through the metropolis straight from the said new palace to St. Paul's, thus practically effecting the union of Church and State;—"A grand street," he says, "which will show St. Paul's at the termination of a vista of two miles in length, and broad in proper proportion. Such a street," he adds, "would resemble in some measure the Long Walk at Windsor, as seen from the Castle, and intended to be terminated by a colossal statue of George III., and would far surpass in magnificence the street proposed by Buonaparte to be terminated by the Parisian elephant; and it would improve, in beauty and in value, a part of the metropolis now occupied by mean streets, lanes, mews, &c."—Upper Grosvenor-street, Berkeley-square, Conduit-street, Golden-square, Covent-garden, the Middle and Inner Temple, &c., to wit. It is true that the gallant projector, in the resolutions of which he has given notice for the first day of next session, does not mention the grand two-mile street, "broad in proportion;" but doubtless when he has got the palace the rest will follow.

---

[1] Thackeray entertained a poor opinion of the arch by Decimus Burton at Hyde Park Corner, and particularly of the colossal bronze equestrian statue of the Duke of Wellington by Matthew Cotes Wyatt which was placed on the arch in 1846. This piece of statuary, which found few admirers, was removed to Aldershot in 1883.

There are some minor points upon which Sir Frederick has changed his mind in process of time, and he announces them with an air of authority and condescension which are quite in keeping with the guardian genius of the Bronze Horse. *Ex. gr.*:—

Imprimis—"I give up all idea of making St. James's Palace a residence for the Monarch, and I limit my views to making a splendid entrance into the park from St. James's-street."

Furthermore—"I give up the idea of selling the gardens of Buckingham House for building."

He will not sell the grounds of Buckingham House, and he shortly tells us why. He proposes giving them to the public in exchange for that portion of Kensington Gardens which is to be taken from them for his new palace. "I would throw them open to the public," he says, "thus affording to the lungs of a densely populated part of the metropolis *an ample compensation* for the small portion (*mem.*: about a hundred acres) of Kensington Gardens which it is proposed to occupy with the new palace, which is situated in a locality where there is not a dense population, and *where nobody but a stray nursery-maid is ever seen!*"

We do not pretend to have studied the statistics and habits of "stray nursery-maids;" sorry we are they should ever go astray at all. But surely when they do stray they stray with their young charge, Master George, Miss Emily, and so forth; and surely if they are to stray in search of fresh air, they would be most likely to find it where there is *not* a dense population in the immediate neighbourhood. Their walk would be the more healthful, as well as more agreeable, for the absence of certain other features which Sir Frederick Trench mentions as inseparably connected with the site of Buckingham Palace and its grounds. Concurring with Mr. Hunt (Radical Hunt), he thus describes these eligible premises:—

> "*A dirty, dismal, unwholesome hole*, the basement below the level of the Thames, surrounded by sewers and stagnant water, and public-houses, and other nuisances, and *subject to inundations which leave behind them a pestilential sediment.*"

In the course of his petition to William the Fourth, the gallant projector describes more at large the advantages of this delicious spot:—

> "Within thirty feet of the Palace stands a great inn and public-house, from whence diverge two rows of mean buildings, containing every species of nuisance.

"A great mound of earth has been constructed to shut out the Mews, but evidently calculated to render the situation more damp, dark, and unwholesome; while for the formation of this nuisance, another nuisance has been created, in the shape of a piece of water, which, however pleasing to the eye on a bright and hot summer's day, must aid the great body of water in front of the Palace in producing *fog and unwholesome vapour, and creating around the Palace a truly Walcheren atmosphere.*

"Again, quite close to the Palace is a steam-engine, and a great brewery; and still nearer (though somewhat removed at a great expense) is a main sewer, which (like the basement of the Palace itself) is below the level of the Thames at high water and spring tides, and, therefore, an incurable evil."

Such is the sylvan retreat, with its "Walcheren atmosphere"[2] and "pestilential sediments," to which Sir Frederick Trench would dismiss the "stray nursery maids," and the little boys and girls, who heretofore have been wont to perambulate in the high, clear, cheerful atmosphere of Buckbern-hill. Such is the medicated atmospheric-bath which, with its attendant "all sorts of nuisances," he would allot for the recreation and restoration of "the lungs of a densely populated part of the metropolis." The gallant baronet, who is tender upon the subject of the "beloved" wife of one sovereign, and "the lovely children" of another, can consign with complacency the children of the gentry, and the wives and children of the hard-working artisan to an atmosphere which he declares to be "pestilential."[3]

Sir Frederick Trench is not a man with whom one would wish to talk seriously, much less severely, upon this or any other matter. He is not the man to understand argument, nor to challenge rebuke. Seriously speaking, we believe that the worst that can fairly be said of him is, that he is one of those shallow, fussy people who may be encouraged by the applause of unkind friends to put themselves forward as champions of all sorts of foolish jobs and projects, upon the terms of reaping a full share of the odium and none of the profit. Let him be wise in time; and if he ever is to be wise it surely is time now, after a quarter of a century of aerial castle, palace, and street-building. Let him reflect upon the past rather than the future: his future with

---

[2] The English campaign against enemy shipping and installations at Flushing and Walcheren in 1809-1810 had come to nothing because fever overtook nearly the whole of the invading force.

[3] Since Thackeray was at this time living at 13 Young Street and walked frequently with his daughters in Kensington Gardens, his hostility to Trench's proposal is understandable.

posterity is not to be envied. Let him contemplate that abominable waste of bronze on Constitution-hill—let him contemplate it in silent awe and astonishment. Let him be proud, if he will and can, of the part he has had in this triumph over common sense and the united wishes of the whole world of taste. Let him, like the poor bronze beast itself, be deaf to the execrations with which passing multitudes assail it;—but let him also, like that quadruped, be silent on matters which he does not understand. Let him rest assured that the people of this country will provide a palace for their Sovereign worthy of her exalted station, and adequate to the requirements of herself and her illustrious family; let him imagine the possibility that this may be accomplished without trenching in the least upon the existing means of recreation of the people; and let him remain thoroughly convinced that the accomplishment of this important national object will be neither promoted nor retarded by any resolutions, speeches, or pamphlets of the honourable and gallant representative of—the Wellington enormity.

....

[14 MARCH 1848]

MEETING on KENNINGTON COMMON.

Yesterday a public meeting of the working classes was held on Kennington Common, for the purpose, it was understood, of adopting a congratulatory address to the French Republicans,[1] and also of denouncing the income-tax, and taking measures to promote the five cardinal points of the "charter." The meeting originated in the abortive demonstration of Trafalgar-square yesterday week,[2] Kennington Common being considered the most

[1] Louis Philippe had abdicated as King of France and the republic had been proclaimed on 24 February 1848. These events, which were the signal for bold manifestations of unrest throughout Europe, set Thackeray to thinking about the political problems of the modern world, particularly as they posed themselves in England. While he said "God save the republic," he was opposed to socialism and communism; and he believed that "the collision of poverty ag[ain]st property is begun in France, but not here as yet" (*Letters*, II, 355-7). Thus alerted, he agreed readily when the *Morning Chronicle* asked him to report on the Chartist meetings which were the chief popular response in England to events across the channel.

[2] Under the heading DISTURBANCES IN THE METROPOLIS the *Annual*

convenient space beyond the boundary prescribed by act of
Parliament for holding open air meetings during the sitting of
the legislature. Serious apprehensions were entertained of a
disturbance of the public peace, but the general indignation and
contempt excited by the Trafalgar-square and Stepney-green
riots appeared to have completely cured the prevailing folly, and
consequently the proceedings yesterday were as dull, tame, and
uninteresting as the "thrice told tale" of the Chartists generally
is, and about as orderly and well conducted as a Borough meeting
at the Town Hall of Southwark, under the presidency of the
High Bailiff. It is true that the police were assembled in great

---

Register, . . . 1848 (II, 35-6) provides the following description of the
Trafalgar Square *émeute* of 6 March: "Mr. Charles Cochrane, late a
candidate for Westminster, had proposed a grand assemblage at noon,
in the open air, as a demonstration against the Income-tax, and had extensively placarded the proposal. The Act 57 George III., c. 19, ex-
pressly prohibits, during the session of Parliament, any open-air meeting
to petition the Legislature for any measure affecting the church or state,
at any place within a mile of Westminster Hall, excepting the parish of
St. Paul's, Covent Garden. This law the Commissioners of Police felt it
their duty to enforce. They advised Mr. Cochrane of the illegality of his
project; and on Monday Mr. Cochrane issued notices of this fact, and
used some means to prevent the meeting. The measures were taken so
late, however, that they only served to excite the indignation of a large
crowd who had already assembled. By one o'clock, 10,000 persons were
gathered in the square; and mob-mischief of a playful sort—'bonneting,'
and pushing people into the fountains—filled up the time. A few orators
then appeared, and made inflammatory allusions to the revolution in
Paris. By the time the speeches were over, the crowd had increased to
some 15,000—artisans and labourers out of work, idle spectators, and
thieves. In so great a multitude, the police were overwhelmed: after
vigorously attempting to resist the crowd with their staves, they were
fain to retreat to the station in Scotland Yard. Meanwhile, the mob tore
up the wooden fence round the Nelson pillar, used the pieces as weapons,
and took possession of the spot. The police, largely reinforced, re-
entered the square, attacked the crowd at various points, and ultimately
regained possession of the place; though without dispersing the crowd.
Fights were frequent and general. These scenes continued, with slight
intermission, until night. Occasionally were heard shouts of '*Vive la
République!*' About eight o'clock, a party, under a lad who wore epaulettes, marched off down Pall Mall 'for the palace,' breaking lamps as
they went. At Buckingham Palace, the guard turned out; and the mob,
alarmed at the sight of the bayonets, evaded them; going round by Westminster to their starting-point, Trafalgar Square. The general intent
seemed to be mere wanton mischief; but on the way, a baker's and a
publican's shop were beset, and oaths of distress and starvation, and
rations of bread and ale were exacted. Several ringleaders were arrested;
among them the hero of the epaulettes — who began to cry! By midnight
all was quelled, and soon afterwards the streets resumed their usual
aspect."

force in the neighbourhood, prepared to prevent or check any
public outrage; but with the exception of the noisy ebullitions
of a sprinkling of blackguard ragamuffins, whose presence is
incidental to, and almost inseparable from such assemblages,
there did not appear the slightest disposition to riot or disturbance. A baker's shop in the neighbourhood was rifled of
some bread and flour by a gang of desperadoes on their way to
the meeting, and a baker's man, who was delivering bread from
a hand-cart in the street, was frightened into the abandonment
of his master's property; but these were the only occurrences of
a disgraceful kind worthy of remark during the day. The number of spectators who lined the roads adjoining the common far
exceeded those who appeared to take a personal interest in the
proceedings of the day; and from the commendable prudence
exercised by the police authorities in keeping the men out of
view, the mob were deprived of the principal incitement to
turbulence which had led to a rupture of the peace at Trafalgar-
square. It was calculated that from eight to ten thousand persons
were assembled in and around the common during the day, but
the numbers who evinced any interest in the proceedings were
comparatively insignificant. The windows of the Horns Tavern,
and of several adjoining shops, had their shutters up; and the
various other taverns along the Kennington-road displayed
similar manifestations of alarm and apprehension. A strong
military force was said to be garrisoned in the neighbourhood,
ready to act at a moment's notice in support of the police, should
their aid be unfortunately requisite; but all unnecessary display
of force, with the exception of a small police horse patrol, was
very wisely avoided. Shortly after twelve o'clock Mr. Reynolds,[3]
who presided at the meeting at Trafalgar-square, accompanied
by several persons forming a sort of committee of management,
proceeded from the Horns Tavern to the common, where a couple

---

[3] George William McArthur Reynolds, author of much sensational
popular fiction. In replying for "the Novelists of England" at the dinner
of the Royal Literary Fund on 10 May 1848, Thackeray referred to
Reynolds's incongruous but persistent political activities when he spoke
of "a great Novelist, a member of my own profession, . . . standing upon
Kennington Common in the van of liberty, prepared to assume any
responsibility, to take upon himself any direction of government, to
decorate himself with the tricolour sash, or the Robespierre waistcoat"
(Lewis Melville, *William Makepeace Thackeray*, 2 volumes, London,
1910, II, 66-67).

of waggons were drawn close together, and formed a kind of platform for the principal performers of the day. Mr. Reynolds was again called on to preside, and proceeded in a temperate speech to open the proceedings, but was shortly afterwards interrupted by the arrival of a van filled with working people, and having a tri-color flag flying, which was afterwards transferred to the waggon in which the chairman presided. This was intended as a grand *coup-de-théâtre*, but the failure was signally ludicrous, for although tolerated during the proceedings, yet on leaving the common at their termination the party-coloured rag was pitilessly pelted with mud and stones, whilst the terror stricken fellows in the van vainly endeavoured to escape to the rear, and ultimately sought shelter in indescribable confusion in the bottom of the vehicle. But this is anticipating the narrative of the proceedings.

Mr. REYNOLDS began by exhorting the multitude to abstain from any disorderly conduct, or anything that could tend to a violation of the peace. He said the meeting had originated from that held at Trafalgar-square on Monday last, and he had written two letters on the subject—one to Mr. Cochrane, and the other to Sir George Grey—both of which he read. To neither of the letters did he receive any answer [groans]. With respect to Mr. Cochrane, he would leave his conduct to the decision of the meeting [groans]. Sir George Grey's conduct was most uncourteous. The people had a right to meet to express their opinions on public matters. If their rulers had a just cause, they would not require any force to put down public meetings; but as their cause was a bad one they were obliged to resort to force. The meeting at Trafalgar-square had been stigmatized as riffraff, and it was most dishonest in the daily, and some of the weekly papers, to characterize that meeting in such a manner. The press was in advance of the Government, but the people were in advance of the press, and he hoped that they would exclude those papers which abused them from the coffee houses. They were met in order to express their sympathy with the brave people of France [groans, cheers, and laughter]. The people of France, if properly governed, were as fine and as righteous a set of people as any on the face of the earth; but the tyrant Louis Philippe had endeavoured to enslave them, and it would be a disgrace to the royalty of England to countenance the expelled royalty of France. The principles of republicanism

195

were making great progress, and would soon be universally established [laughter and cheers]. The income-tax, it had been said, did not affect the working classes, but he contended that it did affect the working man, and they ought not to use their exertions against it, and he hoped all parties would join to get all they required. They were told that they were free, but there were laws existing which enslaved them. The aristocracy had all the power, and two or three of their number were the owners of almost the whole of London. Let them look at the expense of keeping up royalty and the aristocracy. Why should they be paying £400,000 a-year to the Queen, when the American President did the work for £5,000 a year; and so it was with all the expenditure of the state. Her Majesty had lately a large sum granted to her to build an addition to her palace, but she paid no consideration to the families of those who were lodging in cellars [groans]. Surely Buckingham Palace would have been sufficient, but she must have a new palace. Then they gave £100,000 to the Queen Dowager, a foreign woman, who had attempted to persuade William IV. not to grant the Reform Bill. Prince Albert had £30,000 a year, besides £12,000 as field-marshal, a young man who had never seen a shot fired in his life. All the costliness of royalty must therefore be cut down, and he hoped that in future the country would insist on curtailing the royal expenditure [cheers].

Mr. WILLIAMS was the next speaker. He described himself as a working man, congratulated the meeting on having the aid of the talents of a new political leader in the person of Mr. Reynolds, who took the chair at the meeting at Trafalgar-square. That was a glorious meeting; but he regretted some disgraceful persons were encouraged by the police to commit plunder. He had no hesitation in stating the police were at the bottom of it. He hoped that on this occasion no such disgraceful scenes would occur. The middle classes were the enemies of the working classes, and they were beginning to see the evil of that state of things. The resolution which he had to propose expressed the sympathy of the meeting with the people of France, who had so gloriously asserted their rights and obtained that power to which they had a natural right. The French people were not a blood-thirsty people, as they had been represented, and the conduct of the Provisional Government had proved that fact. He called upon the meeting to follow the noble example of the people of France, and to obtain peaceably, if they could, but if not, to obtain by every means in their power the rights which belonged to them. They were at present but a nation of paupers, and when they had such men as Mr. O'Connor and Mr. Reynolds to lead them, they had no occasion to despair; and he hoped they would meet and agitate for their natural rights. The Whig Government had at all times been the enemies of the people. They asked for the six points of the charter, to which no one could object, and although he had not joined the Chartist body, he proclaimed himself an advocate of the six points of the charter. It was said that there would be war with the French people; but he would ask whether they would allow the Government to go to war with the glorious people of France. He hoped all of them would form themselves into associations to carry out the object they had in view. He concluded by moving the adoption of a congratulatory address to the French Republicans.

Mr. SHARP seconded the resolution, and said he hoped it would stimulate the meeting to follow the example of the French. Louis Philippe had for seventeen years acted in a manner to enslave the people, and they had cast him from the throne. Louis Philippe was the last king of France, and he hoped that ere long the expense of kings would be done away with in England as well as in France [cheers]. The Provisional Government that had been installed had restored peace and order to France in four days, Louis Philippe had been unable to do during his reign of seventeen years. The working classes produced, and the aristocracy dissipated: and he hoped they would prove their right to their freedom, and establish liberty, equality, and fraternity, as they had now in France [cheers].

Two men named CLARKE proposed and seconded the next resolution, to the effect "That this meeting demands that the Ministry will immediately introduce a measure for the extension of the suffrage to every male adult having attained the age of 21 years, and who is in the enjoyment of his intellects, with such provisions for securing the efficient working thereof as were contained in 'The People's Charter.' "

Mr. DUNN proposed the third resolution—"That this meeting requires at the hands of the Government the immediate recognition of the rights of labour, and the principle of a fair day's wages for a fair day's work, and of every man who is able and willing to work having work found for him."

Mr. M'GRATH seconded this resolution. He said the operation of the income-tax had pressed heavily on labourers and tradesmen, whose wages had been in consequence reduced 10 and 15 per cent. However, it was not the repeal of one nor half a dozen bad laws that would ameliorate the condition of the people of this country, who had nothing to hope for until they dashed the whole thing into entire annihilation, and reared in its stead the rights of free men. He next alluded to the system adopted by the dock authorities at the east-end of London, who subjected the labourers to the most degrading scrutiny, searching their hats and pockets every time they left the premises, in order to see whether or not they had robbed their employers. This he looked upon as worse than slavery, and should be put an end to [cheers].

This resolution was also carried, and a committee was appointed to communicate with her Majesty's ministers.

A vote of thanks was then passed to the chairman, who again addressed the meeting, exhorting those present to return quietly to their homes, and not to afford any excuse for the interference of the police. The chairman then retired, loudly cheered by the multitude, and followed by a considerable portion of the crowd.

Captain ACHERLEY then mounted the waggon, and harangued the persons remaining at considerable length. He expressed his regret and astonishment at none of the previous speakers having alluded even in the most remote degree to the condition of Ireland. He then called for three cheers for "ould" Ireland, which was warmly responded to. The gallant captain then retired, and a heavy shower of rain coming on not a soul was to be seen on the common in the course of five minutes, with the exception of two or three little boys crouching for shelter beneath the waggons. Thus ended the great Kennington-common demonstration.

....

[15 MARCH 1848]

CHARTIST MEETING.

Last night a numerous meeting of Chartists was held in the Literary Institution, John-street, Tottenham-court-road, for the purpose of receiving the deputation entrusted with the congratu-

latory address to the Republican Government of Paris, and
hearing the report of the proceedings.

Mr. Ernest Jones and Mr. M'Grath, two of the deputation,
attended; but Mr. Harney, the third member, was unavoidably
absent, having, as was explained by the chairman, allowed himself to be carried away to such an extent by his enthusiastic
feelings, that he was laid on a sick bed at Paris, and unable to
return to his constituents.

The chair was taken by Mr. Shaw, whose appointment thereto
was ratified by general acclamation. The theatre of the institution was densely filled by a very well-conducted assemblage of
both sexes, who evinced the utmost anxiety to hear from Messrs.
Jones and M'Grath an account of their travels in France.

The CHAIRMAN first addressed the meeting, detailing the objects
for which it had been convened, and bestowing a glowing
eulogy on the admirable conduct of the deputation. The rest
of his speech was devoted to an advocacy of the salient points
of the charter, which he recommended as the only panacea for
England's misfortunes.

Mr. JONES then advanced to the front of the orchestra, which
served as a rostrum, and delivered a round but not altogether
"unvarnished" tale of the trials he had passed, and "a thousand
hair-breadth 'scapes by flood and field."[1] He spoke of the poets,
philosophers, and historians he had met, and the liberty he had
taken to place himself upon an equality with them by showing
his fraternity. He then invoked the genius of British freedom
to work out for England a similar work of regeneration to that
which was going on in France. The French cried, "Down with
Guizot!" and that, when translated, was, in plain English,
"Down with Russell!" The French cried, "Away with corruption!" That, in English, was nothing else than "Away with
class legislation!" The French cried, "Up with reform!" That,
in English, meant "The charter, and no surrender" [cheers]!
So long as the Government observed towards them a peaceable
and constitutional demeanour, he trusted they would do the same;
but whatever course they chose to pursue, he hoped the day was
not distant when they would be receiving a deputation from the
French Republic in their own Government house [cheers].

Mr. M'GRATH next addressed the assembly, and expressed

---

[1] *Othello*, I, iii, 72, 117.

his satisfaction at hearing that there were a number of Government spies present, and he trusted they would represent fairly to their employers all that occurred on the platform. He then reverted to the object of the meeting, gently retouching Mr. Jones's narrative of their reception by the Provisional Government, and the National Guard of Paris, which he described as "glorious" and "flattering" in the extreme. When they went down at twelve o'clock on Sunday morning to the splendid Hotel de Ville to procure an audience of the French Government, they were met at an outer barrier by a guard, not of mercenaries at a shilling a day [groans], but by citizen soldiers employed to protect the infant liberties of their country. Ten thousand of these noble fellows were, according to Mr. M'Grath, assembled on the occasion; and although they questioned the deputation rather sternly as to the object of their visit, yet Mr. Ernest Jones, who spoke French like a native, so charmed them with his "sweet discourses" that at the next barrier the announcement of "the English Chartists" was an "open sesame," and like magic the three Chartists of England found themselves in presence of the Provisional Government. Here the historian paused to take breath, and to inveigh rather pathetically over the injustice done to the occasion not only by the London daily papers, but even by the *Northern Star*. Whilst Mr. Jones addressed the members of the Government, many of them were standing about nodding their heads in token of assent, and when Garnier-Pagès responded, he did so, not briefly, as stated in the papers, but at twenty minutes length. He told them he felt it an honour to receive a deputation representing so powerful a party as the British Chartists, that he had long watched their proceedings with deep interest and the warmest wishes for their success, and he was sure that if ever England made war against the infant liberties of France, the working men of England would not sanction or allow it [cheers]. The speaker then proceeded to describe the appearance of the streets of Paris—a million of men flushed with victory, but maintaining the strictest order and regularity, and not a single glass window was broken. This was an example worthy of being followed by the English. Mr. M'Grath next proceeded to entertain the meeting with a few lively horrors, in which a rusty old guillotine was made to perform the principal part, and which he produced as a specimen of the ex-King's cruelty, but the description was rather over-charged, and what was intended to excite a thrill ended in a titter. He then adjured them to let their cry be "The Charter and no surrender." Their oppressors consisted only of a few thousands, whilst they numbered millions, and if they were determined, the contemptible thousands must yield. Within three weeks they would have a convention sitting in London to take charge of a petition to Parliament, and 250,000 stalwart men would march with it from Kennington Common to the door of the Parliament house. He hoped they would all sign it, and form a component part of that procession, and that they would swear in the presence of heaven, by the love they bore their country, and by the respect they had for their children, never to desist from agitating for the Charter, until the rights and liberties of the people of England were permanently established [cheers]. He begged of them to repudiate all connection with the vagabonds and pickpockets, and for each man to become a constable for the protection of property. They would thus get rid of the onus which the base press of London imposed on them [cheers].

The CHAIRMAN then announced that a subscription would be received at the doors when the meeting broke up, to defray the expenses of the deputation to Paris.

Mr. CUFFY then proposed a resolution, to the effect that the monopoly of political power exercised by the oligarchy of England was a flagrant invasion of the rights of the British people, and that the meeting thereby covenanted to resort to every available means consistent with the law to abolish it, and to establish the rights of the nation on the basis of the British Charter [cheers].

Mr. Purcell, Mr. Dixon, and others supported this resolution, which was adopted, and thanks having been voted to the chairman, the meeting dispersed at a late hour.

INDEX

All names of actual persons in Thackeray's text are listed below. The listing of proper names in passages quoted by Thackeray, on the other hand, is highly selective. They appear only if additional information needed for full identification is provided in the index, or if the reference is of particular significance. Titles of books are listed under the names of their authors, and names of characters are listed under titles. Where a book is reviewed by Thackeray (a circumstance marked by bold-face type), names of characters mentioned are not given. Titles of paintings are listed under the names of artists only where Thackeray's descriptions are detailed and extended.